TO TAKE PLACE

CHICAGO STUDIES IN THE
HISTORY OF JUDAISM

*Jacob Neusner, William Scott Green,
and Calvin Goldscheider, Editors*

ToTake Place

Toward Theory in Ritual

Jonathan Z. Smith

The University of
Chicago Press

chicago and london

JONATHAN Z. SMITH, the Robert O. Anderson
Distinguished Service Professor of the Humanities
at the University of Chicago, is the author of
Imagining Religion, published by the University of
Chicago Press.

The University of Chicago Press, Chicago 60637
The University of Chicago Press, Ltd., London
© 1987 by The University of Chicago
All rights reserved. Published 1987
Printed in the United States of America

96 95 94 93 92 91 90 89 88 87   54321

Library of Congress Cataloging-in-Publication Data

Smith, Jonathan Z.
  To take place.

  (Chicago studies in the history of Judaism)
  Bibliography: p.
  Includes index.
   1. Ritual. 2. Shrines—Location. 3. Tjilpa
(Australian people)   4. Temple of Ezekiel (Jerusalem)
5. Church of the Holy Sepulchre (Jerusalem) I. Title.
II. Series.
BL580.S64   1987   291.3′5′01   86-30869
ISBN 0-226-76359-5

FOR ELAINE
with love and gratitude in celebration of the place we have built together for more than twenty years

CONTENTS

ILLUSTRATIONS ix

PREFACE xi

ACKNOWLEDGMENTS xv

ONE
In Search of Place 1

TWO
Father Place 24

THREE
To Put in Place 47

FOUR
To Replace 74

FIVE
To Take Place 96

ABBREVIATIONS 119

NOTES 121

INDEX 181

Illustrations

1. The Hierarchy of Power as Displayed in the Spheres of Activity of the Ritual Actors (Ezekiel 40.1–44.3), p. 58

2. The Hierarchy of Power as Displayed in the Three Zones of Relative Sacrality (Ezekiel 40.1–44.3), p. 59

3. The Hierarchy of Status as Displayed in the Spatial Range of the Ritual Actors (Ezekiel 44.4–31), p. 64

4. The Egalitarian Division of the Land (Ezekiel 45.1–8 + 47.13–48.35), p. 67

5. The Egalitarian Central Segment of the Land (Ezekiel 45.1–8 + 47.13–48.35), p. 67

6. The Rectified Movements of the Prince and the People (Ezekiel 46), p. 71

7. Map of the Central Liturgical Sites in Christian Jerusalem in the Fourth Century, p. 92

8. Chart of the Stations for the Christian Liturgy in Jerusalem in the Fourth Century, p. 93

PREFACE

The Jews had a peculiar way of con-
secrating things to God, which we
have not. Under the law, God, who
was master of all, made choice of a
temple to worship in, where he was
more especially present: just as the
master of the house, who owns all the
house, makes choice of one chamber to
lie in, which is called the master's
chamber. But under the gospel there
was no such thing.

John Selden, Table-Talk (1689)

In a previous work I wrote, "for the self-conscious student of religion, no datum possesses intrinsic interest. It is of value only insofar as it can serve as an exemplum for some fundamental issue in the study of religion. The student of religion must be able to articulate clearly why 'this' rather than 'that' was chosen as the exemplum."[1] For a student of religion concerned with generic matters, choice is everything. Such a student is bound neither by the demarcations of a given canon nor by the limits of a historic community in constituting the domain of the argument or the field of the illuminating example. Rather, it is the theoretical issues that determine the horizon. In the work before you, the primary question will be a matter of theory: the issue of ritual and its relation to place. The issue has been raised with uncommon clarity by C. Lévi-Strauss, who writes:

> A native thinker makes the penetrating comment that "All sacred things must have their place." It could even be said that being in their place is what makes them sacred for if they were taken out of their place, even in thought, the entire order of the universe would be destroyed. Sacred objects therefore contribute to the maintenance of order in the universe by occupying the places allocated to them. Examined superficially and from the outside, the refinements of ritual can appear pointless. They are explicable by a concern for what one might call "micro-adjustment"—the concern to assign every single creature, object or feature to a place within a class.[2]

As this quotation makes plain, this understanding carries more of the social and verbal understanding of *place* than does the more familiar substantive *sacred space* in writings by so-called phenomenologists or historians of religion. It is this former sense of *place* in relation to the "microadjustments" of ritual that supplies the focus for these inquiries.

In what follows, the thickest examples will be drawn from the Tjilpa group of Australian aborigines and from the traditions of two places in Jerusalem, the Temple and the Church of the Holy Sepulchre. The Tjilpa were chosen because they stand as a privileged example within one of the more influential contemporary theories of religious ritual. They allow, as well, the raising of questions concerning the enterprise of comparison. The second set was chosen because Jerusalem stands as a center of ritual activity for all the major components of Western religious experience and expression. It, too, raises matters of comparison, both with respect to the two places in the city and with respect to another matter. Through unimaginable labors, Jacob Neusner has made available to the generalist all of the canonical documents of classical Judaism. His central and completed work concerns Mishnah. A proper question then becomes: To what might Mishnah be compared? Neusner has made the task at one and the same time both easier and more difficult by making impossible a search for simple similarities of genre.[3] The comparison cannot be to the literature of gloss and commentary, or to collections of law or wisdom-sayings. Such will fail to address what Neusner has exposed as central to Mishnah, to what he terms its "agendum" and its "generating problematics." The key elements that require comparison recur throughout his work: the destruction of the Temple; the experience of being "in no particular place;" matters of separation, mixture, and taxonomy; the centrality of intention; and the consummate word, *sanctification*. I need only cite the penultimate paragraph of his *Judaism: The Evidence of the Mishnah:*

> The Mishnah's evidence presents a Judaism which at its foundations and through all its parts deals with a single fundamental question: What can man do? The evidence of Mishnah points to a Judaism which answers that question simply: Man, like God, makes the world work. If a man wills it, all things fall subject to that web of intangible status and incorporeal reality, with a right place for all things, each after its own kind, all bearing their proper names, described by the simple word, sanctification. The world is inert and neutral. Man by his word and will initiates processes which force things to find their rightful place on one side or the other of the frontier, the definitive category of holiness. That is the substance of the Judaism of Mishnah.[4]

I will argue, in what follows, that it is the Christian liturgical year that may best be compared to the enterprise of Mishnah; but that argument is a long way off. As the ancient Athenians knew, a straight line is not the route of propriety when treating with sacred matters. Unlike present-day tourists, they circumambulated the Parthenon several times before confronting the statue of the goddess. I, too, shall take a more leisurely and circuitous approach to my themes in ranging from Alice Springs, Australia, to Jerusalem; in conversing with guides along the way, from Eliade to Durkheim, from Wheatley to Lévi-Strauss; and in questioning what might be learned in service of a repositioning of elements toward theory in ritual.

ACKNOWLEDGMENTS

The attempt to think through the implications of place for a theory of ritual has not been a utopian enterprise. It has been the result of a quite specific concatenation of events, each tied to a particular academic locale. Three of these have left their impress on the work.

The first was an invitation to give a presentation entitled "The City as Place" to a symposium, "*Civitas:* Christian Views of the City," sponsored by the Religion and Arts Program at Yale Divinity School, in April 1982. I do not know what the convenors had in mind in framing my topic, but the title proved provocative in setting off a chain of thought. The resulting paper, to be published by Scholars Press in the symposium volume edited by Peter Hawkins, presents the arguments of Chapters 2 through 4 of this book *in nuce.* I was privileged to give varying versions of the paper at half a dozen academic institutions in the subsequent year. I particularly

profited from the comments and criticisms made by colleagues at the fiftieth anniversary of the Canadian Society of
Biblical Literature in Toronto, at the Iowa School of Religion,
and at the Department of Religion of the University of
Pittsburgh.

The second occasion was a "Conversation on Ritual Theory"
among René Girard, Walter Burkert, and me, held for four days
in October 1983 under the sponsorship of Burton L. Mack of
Claremont University and Robert Hammerton-Kelly of Stan-
ford University. (That conversation is to be published by Stan-
ford University Press.) I have seldom taken part in a more intense series of intellectual encounters around a central topic.
Thoughts generated by those discussions have found place in
this volume, especially in the concluding chapter.

The third and most proximate event was the invitation to
deliver the Merril L. Hassenfeld Memorial Lectures, sponsored by the Judaic Studies Program at Brown University, in
March 1985. It is the text of those lectures, somewhat revised,
that makes up the contents of this volume. One could not ask
for a better setting in which to present an essay in thinking
about ritual. The members of the Judaic Studies Program have
been colleagues and conversational partners for years. Although our theoretical resources and our exempla do not always coincide, our enterprise, the shared commitment to the
study of religion in modes appropriate to the academy, has
been, and remains, the same. For those good friends, the occasion was not so much a set of lectures as a series of collo-
quies, moments in a continuing conversation about issues we
share.

I am grateful to Professors William S. Green (University of
Rochester), Burton L. Mack (Claremont University), Hans H.
Penner (Dartmouth College), and Paul Wheatley (University
of Chicago) for their careful reading of an initial version of
this work. For the third time, Jacob Neusner (Brown University) has served as the editor of the series in which a book of
mine has appeared. The root of *editor* carries the notion of
giving. I count my twenty-five-year association with Jack one
of the rare gifts of my life, more often as beneficiary than as
donor.

I have named, in the dedication, the one to whom all language appropriate to *le don* may be applied: gift, obligation, prestation—above all, exchange. Unlike that studied in what follows, here the rituals remain private, only to be hinted at in public places.

ONE

IN SEARCH
OF PLACE

It is the spatial image alone that, by reason of its stability, gives us an illusion of not having changed through time and of retrieving the past in the present. . . . Space alone is stable enough to endure without growing old or losing any of its parts.

Maurice Halbwachs

I

In writing on the category of sacred place in his early work *The Sacred and the Profane*, Mircea Eliade paraphrased a moving Australian aboriginal myth that appeared to be emblematic of the topic.

> According to the traditions of an Arunta tribe, the Achilpa [sc. Tjilpa], in mythical times the divine being Numbakulla cosmicized their future territory, created their Ancestor,

and established their institutions. From the trunk of a gum tree, Numbakulla fashioned the sacred pole (*kauwa-auwa*) and, after anointing it with blood, climbed it and disappeared into the sky. This pole represented a cosmic axis, for it is around the sacred pole that territory becomes habitable, hence becomes transformed into a world. The sacred pole consequently plays an important role ritually. During their wanderings the Achilpa always carry it with them and choose the direction they are to take by the direction towards which it bends. This allows them, while being continually on the move, to be always in "their world" and, at the same time, in communication with the sky into which Numbakulla vanished.

For the pole to be broken denotes catastrophe; it is like the "end of the world," reversion to chaos. Spencer and Gillen report that once, when the pole was broken, the entire clan were in consternation; they wandered about aimlessly for a time and finally lay down on the ground and waited for death to overtake them.[1]

In a later publication, after giving a somewhat more adequate summary of the myth, Eliade remarks, "Seldom do we find a more pathetic avowal that man cannot live without a 'sacred center' which permits him to 'cosmicize' space and to communicate with the transhuman world of heaven."[2]

Eliade's interpretation of the Tjilpa myth focuses on the pole as a "sacred axis" that makes territory "habitable" by maintaining contact with the sky, for him, the "transhuman" realm of the sacred, of transcendence. In Eliade's understanding, the pole functions as a type of "sacred center," the point of contact between heaven and earth, a locus of sacrality that "founds" the world for man. It differs from what he believes to be the analogous symbolism of ancient Indian and Near Eastern temples only in that it is portable.[3] By his interpretation, if such a "center" be destroyed, "chaos" ensues. Under such conditions, human life becomes impossible, and death is the result.[4]

I am tempted to use this episode from Tjilpa myth as an emblem for this series of inquiries as well. We shall be concerned with two sacred centers in Jerusalem that provided rich clusters of symbolic meanings: the Temple and the Church

of the Holy Sepulcher. As with the pole, each was destroyed
or lost. For each, there was a triumphant, ideological literature that perceived in their construction a cosmogonic act. For
each, there was a literature of indigenous lamentation (as well
as derisory polemics by outsiders) that found, in the destruction or loss of the sites, a plunge into chaos. Indeed, for one
of the sites, the Temple, the extreme position has sometimes
been held that the religion which cherished the place has
been, since its destruction, as if dead.[5] But this will *not* be the
stance taken in these inquiries; nor, I think, is it the message
to be derived from the Tjilpa myth.

Before turning to a fresh examination of the Tjilpa myth, I
must clear up one important detail in Eliade's account of it. It
is a simple matter of tenses. The English translation of Eliade's
French (which I have quoted), the first French edition, as well
as the German translation (which was, in fact, the original
publication), all agree on a fundamental confusion: The Tjilpa
do not *now* wander with a pole from which they take their direction. Spencer and Gillen were not providing an eyewitness
report of a group of contemporary Tjilpa who lay down and
died when their pole was broken. To credit the facticity of
such an event would be to align religion with a death im-
pulse around a symbolism that would be a Freudian's delight!
Rather, all the events in Eliade's summary: Numbakulla's creation, his withdrawal, the Tjilpa's wanderings, the breaking of
the pole, the corporate death—all occurred within the myths
of the "Dreaming," that is, within the mythical time of the ancestors. We are dealing with story, not history, as is obvious
from any number of narrative details within Eliade's source,
for example, the passage mentioned shortly before the incident of the broken pole, which begins, "Being now very tired,
the men went underground and followed a northerly course."

Eliade belatedly cleared up this confusion in the second
French edition of his work, "Spencer and Gillen report that
once, *according to a myth,* when the pole was broken . . ." as
well as in his more recent account of the text.[6] To repeat: In
understanding the Tjilpa narrative of the broken pole, it is
with the mythic past, with the "Dream time," that we are concerned, and not with the ethnographic present.

In *The Sacred and the Profane,* Eliade paraphrases the Northern Aranda Tjilpa myth in a single paragraph. It is a remark-

able act of compression. The text he condenses takes up thirty-four closely printed pages in his source—itself, a free paraphrase. The narrative was first recorded in 1896 by Baldwin Spencer and Francis James Gillen, well-known pioneers in Australian anthropology. It was published in 1899 and republished, with some alteration, in 1927.[7] Spencer and Gillen are the sole source for the myth.

Eliade's understanding of the myth requires that the creative activities of Numbakulla be seen as the first set of incidents in a continuous myth. The narrative of creation serves as a prologue to the withdrawal of Numbakulla up the sacred pole (in a manner analogous to Eliade's category of otiose high gods), the same pole that is ritually represented in the Tjilpa cult, that is carried about by the Tjilpa ancestors, and that is ultimately broken, resulting in their death. Is this the case? Has Eliade correctly understood the myth as a cycle containing a continuous narrative from primordial creation through a return of chaos? The Spencer and Gillen text, which served as his source, in no way warrants such an interpretation.

First, there is the matter of the figure of Numbakulla himself. Although Numbakulla is treated as a major divine being in Spencer and Gillen's 1927 version of the myth, as "the great outstanding figure in the traditions of the southern, central and northern groups . . . the supreme ancestor, overshadowing all others,"[8] he was not so understood in their earlier version. They showed no signs of even knowing his name in the text printed in 1899, nor did they mention any of the elements of his mythology. In itself, this is not necessarily disturbing, though it should signal the need for caution. Since the pioneering researches of A. W. Howitt, we have been made aware of the Australian aborigine's "secret mythology,"[9] and Spencer does claim to have received new knowledge from a Tjilpa "headman" before producing the later version.[10] But in this case, such a claim is not sufficient to relax the critical reader. Too many problems remain.

Numbakulla is not a proper name, referring to a single divine individual. It is a generic title. It refers to the autochthonous class of "totemic ancestors"—those who "had been born out of their own eternity" (*altkirana nambakala*).[11]

Numbakulla's creative activities, as described in the 1927 version of the myth (for example, his mode of fashioning the

landscape and the Tjilpa ancestors, his ascent up the bloody
pole) are atypical in comparison to other known Aranda
traditions.[12]

The more usual mode of ancestral disappearance is by a return to the earth whence they sprung. "Their bodies either
vanished into the earth . . . or turned into rocks, trees or
tjurunga objects."[13] That is to say, the usual Australian pattern
is not one of celestial withdrawal, but of terrestrial transformation and continued presence. After their period of creative
activity, the ancestors are depicted as sleeping beneath the
ground at a sacred place, the *pmara kutata,* their "everlasting
home."[14] This ancestral mythologem is utterly different from
that associated with the putative Australian "High God" who
is understood to have withdrawn into the sky. Given this, as
we shall see, there would be no need in the narratives of the
Arandan ancestors for a pole to connect sky and earth. Connection with the ancestors is on the terrestrial plane, and it is
forever available; within such a mythology, there is no "celestial rupture" that needs to be overcome.

To return to Numbakulla. The 1927 version of the myth appears to be an awkward hybrid. A common corporate name
for ancestors has been reinterpreted as the proper name of a
single figure who has been given a number of characteristics
more typical of a celestial high god than of an Australian
totemic ancestor.

Such an odd combination raises the possibility of Christian
influence, of a Christianized reinterpretation of Arandan
myth. This supposition is strengthened by the fact that the
putative deity's full title, as given by Spencer and Gillen in
1927, *Injkara Altkira Njambakala,* was an Arandan phrase created by local Christian missionaries to translate the liturgical
acclamation, "Lord God Eternal."[15] The conclusion that the
1927 version of the myth (on which Eliade relied) is an instance of native-Christian syncretism is made more certain by
the fact that the 1899 version of the myth did entirely without
the Numbakulla prologue and gave a more traditional picture
of ancestral times.[16]

Although the pole is broken in both versions, it is only in
the later, hybrid text that there is the interpretative possibility
of connecting that pole with motifs of creation and withdrawal. What, then, of the sacred pole?

It would carry us far from our theme to undertake a detailed discussion of sacred poles among the various Aranda groups. Suffice it to say that the poles take many forms, under a diversity of names, and that they play important roles in both the myths and the rituals.[17] Our concern is with one particular pole—the *kauaua* broken in ancestral times in the Tjilpa myth as paraphrased by Eliade.

In his interpretation, Eliade focuses on nine elements in the Tjilpa myth.

1. The pole was fashioned by Numbakulla from a gum tree.
2. After anointing the pole with blood, Numbakulla climbed up the pole and disappeared into the sky.
3. The pole is a "cosmic axis."
4. Following Numbakulla's withdrawal, the pole plays a ritual role.
5. The pole is always carried about by the ancestors in their wanderings.
6. The ancestors determine the direction in which they travel by the direction toward which the pole bends.
7. The pole is broken by accident.
8. The ancestors die because the pole has broken.
9. This is because the breaking of the pole is like "the end of the world."

Is Eliade correct? Only one element (item 7) can be verified without ambiguity in Spencer and Gillen's text—the pole was broken by accident. None of the other items can be accepted as Eliade has proposed them. Three must be rejected entirely (items 3, 6, and 9); they do not occur in the text. Five must be subjected to revision (items 1, 2, 4, 5, and 8); Eliade has misread the text.[19] If this assessment of Eliade's interpretation of the text is correct, an alternative understanding of the myth must be proposed.

To do so, the incidents of the broken pole and the subsequent death of a group of Tjilpa ancestors must be set within their narrative frame. Putting aside the misleading and extraneous prologue of the myth of Numbakulla and his ascent up the pole, we find the mythical events in their context as the seventy-eighth and seventy-ninth incidents in a long and complex Tjilpa ancestral narrative constituting a series of ninety-four incidents in the Spencer-Gillen text.

The form of the ancestral narrative is one that is widely distributed in Australia. It is an itinerary: the ancestors journeyed from this place to that; something happened; for this reason, the place is called "so and so"; a feature in the present topography either was formed by or memorializes this event; the ancestors moved on to another place.[20] In its simplest form, this pattern may be illustrated by two incidents from the Tjilpa narrative cycle.

> The Tjilpa ancestors crossed the Mount Sonder Range. While doing so they saw an old Bandicoot man making large wooden *pitchis* [wooden troughs], and therefore they called the place Uritchimpa, which means "the place of the *pitchis*."[21]
>
> Then they [the ancestors] went on to Ulirulira which means "the place where blood flowed like a creek" . . . . The young men opened veins in their arms and gave draughts of blood to the old men who were very tired. Ever afterwards the water at this spot was tainted with a reddish color; indeed it is so at the present day.[22]

A number of the incidents exhibit a more complex form. The Tjilpa ancestors come to a place. They meet an individual or another group that has a sacred pole and/or other sacred objects. (Indeed, the lack of a pole is thought worthy of notice.)[23] These objects are shown to the Tjilpa. Some mode of social interaction transpires between the wandering Tjilpa and the indigenous inhabitants—most usually a ceremony, but sometimes acts of violence or sexual intercourse. The Tjilpa ancestors then move on. At Poara, for example, the Tjilpa perform two ceremonies and meet several women from another goup. The women have a sacred pole (*tnatantja*) and own several ceremonies which they show the Tjilpa. The Tjilpa men have intercourse with them and continue on their way.[24] At Alpirakircha, the Tjilpa ancestors meet an old Tjilpa man who has a large *tnatantja*. Both the wandering and the indigenous Tjilpa men perform two ceremonies before the former resume their journey.[25]

This common Australian pattern is highly developed among the Tjilpa, who have complex cycles of ancestral wanderings of a variety of "Tjilpa hordes" among a diversity of groups.[26]

I have reviewed these well-known features of Australian ancestral mythology as they relate to the Tjilpa legends in

order to set the incidents of the broken pole and the ancestors' death within a context. The incidents take place within a
narrative cycle that consists of a set of isolated events, connected only by itinerary—"they came," "they camped," "they
went"—each elaborated to a greater or lesser degree depending on the narrator and the "ownership" of the traditions
being described.[27] Within the series, the incidents of the broken pole and the ancestors' death appear as typical narrative
units. They are not extraordinary, highly dramatic events to be
lifted out and focused upon as having special cosmic significance. They are commonplace happenings within the myths
of ancestral times. Furthermore, the breaking of the pole and
the death of the ancestors are the last incidents in the cycle of
events that make up the narrative of the third Tjilpa ancestral
band. The narrative of *each* band in the Spencer-Gillen text
characteristically ends with either the death of the ancestors
or the band being split into two groups that continue to journey their separate ways. Even on the level of narrative and
plot, as the final events of a subcycle, the two incidents appear typical and unremarkable.

Having observed this much by way of general orientation,
we may turn to the text as given in Spencer and Gillen, recognizing that their version appears to be a glossed paraphrase
rather than a transcription of an oral narrative.

[INCIDENT 78] At a place called Okinyumpa an accident
befell them which made them all feel very sad; as they
were pulling up the *Kauaua*, which was very deeply
implanted, the old *Oknirrabata* [a wise elder], who
was leading them, broke it off just above the ground;
and to this present day a tall stone standing up above
the ground at this spot represents the broken, and
still implanted, end of the pole.

[INCIDENT 79] Carrying on the broken *Kauaua* they came
to Unjiacherta [sc. N'tjuiatja:tua] which means "the
place of the Unjiamba [sc. Ntjuiamba, or honeysuckle-
totem] men" and lies near to the Hanson Creek. They
arrived here utterly tired out, and found a number of
Unjiamba men and women of all classes. They were
too tired and sad to paint themselves, their *Kauaua* in

its broken state was inferior to many of those which the Unjiamba people had, so they did not erect it, but, lying down together, died where they lay. A large hill, covered with big stones, arose to mark the spot. Their Churinga, each with its associated spirit individual, remained behind. Many of them are very large and long and are now in the *Pertalchera* [sc. *pmara kutata*, or the "everlasting home" of the *tjurunga*] or storehouse at Unjiacherta.[28]

As is typical, the two incidents are marked by movement from one camp to another—from Okinyumpa to N'tjuiatja: tua in the Hanson River region, a distance, on a present-day map, of some ten miles. There is an implied causal relationship between the two incidents, but not that posited by Eliade. The ancestors do not die because their pole was broken. They are embarrassed because the broken portion of their pole is no longer as splendid as the many poles of their hosts, and they are "utterly tired out." This latter motif, that of being "tired," is a frequent cause of ancestral death, in this narrative cycle and in others.[29]

By focusing on the false causal relationship—from broken pole to corporate death—Eliade has missed the actual structure of the narrative. Each incident has two parts (again, typical of ancestral narratives): event and memorial. In incident 78:

[EVENT] The pole is broken.
[MEMORIAL] "And to this present day a tall stone standing up above the ground at this spot represents the broken, and still implanted, end of the pole."

In incident 79:

[EVENT] The Tjilpa ancestors die.
[MEMORIAL] "A large hill, covered with big stones, arose to mark the spot." Furthermore, their *tjurunga* "remained" behind and are "now" in their "storehouses," accessible at ceremonial occasions.

In Eliade's abridgment, there are no memorials; there are only events. The pole is broken; the ancestors die.[30]

When the pole was broken, the entire clan were in consternation; they wandered about aimlessly for a time
[note: this is not in the Spencer-Gillen text] and finally
lay down on the ground and waited for death to overtake them.

By dissevering the double structure of event/memorial, Eliade
has missed the generative element in the myth. It is, above all,
an etiology for a topographical feature in the aboriginal landscape of today. It is the memorial that has priority.

Although there are other elements in the myth that may
well be employed to increase our understanding of these two
brief narratives,[31] for our purposes, the pattern of event/
memorial is paramount. It will allow us to juxtapose two quite
different understandings of the Tjilpa myth and, by extension, two quite different ways of conceiving of place within
the study of religion.

By homologizing the *kauaua* of the Tjilpa ancestral band
with that of Nambakulla, by emphasizing the "rupture" between the world above and the world below brought about
by the breaking of the pole, Eliade has placed the Northern
Aranda tradition within a celestial and transcendental context, within the framework of his universal symbolism of the
"Center." Within such a frame of reference, place is established by its connection with cosmogony and by its "opening
toward a world which is superhuman" and remote. In Eliade's
understanding of the Tjilpa pole, the *kauaua* permits the Tjilpa
to "cosmicize space and to communicate with the transhuman
world of heaven."[32] For this reason, he insists, to break the
pole is to "end the world."

I do not doubt that such understandings of place can be
found within the history of religions, and that there are traditions in which poles (or world-trees, or mountains) sometimes play such connecting roles; but they are not present in
the Tjilpa myth. The horizon of the Tjilpa myth is not celestial, it is relentlessly terrestrial and chthonic. The emphasis is
not on the dramatic creation of the world out of chaos by transcendent figures, or on the "rupture" between these figures
and men. Rather, the emphasis is on transformation and continuity, on a world fashioned by ancestral wanderings across
the featureless, primeval surface of the earth.[33]

In the ancestral "Dream time," when the ancestors emerged from their "sleep" beneath the surface of the earth, their activities transformed the primeval earth into its present topography. Every feature of the contemporary landscape represents a "track," a deed, a work, of these ancestors. Likewise, when the ancestors died, they returned to "sleep" under the earth, leaving behind the marks of their places of departure. In the majority of the ancestral myths, the ancestors are, themselves, transformed into rocks, trees, or *tjurunga* objects as well as into the "stuff" of the individual tribespeople. Each feature of the landscape, as well as each living Tjilpa, is an objectification of these ancestors and their deeds.[34] Géza Róheim caught the point with precision when he wrote:

> Looking at the kernel of these frequently tedious [ancestral] narratives we are struck by one feature: in all of them *environment is made out of man's activity.* . . . This is a man-made world. Environment is regarded as if it were derived from human beings.[35]

It is anthropology, not cosmology, that is to the fore. It is the ancestral/human alteration of and objectification in the landscape that has transformed the undifferentiated primeval space during the Dream-time into a multitude of historical places in which the ancestors, though changed, remain accessible. This is expressed in the myths. It is expressed as well in the extreme localization of the Aranda *njinanga* sectional organization, with its demarcated structures of homeland and birthplace.[36]

In a recent, important study of the notion of ancestral transformation among the neighboring Walbiri and Pitjantjatjara tribes, Nancy Munn has provided a precise typology of such transformations, as well as a trenchant statement of their significance:

> Three types of transformations are prominent . . . (1) metamorphosis (the body of the ancestor is changed into some material object); (2) imprinting (the ancestor leaves the impression of his body or some tool he uses); (3) externalization (the ancestor takes some object out of his body). Of the three, externalization is more specialized . . . [and] the first two are most common. . . . The Ab-

origines relate the ancestor to his transformations either
by referring to the process of transformation itself (e.g.
A becomes *B*) or to the state of identification which results (e.g. *A* and *B* are "the same thing"). The identification expresses the permanence of the incorporation of
the ancestor or subject in the object; the processual
statements [that is, the transformations] express the primary grounding of these permanent properties in a dy-
namic relationship between subject and object, sentient
being and c :ternal object world.[37]

In discussing the Aranda traditions concerning their ancestors, I have used three terms to express the relationship between the ancestors and present-day life and land: "memorial," "transformation," and "objectification." Although there
is some debate in the scholarly literature concerning their relative adequacy, I do not intend to choose among them.[38] Each
captures an aspect of the contribution the Tjilpa myth might
make to an initial reconnaissance of our theme. For we have
learned, from the Tjilpa narratives, that loss does not necessarily represent a "rupture," a "fall," a plunge into the "chaos"
of "nonbeing." Instead, loss can provide the beginning for a
complex process of modulation and change in that which was,
but is no longer, and yet remains present. The transformation
of the ancestor is an event that bars, forever, direct access to
his particular person. Yet through this very process of change,
through being displaced from his "self" and being emplaced
in an "other"—an object, a person, or a mark—the ancestor
achieves permanence. He remains forever accessible.

Furthermore, there is in this network of ancestral presence
and transformation no economy, no condensation. In principle, the only limitations on the number of "places" of ancestral objectification are the attention and memory of the
Aranda, the ability of men of the proper group who are related to the specific ancestor to be attentive, to recall the ancestral deeds and experience the ancestor's continued presence. As Strehlow reports:

> The body of the Ulamba ancestor is shown at many
> points of the route which he once travelled: the main
> peak of Ulamba, the rock from which he sprang into life,
> the sharp hill near the mountain pass south of Ulamba,

the great boulder which forms the lower portion of the
Ulamba sacred cave, and many other rocks elsewhere,
are, each one individually, stated to be "the body of the
Ulamba ancestor." In addition, there is a *tjurunga* in the
cave, which represents the ancestor: indeed, there could
have been several *tjurunga* of him at Ulamba and others
in different storehouses, and the native still would not
have been troubled for even a moment by their number. . . . For the Northern Aranda native (and indeed all
Aranda natives) believes in the simultaneous presence
of the ancestor at each of the many scenes which once
witnessed the fulness of his supernatural powers. . . .
Today . . . [the ancestors] are present wherever men of
the . . . [appropriate] group may happen to perform ceremonies in their memory. . . . The Northern native believes in the presences of his revered and dreaded ancestor wherever and whenever ceremonies are being
given in his honor and his remembrance.[39]

The central ritual connection between the ancestor and his
"place," between the ancestor and the individual Aranda, the
central mode of celebrating and signifying objectification, is
not dramatization, but recollection. In the words of Gurra,
one of Strehlow's most important informants, "My elders kept
on repeating these ceremonies time and time again in my
presence: they were afraid that I might forget them. . . Had I
forgotten them, no one else would now remember them."[40] In
such a system, rupture does not occur by breaking poles link-
ing heaven to earth; rupture occurs through the human act of
forgetfulness.[41]

II

In the first portion of this inquiry, I sought to provide an alternative understanding of a particular text interpreted by Eliade
in a characteristic manner by rereading the same sources on
which he depends. But the issues cut deeper than a difference
between us over how to read Spencer and Gillen's account of
the Tjilpa and their pole. What is at stake, finally, is a question
of the comparative enterprise itself.

It is axiomatic that comparison is never a matter of identity. Comparison requires the acceptance of difference as the grounds of its being interesting, and a methodical manipulation of that difference to achieve some stated cognitive end. The questions of comparison are questions of judgment with respect to difference: What differences are to be maintained in the interests of comparative inquiry? What differences can be defensibly relaxed and relativized in light of the intellectual tasks at hand?

In the particular example under discussion, we can infer a set of decisions Eliade has made. He has chosen here, as elsewhere in his work, to read the Tjilpa texts in terms of a pattern largely developed from ancient Near Eastern and Indic materials—a temple pattern that focuses on cosmogony and its replication in the symbolism of the "Center." In a variety of his works, Eliade has summarized this symbolism as "expressing itself in three connected and interrelated" notions:

1. the "sacred mountain," where heaven and earth meet, stands at the center of the world;
2. every temple or palace, and, by extension, every sacred town and royal residence, is assimilated to a "sacred mountain" and thus becomes a "center";
3. the temple or sacred city, in turn, as the place through which the Axis Mundi passes, is held to be the point of junction between heaven, earth, and hell.[42]

It is in the context of his attempt to establish the pattern of the "Center" as a primary mode of human symbolism that the Tjilpa and their pole take on crucial, evidentiary significance for Eliade. He admits that the pattern is most prevalent and best developed among "all the Oriental civilizations—Mesopotamia, India, China, etc.,"[43] and through his investigations of shamanism, he has claimed to find elements of the same pattern in the tertiary, nomadic, hunting, and pastoral cultures of the Americas, northern and central Asia, and Africa.[44] But in both his earliest and latest discussions of the topic, the Tjilpa and their pole remain the *sole* example for the presence of the pattern of the "Center" among truly "primitive" peoples.[45]

Common sense would suggest that there are distinctions and differences here that cannot be so readily relaxed. At the very least, we would expect some principles of translation to be announced. The symbolism of the "Center" is, above all, a complex ideology of building—a matter of temples, palaces, and the like. In this sense, the Tjilpa do not build. The Tjilpa have been characterized as "pure nomad(s)" who occupy "a lean-to shelter of shrubs so placed as to shield the occupants from the prevailing wind."[46] They have no built shrines. For the Tjilpa, there are sacred topographical features that form a map of the "totemic landscape."[47] The *tjurunga*, and other sacred objects, are hidden in natural crevasses in rocks, in caves, or in hollow trees.[48] In less mountainous regions, they are hidden in brush platforms in the forks of trees.[49]

The literature on the Australian "aborigines" has often used this fact to establish their "primitivity," whether in a derisory sense or to establish their scientific value as "contemporary Stone Age" peoples. Thus, an early report from 1699 declared the Australians to be:

> the most miserable people in the world. Hodmadods [that is, "Hottentots"] though nasty people . . . are Gentlemen [compared] to these [Australian natives]: who have no houses and skin garments, Sheep, Poultry, Fruits, etc. . . . They differ little from brutes.[50]

Spencer and Gillen introduce their work with the claim that "it has been possible to study in Australia human beings that still remain on the culture level of men of the Stone Age."[51] Neither of these sorts of conclusions is true, but the fact remains: the Tjilpa do not build constructions of the sort implied by the symbolism of the "Center." This is a significant difference, one that cannot be relativized in a casual fashion.

The crucial elements in Eliade's symbolism of the "Center"—the cosmological world-mountain where heaven, earth, and underworld are linked, and the replication of this pattern in human acts of construction, in temples and palaces—he largely borrowed from the so-called Pan-Babylonian School.[52] These authors developed this pattern on the basis of their reading of the then newly deciphered Babylonian and Akkadian texts, and they insisted on a radical difference between their view of ancient Near Eastern ideology and the "primitive world view" as reconstructed by anthropologists.[53] Eliade has consistently collapsed this difference.

In light of the nearly hundred years' progress since the

Pan-Babylonians in understanding and interpreting the literature of the ancient Near East, we may fairly ask: Does the pattern hold? Did they correctly represent ancient Near Eastern
ideology? Only then can we inquire whether it is legitimate to
ignore their insistence on difference, whether it is possible to
apply their pattern to "primitive" materials as well.

Without laboring the point, a blunt answer to our question
must be negative. There is no pattern of the "Center" in the
sense that the Pan-Babylonians and Eliade described it in
the ancient Near Eastern materials. The generating notion of
the pattern is that of the world-mountain; it is this cosmogonic
element upon which everything else depends. The most recent study of this theme asserts, without equivocation:

> The term "cosmic mountain," as it has been used in the
> study of Ancient Near Eastern religion, has been based
> in large measure on an assumed Mesopotamian *Welt-
> berg*. . . . The *Weltberg*, as it has been understood by an
> earlier generation of scholars, does not exist.[54]

The philological evidence the Pan-Babylonians relied on has
all but evaporated. Not one of the terms, understood by them
to refer to a central mountain with its roots in the underworld
and its summit in the heavens, has survived scrutiny.[55]

The effect of this reevaluation cannot be minimized. If
there is no evidence in ancient Near Eastern materials for a
central cosmic mountain that served as an *axis mundi*, there
can be no assimilation of such a mountain to the temple, as
Eliade's pattern requires. This calls into question the notion of
the temple as the "Center" of the cosmos.

The particular temple title on which Eliade builds his case,
Dur-an-ki, which he renders, "the bond of heaven and earth,"
is a particularly unfortunate choice. The Babylonian term
means the opposite of what he suggests. It does not refer to a
link between heaven and earth, but rather to the scar left
when they were separated by the king-god. As with the human navel, so with the temple. The *Dur-an-ki* marks the place
of permanent disassociation, rather than of conjunction and
access between the celestial and terrestrial realms.[56]

This is not to argue that there are not ideological statements and titles, particularly in societies that have been labeled examples of "oriental despotism," that claim the status of "center" for various temples, palaces, and capitals. It is to insist, only, that such titles may not be easily or universally homologized to world-mountains, as Eliade's model requires. The language of "center" is preeminently political and only secondarily cosmological. It is a vocabulary that stems, primarily, from archaic ideologies of kingship and the royal function. In any particular tradition, it may or may not be tied to cosmological and cosmogonic myths.

We are left with what appears to be a wholly negative set of results. In the first part of this chapter, we have seen that the Tjilpa and their pole may not be interpreted, as an example of Eliade's pattern of the "Center." In this second part, we have seen that a reconsideration of the ancient Near Eastern materials from which the pattern of the "Center" was first generated will not support such an understanding. Without examining each and every instance, it cannot be claimed that the pattern of the "Center" is a fantasy, but it is clearly far from a universal (or even dominant) pattern of symbolization. At the very least, the burden of proof has shifted to those who will claim that a particular cultural construction represents a "Center." The "Center" is not a secure pattern to which data may be brought as illustrative; it is a dubious notion that will have to be established anew on the basis of detailed comparative endeavors. Nevertheless, the difference with which we began this second moment of our inquiry remains. The Tjilpa do not build; Mesopotamia did. Indeed, it is tempting to suggest that Mesopotamian religion was built on building.

The ancient Near Eastern temple (which, we must recall, was nowhere marked by a special word, but rather was denoted by a generic noun meaning "house") was not only a center of political and economic power. It was, as well, the focus of a complex set of notions related to the view of creation as an activity, as a building on or reshaping of a previous order. This, in itself, invites initial comparison with the Australian traditions as represented by the Tjilpa.

As we have seen, the Tjilpa conceive of the world as a landscape whose distinctive features were formed by ancestral activity. I have already cited Róheim's remark that, for the Australians, the world was a "man-made world" and summarized the mythology. Let me repeat its essential details:

> At the beginning of time the earth had looked like a featureless, desolate plain. No mountain ranges, sand-hills, swamps or river courses existed on its barren sur-face. . . . Only below the surface of the earth did life already exist in its fulness, in the form of thousands of uncreated supernatural beings that had always existed; but even these were still slumbering in eternal sleep. Time began when these supernatural beings [ancestors] awakened from their sleep. They broke through to the surface of the earth; and their "birthplaces" became the first sites on the earth to be impregnated with their life and power. . . . After emerging from their eternal slum-bering places, these supernatural beings . . . moved about on the surface of the earth. Their actions and their wanderings brought into being all the physical features of the Central Australian landscape. Mountains, sand-hills, swamps, plains, springs, and soakages, all arose to mark the deeds of the roving totemic ancestors and an-cestresses. In the scores of thousands of square miles that constitute the Aranda-speaking area there was not a single striking physical feature which was not associated with an episode [of ancestral activity] in one of the many sacred myths.[57]

What does activity mean in such a context? It is clearly more a matter of marking than of making, of memorializing than of constructing. It is not a language of edifices, but of "tracks," "paths," "traces," "marks," and "prints."[58] A topographic fea-ture was not deliberately constructed by the ancestors. In most cases, it appears as a sort of accidental by-product of their journeys. The feature records, permanently, the transi-tory act of their passing-through in a manner similar to a photograph of the movement of charged particles in a cloud chamber—a solemn and important graffito, "Kilroy was here." By contrast, the ancient Near Eastern materials seem relent-lessly intentional and constructivist. A few examples will suf-fice to establish the difference.

The state of the cosmos prior to the king-god's creative ac-tivity, narrated with the formulaic, "When there was not yet

. . . ,"[59] can be described in terms of a lack of buildings; be
they houses, temples, or cities.

> *A holy house, a house of the gods in a holy place, had not*
> *been made;*
> *A reed had not come forth, a tree had not been created;*
> *A brick had not been laid, a brick mould had not been built;*
> *A house had not been made, a city had not been built*
>
> .   .   .   .
>
> *Nippur had not been made, Ekur had not been built;*
> *Uruk had not been made, Eanna had not been built;*
> *The* Apsu *had not been made, Eridu had not been built;*
> *A holy house, a house of the gods, its dwelling, had not been*
> *made.*[60]

Each of the subsequent creative acts in the text is a verb of
building: Marduk "made," "built," "constructed," "laid foundations," "poured [dirt]," "piled up a dam," and "laid brick."

This particular cosmogonic text was part of a ritual for the
purification of a temple (Ezida at Borsippa). Similar building
cosmogonies appear in other texts associated with the repair
or restoration of temples.[61]

In a more complex and extended form, *Enuma elish,* the
best known cosmogonic text from the ancient Near East, is
dominated by building. Indeed, in many respects, it is improper to term this text a cosmogony. It is, essentially, a
narrative of the creation of the holy city of Babylon and the
construction of its central shrine, Esagila.[62] Here, there is language of "center," but in a quite specific political sense.

In *Enuma elish,* only the first generation of the gods do not
build, they procreate the second generation of deities and the
distinctive features of the cosmos. The king-god of the second
generation, Ea, marks his kingship by constructing. On the
body of his vanquished father, Apsu (the primordial sweet
water), "he establishes his dwelling," his "cult hut"—also
called Apsu (1.71–77). This same action is elaborately repeated by the king-god from the third generation, Ea's son,
conceived in the Apsu, the powerful Marduk.

We have known the bulk of *Enuma elish* since 1876, but for
most of that time we have known only the world-construction

activities of Marduk as narrated in the fourth tablet and severely damaged fifth tablet of the series (only twenty-six lines
were recovered). In those texts, Marduk, the newly appointed
king-god, after defeating his grandmother Tiamat, refashioned
the cosmos by splitting her body in half. "Half of her he set in
place and formed the sky as a roof," measuring it to be equal to
Ea's building, the Apsu (4.140–46). He then established the celestial bodies as the "stations" of the gods (5.1–22).

In 1961, the missing lines of the fifth tablet were published
for the first time (lines 23–156).[63] They have caused a thorough reevaluation of the text. Thirteen lines are devoted to
Marduk's fashioning of the earth (5.52–65); twenty-three lines
tell of gift-giving among Marduk and the other gods (5.66–
89); thirty-two lines tell of Marduk's enthronement (5.85–117),
ending with the gods declaring, "whatever you command we
will do." Marduk's response is a complex act of construction.
He will build Babylon, "the homes of the great gods," the
"counterpart" (*mi-ih-rit*) of the heavens, halfway between the
heavens and the Apsu. It will be a "resting place" for the gods
when they descend from the assembly on high to their home
in the Absu below. But it will also be Marduk's house and
his capital. He will "build it with the craftsmanship [of the
mas]ters" (5.119–30).

In the sixth tablet, this complex ideological language of enthronement, building, and counterparts is continued. After
creating man (primarily as the temple-servant of the gods),
Marduk orders as a "homage" and "throne room" the construction of the central shrine of Esagila. It is to be a building
"like the building of lofty (?) Babylon," and made of bricks.

> For one whole year they (the gods) molded bricks,
> And when the second year arrived,
> They raised on high the top of Esagila, the counterpart [mehret]
> of Apsu. . . .
> For Marduk, Enlil and Ea, they established his temple as a
> dwelling. (6.60–64)[64]

And a divine banquet is held to establish his installation.

Other instances might be brought to bear to illustrate these
themes: that regardless of the context (cosmic or historic)
temple and temple building are less connected with cos-

mogony than they are with kingship.[65] (For a further example, one need think only of the complex, second millen-
nium cylinder inscriptions of Gudea of Lagash.)[66] But these
are sufficient to establish the point of difference, the radically
disparate horizons, between the traditions of the Tjilpa and
those of the ancient Near East.

I know of only one work that systematically and explicitly
reflects on this difference, an article by the geographer Erich
Isaac.[67] He attempts to classify religions according to a "polarity between religions which tend to extreme landscape transformations and those which tend to minimal transformations." Unfortunately, he grounds the distinction in a murky
and overly theological differentiation, one that owes not a
little to disreputable biblical apologetics, arguing that those
religions which transform the landscape are "religions that
conceive of the process of world creation as providing the
meaning of human existence," whereas those which are characterized by little landscape transformation "are religions
which conceive the meaning of human existence to derive . . .
from a divine charter granted to them, e.g. the beginning of
hunting or cultivation, the Crucifixion, Israel's covenant." His
subsequent comparison of the Shona-Budja of Southern Rho-
desia and the ancient Mesopotamians does little to clarify the
distinction, even if I were persuaded by his ethnography.[68]
The issue for comparison is one of avoiding all such simple
dualisms.

For example, in the materials under discussion, we need to
note a range of taxonomic possibilities. While, unlike Martin
Heidegger, whose lecture on building remains a philosophic
classic,[69] I place no probative confidence in the revelatory
power of hypothetical etymological roots, it would be possible, in principle, to locate any particular building ideology
along a continuum from the sphere of "nature"[70] to that of
"culture." In terms of vocabulary, one might associate the former pole with the word *building* itself, containing, as it does,
the root metaphor of organic growth;[71] and the latter pole with
the word *construction*, enshrining the notion of an intentional,
artificial activity.[72] All other terms might be ranked along such
a continuum, while recognizing that most Indo-European
terms for building are relentlessly social. Thus, the Latin *aedēs*
(English *edifice*), with its notion of fire, hearth, and home,

would stand at the division between the natural and the social;[73] the Greek *oikos*, with its sense of family and clan, would
be clustered at the far end of the social spectrum.[74]

Following such a clustering, the traditional Indian temple,
ideologically considered in some traditions to have "grown"
from a "seed,"[75] would be associated with the organic end of
the continuum, whereas the Near Eastern temple would be
associated with its opposite, constructivist end. For purposes
of comparison, this distinction might suggest that the Indic
and Near Eastern temples may not be easily joined together
(as Eliade's pattern of the "Center" requires), but that the
Aranda notion of ancestral spots (even though lacking building) might be fruitfully juxtaposed to the Indian temple.

Alternatively, we might seek to classify and compare differences with respect to place. In the Arandan traditions, it is
clear that all significant places are the result of ancestral activity. Although each place might, in the myths, be the accidental by-product of their wanderings, once marked, each
place is precisely where the event occurred—it cannot be another. The specificity of place is what is remembered, is what
gives rise to and is perpetuated in memorial.

Here again, there is a remote parallel to the Indic and a
sharp contrast to the Near Eastern. Although there are a multitude of temple places in India, each, in some theories, is
built over a portion of the fallen and dismembered body of a
deity.[76] That is to say, while the distribution of the pieces (the
locales) might *once* have been accidental, a given temple can
now have been built only on such and such a place (as determined by, among other things, rituals of divination).

In the Near East, whether temple building be by gods or by
kings, one gets a much greater sense of the arbitrariness of
place. A temple is built where it happens to have been built.
A temple is built at a central place, the place where a king or
god *happens* to have decided to take up residence. Perhaps
this is because temple here is always a royal function, and the
power of kingship is such that it constitutes a place as central
sheerly by being *there*. As one late omen interpreter reminds
Assurbanipal:

> If an eclipse occurs, but it is not observed in the capital,
> such an eclipse is considered not to have occurred. "The

capital" means the city in which the king happens to be staying.[77]

Clearly, as we move closer to a consideration of a major Near Eastern temple—that in Jerusalem—we must gain a better and broader understanding of such a notion of place and its relationship to royalty. To that end, the second and third chapters are dedicated.

TWO

FATHER PLACE

Place is the beginning of our existence, just as a father.

Roger Bacon

I

In 1937, at the age of eighty-one, Sigmund Freud, addressed an open letter to his younger friend Romain Rolland on the occasion of Rolland's seventieth birthday. Entitled "A Disturbance of Memory on the Acropolis," it is an ingenious meditation on an experience Freud had in 1904 when he first stood, with his brother, on the Acropolis in Athens. For our purposes, we may set aside Freud's particular interpretative schema—his notions of guilt, ego defense, "derealization," and the like—and focus only on his one-sentence description of the experience.

24

When, finally, on the after-
noon of our arrival, I stood on the Acropolis and cast my
eyes around on the landscape, a remarkable thought
suddenly entered my mind: "So all this really *does* exist,
just as we learnt at school!"[1]

Compressed within this little anecdote are themes that will
preoccupy us in the pages to come: place, memory, and myth,
as well as processes of confirmation and disconfirmation.

Freud's text is deceptively simple, as is memory itself. It is
probably deceptive as well. It is a reminiscence in 1937 by an
old man in Vienna of an experience he had in Athens at the
age of forty-eight, juxtaposed to his recollection of what
he learned as a teen in Vienna's Sperlgymnasium. Freud
got some of the chronological details of his Athen's journey
wrong,[2] and the landscape of the Acropolis could not have ac-
corded with what he had learned at school. Between 1873,
when Freud left the Gymnasium, and 1904, when he first visited Athens, the Acropolis underwent the series of major excavations (begun in 1885) that thoroughly altered its topography.[3] At best, Freud carried with him a mental pastiche of
literary accounts that held as simultaneous a number of incongruous elements, a "condensation," a "palimpsest," rather
like his later thought experiment with Rome:

> Now let us make the fantastic supposition that Rome
> were not a human dwelling place, but a mental entity
> with just as long and varied a past history: that is, in
> which nothing once constructed had perished, and all
> the earlier stages of development had survived alongside
> the latest.[4]

Or, like the spatiotemporal juxtaposition in Jensen's novella,
Gradiva: A Pompeiian Fancy, which Freud later analyzed.[5]

So it is with memory: it is a complex and deceptive experience. It appears to be preeminently a matter of the past, yet it
is as much an affair of the present. It appears to be preeminently a matter of time, yet it is as much an affair of space.

For more than two thousand years, philosophers in the
West, working primarily within the limits of a re-presentative

theory of memory, have wrestled with the dilemma first posed
clearly by Aristotle. If memory of a past experience is, through
the processes of memory, experienced only in the present,
how can that present memory be an awareness of the past?
How does memory differ from perception on the one hand
and fantasy on the other?[6] The classical solution to this co-
nundrum often gave rise to a second, the insistence that memory was a sort of mental place (as, for example, in John Locke's
"storehouse" metaphor).[7] But, rather than offering an escape,
this immediately landed the philosopher back in the former
difficulty. As Thomas Reid, among others, was to ask: How
does the ability to "revive" a stored memory differ from a
fresh and present impression?[8]

Despite a number of gallant attempts, one must conclude
that the re-presentative theory of memory is fatally flawed
(though it remains a central assumption of most students of
religion in treating such topics as myth and ritual). It must
further be observed that no subsequent proposal as to memory has enjoyed wide consensus.

Nevertheless, the postulation of an intimate connection between memory and place is intriguing, and offers an initial
point of entry for our inquiries. The connection is enshrined
in those handbooks of mnemotechnics, so carefully studied
by Frances Yates and others, that constituted a major mode of
Western intellectual discourse and transmission from the an-
cients through the seventeenth century.[9] It is recalled as well
in our use of such cognitive terms as *locus, topic,* and *commonplace* and in such phrases as "I can't place it" to refer to lapses
of memory.

In each of these examples, the notion appears the same.
Space is conceived as being already existent, as being divided
up into empty loci into which the images by which memories
would be recalled are placed. The loci are thought both to
preexist and to survive the memories (the point of the oft-
repeated analogy to a wax tablet). But what if matters be reversed? What if space were not the recipient but rather the
creation of the human project? What if place were an active
product of intellection rather than its passive receptacle?

In the history of Western philosophy, this understanding of
space is associated with the towering figure of Immanuel

Kant—already in his inaugural dissertation *De mundi sensibilis atque intelligibilis forma et principiis* (1770); most familiarly, in the striking conclusion to the first section on space in the "Transcendental Aesthetic," which stands at the head of the *Critique of Pure Reason:* "It is, therefore, solely from a human standpoint that we can speak of space." [10]

Kant was concerned with spatial matters not merely as an aspect of epistemology, or solely as an attempt to mediate the debate between Newton and Leibniz over "absolute space," [11] but as a reflection of other interests as well. For Kant was not only one of the most significant philosophers of all time, he was a major figure in the history of geography was well. [12]

Kant introduced the study of geography into the curriculum of the University of Königsberg in 1756 and offered a course on geography forty-eight times during the subsequent forty years. Indeed, "he lectured more often only on logic and metaphysics." [13] It is not so much his general geographical theories that concern us, but his work on a particular topic that will prove important to later theories of space conceived by both social anthropologists and students of religion: the topic of orientation, [14] or how we "place" ourselves.

The text I have in mind is one of Kant's so-called precritical essays, his 1768 paper "On the First Ground of the Distinction of Regions in Space." [15] Kant sets out to demonstrate the claim that "the positions of the parts of space in relation to one another" presuppose "universal" or "absolute" space. [16] The essay falls far short of achieving this proposition; indeed, it is exceedingly flawed. [17] But a portion of his endeavor remains useful for our purposes. Kant begins by making a set of what he terms "preparatory observations," [18] the first of which is of most direct interest. Here, Kant argues that orientation is always in relation to our bodies. Maps, charts, or cardinal directions are useless unless they be oriented with respect to the individual's body, especially to the left and right sides and hands.

> Our geographical knowledge, and even our commonest knowledge of the position of places, would be of no aid to us if we could not, by reference to the sides of our bodies, assign to regions the things so ordered and the whole system of mutually relative positions. [19]

It is the relationship to the human body, and our experience of it, that orients us in space, that confers meaning to place.[20] Human beings are not placed, they bring place into being.

It is at this point that we ought to turn to our colleagues in geography who deserve to have their say. After all, in the economy of the academy's disciplinary labor, they are the ones charged with understanding place. In the words of the Committee on Geography of the National Academy of Sciences, "The modern science of geography derives its substance from man's sense of place."[21] How is that sense understood by contemporary theorists of geography?

For this sense, we must turn to the so-called humanistic geographers[22] rather than to those more econometrically inclined geographers who have created such important notions as "central place" and "locational analysis," which presume a rational and efficient distribution of places for largely economic reasons.[23] In sharp contrast, the humanistic geographers have insisted that "to interpret the meaning of places . . . is to interpret the subjective meaning of persons."[24]

It has been the persistent claim of the humanistic geographers that place is best understood as a locus of meaning. Allow me to summarize the conclusion of one such geographer, Yi-Fu Tuan, as a point of entry into a consideration of this claim.

> Space is more abstract than place. What begins as undifferentiated space becomes place as we get to know it better and endow it with value. . . . If we think of space as that which allows movement, then place is pause; each pause in movement makes it possible for location to be transformed into place.[25]

Tuan defines place, broadly, as "a focus of value" and of "intimacy."[26] "When space feels thoroughly familiar to us, it has become place."[27] Thus, "abstract space, lacking significance other than strangeness, becomes concrete place [only when it is] filled with meaning."[28]

Given this sort of definition, it is no surprise that much of the value-laden, intimate, and meaningful experience of place has been derived by these geographers from reflection on the

"home place." It is, perhaps, an irony that home is most frequently perceived as meaningful from the perspective of distance. "Country road, take me home / To the place, I belong . . . ," as the bard of country popular music would have
it. Place as home-place appears to be preeminently a category
of nostalgia (a word derived from the Greek *nostos*, "to return
home"), of *Heimweh* ("homesickness"). It is built on the sort
of recollections so effectively celebrated in William Goyen's
poetic novel, *The House of Breath*.

> That people could come into the world in a place they
> could not at first even name and had never known be-
> fore; and that out of a nameless and unknown place they
> could grow and move around in it until its name they
> knew and called with love, and call it HOME, and put
> roots there and love others there; so that whenever they
> left this place they would sing homesick songs about it
> and write poems of yearning for it, like a lover; remem-
> bering the grouping of old trees, the fall of slopes and
> hills, the lay of fields and the running of rivers; of ani-
> mals there, and of objects lived with; of faces and names,
> all of love and belonging, and forever be returning to it
> or leaving it again![29]

The nostalgic literature of home is filled with these sorts of
reveries: moments of significance, private or shared, incom-
prehensible to those outside. Home is perceived as the condensation of such reveries. Home is not, from such a point of
view, best understood as the place-where-I-was-born or the
place-where-I-live. Home is the place where memories are
"housed."[30] As such, home is unique: "There's no place like
home."

In the geographical literature, home has been extended to
other modes of human habitation and to other sorts of locales
following the assumed principle: "All really inhabited space
bears the essence of the notion of home."[31] Hence, the development of the subdiscipline of perceptual geography, which
has resulted in a body of literature, from Charles Trowbridge
through Kevin Lynch and Peter Gould, concerned with dis-
cerning the "mental maps" of city folk, the perceptions of loci
of meaning and information within the urban landscape held

by citizens as they orient themselves from home to city in
their daily lives.[32]

Common to all these various attempts to define place from
the originating perception of home-place in the current geographical literature is a focus on the individual and his or her
subjective experience as constituting home and, by extension, other modes of human place. Alan Gussow has been
most succinct:

> The catalyst that converts any physical location—any
> environment if you will—into a place, is the process of
> experiencing deeply. A place is a piece of the whole en-
> vironment that has been claimed by feelings.[33]

We may pause, at this point, to make several different sorts
of comments. The first, and most obvious, reflects some suspicion as to the parochialism of such notions. Are we, in fact,
convinced that the perception of home and place, indigenous
to our culture, can be so readily generalized? At one level, this
is a linguistic issue.[34] As George Steiner reminds us, "Any bilingual translator is acquainted with the phenomenon of 'false
friends' . . . mutually untranslatable cognates such as English
home and German *Heim.*"[35] Indeed, in a critical paper, the
geographer David Sopher has gone so far as to argue that the
"rich meaning of the English lexical symbol [home] is virtually
untranslatable into most other languages" and that there is a
"uniquely complex significance of home in the English language."[36] At another level, it is impossible to escape the suspicion that such recent celebrations of nostalgia for home-place
in the geographical literature are, at least in part, reactions to
the perceived contemporary phenomenon of urban rootless-
ness and anomie.[37]

A second sort of comment is historical. The approach taken
by present-day humanistic geographers stands in sharp contrast to the mainstream of geographic theories of place in
most of Western history. To state the opposition bluntly: the
traditional theories held that it is place that creates man and
his culture as well as his character, rather than the other way
round. *Topos* or *physis* is what shapes, what gives form and
content to *nomos* and *ethos*. This is the dominant European intellectual tradition often oversimplified under the rubric "en-

vironmental determinism" (since the Enlightenment, perhaps better labeled "environmental relativism"). Fortunately, it is not necessary to rehearse the history of this tradition; that task has been masterfully accomplished by Charles J. Glacken in his *Traces on the Rhodian Shore*.[38] But it is worth reiterating the implication of the classical theory that is central to our theme: place is not the creation of personality; it is what forms or imprints personality. In the writings of the humanistic geographers, it is assumed that this principle is wrong. Is the rejection of the classical notion of place based on theoretical or methodological grounds? Or is it politically motivated, a discomfort with the close association of the classical notion with twentieth century forms of totalitarianism and racism?

A third sort of comment stems from a more theoretical perspective—the degree to which the focus on the unique and meaning-laden experience of home-place represents a new modulation of the older, thorny geographical claim of "exceptionalism," combined, perhaps, with environmentalist notions of *Heimat*. The claim of exceptionalism, which many trace back to Kant, is primarily concerned with the place of geography in a classification of the sciences, but it has as well to do with the object of geographical inquiry and its putative "uniqueness."

The foundation document of exceptionalism is a passage from the introduction to Kant's *Lectures on Physical Geography*.

> We may classify our empirical knowledge in two ways: either according to conceptions or according to time and space in which they are actually found. The classification of perceptions according to concepts is the logical classification, that according to time and space the physical classification. Through the former we obtain a system of nature (*Systema naturae*), such as that of Linnaeus, through the latter, a geographical description of nature. . . . Description according to time is history, [description] according to space is geography. . . . Geography and history fill up the entire circumference of our perceptions: geography that of space, history that of time.[39]

There is much in this statement that would repay careful study from a Kantian perpsective: not only the epistemologi-

cal framework, but also, more specifically, the issue of the relationship of Linnaean systematics to the Kantian enterprise
as disclosed in the *Critique of Judgement*.[40] But this is not the
way in which the passage has been used by a variety of geographical theorists. Instead, loosely basing themselves on
what they believe to be the implications of the passage, they
have argued a series of methodological propositions. These
propositions may be grouped into three clusters.[41] The first
seeks to establish the characteristics of geography as a discipline; the second, the characteristics of the objects of geographical inquiry; the third, the characteristics of the nature
of geographical inquiry.

1. If, as Kant states, geography treats the "entire circum-
ference" of our spatial perceptions, then there can be no limits placed on the class of objects geography studies. To cite
Richard Hartshorne, the most distinguished and sophisticated of the American geographical exceptionalists:

> Geography does not claim any particular phenomena as
> distinctly its own . . . regardless of the fact that those
> phenomena may be of concern to other students from a
> different point of view. . . . Geography does not distin-
> guish any particular kinds of facts as "geographic facts".
> . . . In the broadest sense . . . all facts of the earth's sur-
> face are geographical facts.[42]

For this reason, geography, as a discipline, is not defined
by its subject matter, but rather, citing Hartshorne, "geography is to be defined essentially as a point of view, a method of
study."[43]

2. In defining this "point of view," Kant's parallelism between history and geography—geography as the spatial concomitant of history—becomes decisive. It leads to the syllogism: If history deals with the unique event, and if geography
is like history, then geography likewise deals with the unique.[44]
Citing Hartshorne again, "The degree to which phenomena
are unique is not only greater in geography than in many

other sciences, but the unique is of the very first practical importance."[45] This leads to the postulation of unique areas, regions, or locations as the proper objects of geographical study. In Hartshorne's terms:

> The uniqueness of a region is of a very different order from the uniqueness . . . of each pea in a pod. Each of these is unique in characteristics that can unquestionably be called minor while major characteristics are identical, whereas a region is unique in respect to its total combination of major characteristics.[46]
>
> Areas, as such, cannot be studied in terms of generic concepts, but can only be regarded as unique in their *einmalige* combinations of interrelated phenomena.[47]

3. The third cluster of propositions is genetically more complex, as it does not take off directly from Kant's statements about geography (indeed, in some ways it contravenes them), but rather from the murkier world of German Neo-Kantianism, especially that of the Heidelberg (or Baden) school, primarily associated with Wilhelm Windelband and Heinrich Rickert,[48] as carried over into geographical theory by Alfred Hettner[49] and popularized, in this country, by Hartshorne.[50] At issue was dualism, both in its Kantian and Neo-Kantian Idealist forms. The Heidelberg school claimed to resolve this dilemma by focusing attention not on the objects of knowledge but on their methods. One set of methods, to be associated primarily with the natural sciences, was generalizing and lawful—in Heidelberg terminology, the nomothetic sciences. The other, to be associated primarily with the historical and cultural sciences, was individualizing, concentrating on the distinctive "physiognomy" of the phenomenon and on those particular relationships which bound the phenomenon to its environs—in Heidelberg terminology, the idiographic sciences. Both the nomothetic and the idiographic are possible ways of conceiving the same object; neither is reducible to the other. "Reality becomes nature if we consider it in regard to what is general; it becomes history if we consider it in regard to the particular or individual."[51] From such a perspective, geography, while having generalizing (nomothetic)

aspects, is essentially an idiographic enterprise.[52] As one distinguished philosopher and historian of science has noted:

> The end product of geographic research still has been contemplation of the unique. . . . The only way of integrating unlike entities has appeared to be through an intuitive process.[53]

There are many elements in this disciplinary debate that invite comment. Indeed, the attentive reader will have caught the parallels to arguments in the social sciences (usually deriving from Dilthey) and to those in religious studies. *Mutatis mutandis*, what is said here about geography applies to these other arguments of disciplinary identification as well.

For our purposes, we need focus only on the claim that place be conceived as "individual," as having a "unique physiognomy" that is best captured by the pictorial character of idiographic method.

At one level, this appears to be a trivial claim. Simply as a function of its specific location mapped on a system of spatial and temporal coordinates, any place is, by definition, individual. To cite a philosophical discussion of the notion: "Its position in space-time is of the essence of an individual. Two individuals are identical if and only if they have the same position."[54]

In geographical discourse, however, this space-time language has often been thoughtlessly joined to a quite different, and more problematic, language: that of individuation or uniqueness by virtue of attributes or properties.[55] The result is the hybrid, muddled language of a "unique *Erdstelle* . . . stamped as an individual," a "particular *Erdstelle*" with a "complete individuality or character of its own."[56] Location has been translated into character without warrant or procedural rules. Furthermore, such hybrid language persistently confuses the "unique" with the "individual." Uniqueness denies the possibility of comparison and taxonomy; the individual requires comparative and classificatory endeavors. Uniqueness prevents science and cognition; the individual invites the same.[57] To put this another way, absolute difference is not a category for thought but one that denies the possibility of thought. In the words of a distinguished historian:

> This word "unique" is a negative term signifying what is mentally inapprehensible. The absolutely unique is, by definition, indescribable.[58]

II

In the preceding pages, a number of topics and figures have been rapidly reviewed, ranging from Freud and notions of memory to Kant and the work of some contemporary geographical theorists. Each has been subjected to implicit or explicit criticism, and that criticism has revolved around a single point: the extraordinary priority granted to the autonomy of the singular mind and experience, whether in the cognitive or the affective mode, and the difficulty that priority presents for matters of theory. In particular, we need to focus on the issues raised by this preoccupation for classificatory and comparative endeavors. From our perspective, this issue was most effectively joined by Durkheim and the French sociological school. For, as Marx with Hegel, Durkheim can be described as having "stood Kant on his head."[59] As Durkheim averred in an early article, written in the tormented context of the Dreyfus Case, individualism is:

> itself a social product, like all moralities and all religions. The individual receives from society even the moral beliefs which deify him. This is what Kant and Rousseau did not understand. They wished to deduce their individualistic ethics not from society, but from the notion of the isolated individual.[60]

Because this reversal will provide the theoretical perspective on all that follows—both the general theory of ritual toward which these studies aim and the specific comparisons with respect to Jerusalem that serve as exemplars of this theoretical concern—the remainder of this chapter will be devoted to an elucidation of its consequences.

I do not wish to be misunderstood at this point. I am not suggesting a Durkheim redivivus. It is impossible to accept the answers Durkheim set forth to the questions he posed. But the questions and, of even greater import, the reversal that gave rise to them are central to our concerns. We shall therefore need to be more attentive to their modulations and implications in the workings of other scholars; nevertheless, I would insist that their first formulations in Durkheim have more than merely chronological priority. His works establish our agendum.

Although earlier hints may be found, the Durkheimian program with which we are concerned was first announced in a collaborative effort between Durkheim and Marcel Mauss, published in 1903, "On Some Primitive Forms of Classification: A contribution to the Study of Collective Representations."[61] In this essay, classification is taken to be a primary logical operation with two (essentially spatial) characteristics: classification forms groups that are distinct from one another; and it arranges these groups in hierarchies. In contradistinction to their philosophical and psychological predecessors, the authors insist that classification is neither natural nor the result of the workings of innate, individual mental capacities.[62] This poses the question:

> Far from being able to say that men classify quite naturally, by a sort of necessity of their individual understandings, we must on the contrary ask ourselves what could have led them to arrange their ideas in this way, and where they could have found the plan of this remarkable disposition.[63]

Durkheim and Mauss postpone the answer by first undertaking three probes of traditional classificatory systems: the Australian, the Amerindian, and the classical Chinese.

After these, which occupy the bulk of the essay,[64] four brief conclusions follow. (1) These classification systems are nonutilitarian. "Their object is not to facilitate action but to advance understanding, to make intelligible the relations which

exist between things." As such, they may be said "to consti-
tute a first philosophy of nature." [65] (2) The origin of this system is social. Men "classified things because they were divided into clans."

> Society was not simply a model which classificatory
> thought followed; it was [society's] own divisions which
> served as divisions for the system of classification.
> The first logical categories were social categories; the
> first classes of things were classes of men, into which
> these things were integrated. It was because men were
> grouped, and thought of themselves in the form of
> groups, that in their ideas they grouped other things.
> . . . Moieties were the first genera; clans, the first
> species. [66]

(3) Not only groupings, but also relations of unity and hierarchy "are of social origin."

> It is because human groups fit into one another—the
> sub-clan into the clan, the clan into the moiety, the
> moiety into the tribe—that groups of things are ordered
> in the same way. . . . Logical hierarchy is only another
> aspect of social hierarchy, and the unity of knowledge is
> nothing else than the very unity of the collectivity, ex-
> tended to the universe. [67]

(4) By tracing such divisions to society, Durkheim and Mauss
can make one further argumentative move. The peculiar authority that such classifications have, the conviction that they
"represent" the world (thus giving rise to the naturist fallacy),
is the result of their being "affective" as well as cognitive
systems.

> Religious emotions, notably, not only give it [the repre-
> sentation] a special tinge, but attribute to it the most es-
> sential properties of which it is constituted. Things are
> above all sacred or profane, pure or impure, friends or
> enemies; i.e. their most fundamental characteristics are
> only expressions of the way in which they affect social

sensibility. The differences and resemblances which determine the fashion in which they are grouped are more
affective than intellectual. . . . And it is this emotional
value of notions which plays the preponderant part in
the manner in which the ideas are connected or separated. It is the dominant characteristic in classification.[68]

It is this last characteristic which distinguishes traditional
from scientific classification. Over time, "this element of social affectivity has progressively weakened, leaving more and
more room for the reflective thought of individuals."[69]

The essay is not satisfactory. In the words of its most careful
student, Rodney Needham, "Durkheim and Mauss's argument
is logically fallacious and . . . it is methodologically unsound.
There are grave reasons, indeed, to deny it any validity what-
soever."[70] Yet all is not negative, only confidence misplaced.
Durkheim and Mauss have persuasively moved the issue from
nature to culture, from the individual to society. They correctly saw a relationship between the organization of society
and the operations of a classification; their error lay in seeing
the relationship as a causal or genetic one, as a matter of origins: "[people] classified things *because* they were divided by
clans."[71] But there is concealed within this causal language
another mode of expression. To cite just two examples: "the
classification of things *reproduces* this classification of men";
"the two types of classification which we have just studied
merely *express under different aspects* the very societies in which
they were elaborated; one was modelled on the jural and religious organization of the tribe, the other on its morphological
organization."[72] That is to say, the two systems may be isomorphic without being genetically related. In Needham's
terms, "these two orders of facts may be regarded as aspects
of one conceptual order, one mode of classification. This concordance need not be a formal correspondence, such as Durkheim and Mauss supposed, but may subsist in a structural
sense, institutions of different forms being seen as based on
the same mode of relation."[73]

It is tempting, at this point, to launch into a detailed review
of Durkheim's masterwork *The Elementary Forms of the Religious*

Life,[74] originally and significantly entitled *The Elementary Forms of Thought and the Religious Life*,[75] which seems, in the bulk of its text, to be largely a commentary on Australian aborigines, but which is, in fact, as its footnotes amply illustrate, a sustained and brilliant argument with Kant (perhaps modulated through Durkheim's lifelong preoccupation with the works of the French Neo-Kantians, Charles Renouvier and Octave Hamelin).[76] But I shall resist. I will consider only those issues, relevant to our concerns, that were raised by the essay and that find some satisfaction in *Elementary Forms*.

The first is the issue of the dual. In the essay, Durkheim and Mauss raise the matter at several points in a strikingly inconsistent fashion. At the outset, they appear to concede that there is some innate mental capacity for dual classification.[77] In their conclusion, the same polarities are identified as being specifically the products of "religious emotion"—hence, neither innate nor individual.[78] In between, duality is held to be logically (and, alas, chronologically) simple. It is a mode of classification that cannot be further reduced (that is, classification, by definition, requires at least two classes).[79] But there is a danger here: By failing to give an account of the origin of social dualism, Durkheim and Mauss give unwitting comfort to those who would hold dualism to be "natural"—male/female, night/day, up/down, right/left. In *Elementary Forms*, this is explicitly denied through the turn to religion as the central object of theoretical interest.[80]

As is well known, Durkheim initially defines religion as the absolute distinction between the sacred and the profane,[81] an essentially spatial definition in that "the sacred thing is par excellence that which the profane should not touch, and cannot touch with impunity."[82] This leads to the question that puts to rest "naturism":

> For we must first of all ask what has been able to lead men to see in the world two heterogeneous and incompatible worlds, though *nothing in sensible experience* seems able to suggest the idea of so radical a duality to them.[83]

The answer is delayed for some 250 pages in the original French. It is, Durkheim argues, the alternation between the

repetitiveness of ordinary life and the "effervescence" of cele-
bratory ritual that gives rise to the duality.

> How could such experiences as these fail to leave in him
> [the aborigine] the conviction that there really exist two
> heterogeneous and mutually incomparable worlds? One
> is that where his daily life drags wearily along; but he
> cannot penetrate into the other [ritual life] without at
> once entering into relations . . . that excite him to the
> point of frenzy. The first is the profane world, the sec-
> ond, that of sacred things.[84]

In other words, it is a distinction in the social experience of
the quality of time that stands at the origin of the absolute spatial dichotomy of sacred and profane, which, in turn, gener-
ates the other cognitive dualities on which intellection rests.[85]

Having given extraordinary priority to the dual, Durkheim
and Mauss have difficulties dealing with classification systems
that are more complex (or compound), be it a case of number
or of hierarchy. In these cases in their essay, their arguments
become both desperate and disparate. At different points,
when confronting complexity, they suggest that there is, perhaps, "uncertainty" in the ethnographic reports; in another
instance, they view these "more differentiated organizations"
as atavistic throwbacks, a return to "the state of original confusion from which the human mind has developed"; at other
times, they argue that complexity is the result of historical
processes, a "segmentation," a "crumbling," a "disintegra-
tion" and "fragmentation," an "altered form of earlier [dual]
classifications."[86] What this uncertainty and irritation reveals
is a stunning fact. Durkheim and Mauss fail to perceive the
issue of ideology: that the tribe as observed need not correspond in fact to their own systematic statements about themselves. There is simply no hint of suspicion, no room for
discrepancy, in Durkheim and Mauss's account of the "primitive." (Indeed, to my recollection, this point is only briefly
touched on once in *Elementary Forms*.[87])

In the above, I have used the term *ideology* in the way it is
employed in the magisterial work of Georges Dumézil (perhaps the most significant contemporary student of religion
whose work can be related to the Durkheimian enterprise),

when he writes of the "Indo-European tripartite ideology." In a charming, autobiographical sketch, he reveals what the word connotes for him. He writes of the "decisive progress" that he made in his thinking in the 1950s:

> the day that I realized . . . that the tripartite ideology was not necessarily accompanied, in the life of a society, by a *real* tripartition of that society, as is the case following the Indian model; on the contrary, I recognized that, wherever one could establish its presence, [the ideology] is nothing (or is no longer, or perhaps never was [anything]) but an ideal and, at the same time, a means of analyzing, of interpreting the forces which are responsible for the course of the world and of human life.[88]

What makes all the difference is that Dumézil has available to him, even if he rarely draws explicitly on it, the "linguistic turn," theories of the social, world-constructing role of language—an enterprise of fabrication in both senses of the term: an affair of both building and lying. (But it might be noted, as will be discussed below in chapter 5, that Durkheim came exceedingly close to stating such a theory in his discussion of the totemic "emblem" in *Elementary Forms.*[89])

What is at stake in raising such questions concerning the dual, complexity, ideology, and language is the issue of discrepancy: the perception of a gap between the "socially ideal" and the "socially real." A more active and political name for such an essentially cognitive gap is conflict. This is an issue clearly recognized by Durkheim as arising in modern, industrial societies (the point, after all, of his early work on *The Division of Labor*)[90]; it is less clearly recognized (if at all) as arising in so-called simple societies. For there is a specious symmetry to language of the dual—the implication of equality, balance, and reciprocity. And yet, this is clearly not the case. *Up* and *down, front* and *back, right* and *left* are almost never dualities of equivalence; they are hierarchically ranked in relations of superordination and subordination with radically different valences.[91] If our bias is to see equality in such arrangements, the *tendenz* of the social documents from which we extract our notion of the dual is clearly toward hierarchy.

There is a second feature, no less important than the first.

Alongside the tension between equality and hierarchy must be placed that between polarity and continuity. Both egalitarian and hierarchical dualisms conceal a far less highly profiled "reality." What appears, ideologically speaking, as dual is a radical reduction of an extended plenum of graduated positions. (One need think only of the endless distinctions in the literature on socioeconomic classes.[92])

Both of these issues, and their implications, may be illustrated by a telling example in Claude Lévi-Strauss's controversial article "Do Dual Organizations Exist?"[93] drawn from Paul Radin's monograph on the Winnebago.[94]

The Winnebago are divided into two exogamous moieties: "Those Who Are Above" (*wangeregi herera*), and "Those Who Are on Earth" (*manegi herera*)—to be referred to as *A* and *B*, respectively, in what follows. Radin noticed a "curious discrepancy" in the native accounts of the relationship between this dual social organization and an idealized map of Winnebago village structure. The majority of his informants described a circular village with equal areas belonging to the two moieties, divided from each other by an "imaginary diameter running northwest and southeast." The lodge of the Thunderbird clan, the first of the four clans of the *A* moiety, stood at the southern extremity within the one half, with the other lodges belonging to *A* scattered throughout the moiety's "territory." The lodge of the Bear clan, the first of the eight clans of the *B* moiety, stood at the northern extremity within the other half, with the remaining lodges belonging to *B* scattered throughout the moiety's "territory."[95] Several informants insisted on a different model, however. Here, there was no distinction between the two moieties. The ruling lodges (those of the Thunderbird and the Bear clans) were in the center, with the other lodges clustered around them. The contrasts were between the village and the cleared land surrounding it and between the cleared land and the encompassing forest. The first model, which Lévi-Strauss terms a "diametric structure," and which is symmetrical and reciprocal (the one moiety's territory being the mirror image of the other), was "always given" by members of *A*. The second model, which Lévi-Strauss terms a "concentric structure," is hierarchical. It collects the ruling functions in the center in distinction to the other lodges (regardless of moiety) and then distinguishes the human and inhabited realm from the cultivated land, and the cultivated land from the wild land. This latter diagram was described only by members of *B*.[96]

Lévi-Strauss's first interpretative comment is apt:

> Radin did not stress this discrepancy; he merely regretted that insufficient information made it impossible for him to determine which was the true village organization. I should like to show here that the question is not necessarily one of alternatives. These forms, as described, do not necessarily relate to two different organizations. They may also correspond to two different ways of describing one organization too complex to be formalized by a single model, so that the members of each moiety would tend to conceptualize it one way rather than the other, depending upon their position in the social structure. For even in such an apparently symmetrical type of social structure as dual organization, the relationship between moieties is never as static, or as fully reciprocal, as one might tend to imagine.[97]

He further notes that the "diametric structure" is inherently that of a "balanced and symmetrical dichotomy," whereas in "concentric structures, the inequality may be taken for granted, since the two elements are, so to speak, arranged with respect to the same point of reference—the center—to which one of the circles is closer than the other." He goes on to raise the central question: "How can moieties involved in reciprocal obligations and exercising symmetrical rights be, at the same time, hierarchically related?"[98] Lévi-Strauss provides, in effect, a logical answer that, even though the available Winnebago evidence does not fully support his claim, is methodologically far superior to Radin's conjectural process of historical accretion.[99] The Winnebago system, Lévi-Strauss contends, is composed of "triads, disguised as dyads through the logical subterfuge of treating as two homologous terms a whole that actually consists of a pole and an axis which are not entities of the same nature"—in this case, a water-land pole and a sky axis.[100] Lévi-Strauss never quite returns, however, to explore his initial observation that "the members of each [Winnebago] moiety would tend to conceptualize it in one way rather than the other, depending on their position in the social structure." It is this issue which requires further comment.

Although Radin insists that the terms "upper" and "lower" for the two moieties "have no connotation of superior and inferior," [101] the details he supplies for Winnebago social organization suggest otherwise. There is reciprocity between A and B, but it is asymmetrical. The chief is always selected from A. "They call the Thunderbird people chiefs and it is from among their ranks that they select the chief of their tribe." [102] The entire moiety A is sometimes termed "chiefs" in contradistinction to B, which is called "soldiers." [103] Members of B "acted as servants to the Thunderbird clan on various occasions." [104] A's powers clearly define the external boundaries of the tribe. A is responsible for war, for preserving peace, and for acting as intermediary with other tribes. B's powers are more internalized. B is responsible for the internal order and discipline of the tribe. One of its clans serves as "public crier and intermediary between the chief and his people." [105] Thus, A can be seen as having a less ambiguous range of power than B has. It is largely directed against external threats. B's range is more ambivalent. Its power is directed internally, against fellow tribesmen. This ambivalence is concentrated in the paramount clan of B, the Bear, which "next to the Thunderbird clan [is] the most important in the village." [106] The ambivalence is expressed in an informant's account, quoted by Radin, that if a member of the tribe sought "to kill game on his own account," the Bear clansmen would destroy his lodge and break his dishes. If the offender resisted, he would be severely whipped. If the offender attempted to resist this by force, he would be killed. "If, on the other hand, he submitted to whatever punishment the Bear clansmen inflicted upon him without resistance and apologized to them, then they would build him a new lodge and supply it with better goods than those which they had been compelled to destroy." [107] Thus, it is from a perspective of power that A sees the village as symmetrical and reciprocal; it is from a position of subordination that B pictures the village as hierarchical. A's position is one of relative clarity; hence, the mirror-image character of its picture of the tribal organization. B's position is ambivalent; hence, its more highly valenced "concentric" diagram.

The same pattern of clarity and ambiguity obtains for the classificatory logic of the two moieties.[108] *A* is unambiguously linked to sky. It contains four clans, each of which is associated with a bird. *B* is more ambiguous, being linked both to earth and to water. It consists of eight clans, five or six of which are associated with land animals, two or three of which are associated with water animals.[109] In other words, there is taxonomic unity to the powerful *A* moiety and relative "fuzziness"[110] to the subordinate *B* moiety. This fuzziness extends further within *B*. Some lists omit two of the three water clans (Fish and Snake [?]).[111] There are no political functions associated with these two clans, and they partake in no relations of special reciprocity (*hitcak'oro*, "friendship") with other members of their moiety.[112] The remaining water-related clan (Water-spirit) is the only one to have a "term of respect," to have a "minor" political function, and to participate in "friendship" relations of special reciprocal obligations.[113]

Combining these observations on the dual organization of the Winnebago, we may venture a postulate. The taxonomic clarity of *A* and its position of superordination are what enables it to perceive the relations between the moieties as symmetrical; the classificatory fuzziness of *B* and its position of subordination are what leads it to perceive the relations between the moieties as hierarchical and asymmetrical.[114] These opposing positions give rise to two discordant ideological maps of geographical and social space.

The notion of hierarchy, the Durkheimian reversal, all point in the same direction: that place is not best conceived as a particular location with an idiosyncratic physiognomy or as a uniquely individualistic node of sentiment, but rather as a social position within a hierarchical system. What we are concerned with is the connotation of *place* that always accompanies its use as a verb in English[115] and is revealed in phrases such as *keep your place*. It is a sense that has been overshadowed, in English, by a more civic understanding of *place* (as in its cognate, *piazza*), but which is embedded in some forms of Indo-European usage.[116]

Nevertheless, the connection between place in its social, hierarchical sense and the city is suggestive. It will provide the point of departure for the next chapter. There, we shall turn our attention to a specific and exceedingly difficult civic and temple-text, Ezekiel 40–48, using as interpretative tools a general theory of hierarchy (as set forth by Louis Dumont), of urbanism (as argued by Paul Wheatley), and of hierarchical building (as adumbrated by Clifford Geertz). In so doing, we may come to appreciate the full force of Roger Bacon's observation that "place is the beginning of our existence, just as a father"[117]—not simply in the sense of environmental generation, but also in the sense of social location, of genealogy, kinship, authority, superordination, and subordination.

THREE

TO PUT
IN PLACE

*A noble, logical diagram once re-
corded will never die, but long after
we are gone will be a living thing,
asserting itself with ever-growing
insistency.*

Daniel Burnham

I

Perhaps the chief of the systems
layout branch at NASA is right after all. If so, he might have saved
old Hanina b. Hezekiah at least
one measure of oil (b. *Menaḥot* 45a
and parallels).

Ezekiel begins his book with
the description of the final
phase of a spaceship's de-
scent from a circular orbit to
the earth and of its subsequent landing. This narrative
is accompanied by a description of the main parts of the

> spacecraft. . . . Ezekiel also speaks of the commanders
> of the spaceships; he hears them talk, he observes their
> movements; on one occasion he witnesses a peculiar
> event involving the participation of a ground crew sum-
> moned by the commander. He takes part himself in
> flights in these spaceships: two flights take him to tem-
> ples whose location and significance are still unsolved
> mysteries.[1]

An eccentric understanding of the biblical text, to be sure; but
one no stranger than some of the critical theories that have
been advanced to explain Ezekiel, or odder, for that matter,
than the text itself. Yet even with space travel as a "key to the
clear understanding of Ezekiel's report," Blumrich must admit
that the "location and significance" of the temples "are still
unsolved mysteries."[2]

It is to this most difficult text, the temple visions of Ezekiel
40–48, that we shall turn our attention in this third chapter.[3]
We know far less than we should like about this text. It is not
so much a part of the composite work attributed to Ezekiel as
it is a document from that vast, largely postexilic, priestly literary and intellectual endeavor that has had far greater impact
outside of the biblical canon than within. Nevertheless, of all
the texts preserved within the biblical canon, it is, perhaps,
the most articulate in offering a coherent ideology of place: of
temple and city, with focus on the temple.

We cannot judge from our present vantage point how representative that ideology was (or, better, for whom it was representative), just as we cannot now, if ever, identify the temple
with any known building, or the city, as described, with any
known city; but we can judge the consistency and force of its
ideological principles. While drawing heavily on archaic Zion
traditions, rather than on the city-centered and king-focused
Jerusalem traditions, Ezekiel 40–48 is an endeavor in mapping
the social configurations of an ideal cultic place. It is this social
map, rather than artifacts of mortar and stone, with which we
are concerned. As Clifford Geertz argued with respect to the
Southeast Asian temple-state, so here with Ezekiel, "to understand the *negara* is . . . to elaborate a poetics of power, not
a mechanics."[4]

The rudimentary elements of this map are announced in

the introduction to the first set of visions (Ezekiel 40.1–2, 5). In the "fourteenth year" after the destruction of Jerusalem and its temple, the prophet was transported "by the hand of YHWH" from his place of deportation in Babylonia to "the land of Israel," where he is "set down upon a very high mountain, on which was a structure like a city."[5] The structure's most immediate distinctive feature is its surrounding wall—it is more than ten feet thick.[6]

With this, we are given the fundamental coordinates of the map and a clear indication of its status. The "structure" (correlated with "temple" in Ezekiel 40.5) is not any extant building. It is an ideal construction, unconstrained by the pragmatics of architecture or the accidentalities of history. It is organized around two axes. It has imposing verticality ("a very high mountain"), and it is enclosed, marked off from its surroundings by a very thick wall ("and see, a wall ran round the temple on the outside"). It is a building conceived of as a city, unlike the more open Winnebago village briefly considered in chapter 2. Its primary language is one of "gates" and "entering." Like the Winnebago example, the maps of this place are primarily conceptual.

For some understandings of city, the enclosing, sheltering, and delimiting presence of a wall serves as its chief (at times, defining) characteristic.[7] Certainly, one can think of a variety of relentlessly urban, ancient Near Eastern texts in which city walls are prominent objects of celebration: the stunning repetition of the invitation to survey the walls of Uruk that begins and ends the late redaction of the Gilgamesh epic (1.1.11–19; 11.303–7),[8] or the analogous encomium in Psalm 48 in the Hebrew Bible from the Zion tradition.[9] Royal chronologies were established by the dates on which city walls were built,[10] and the construction of walls around a royal palace were worthy of annalistic note.[11] Boasts[12] and lamentations[13] over the destruction of cities—from Ur to Jerusalem—focus attention on the tearing down of their walls. But there is a danger in rehearsing these well-known traditions: that the city wall (correlated, at times, with elements such as height) be reduced to a primary function of defense. This function is there. But as the examples already given make clear, the possession of a wall might equally be thought of in terms of prestige and status. Such a view allows us to join with a body of recent social theory on cities. It allows us, as well, to begin to sort out the alternative understanding of walls that has figured prominently in scholarship on religion—that which sees them as a marking off of the "sacred." [14]

In what follows, I shall assume the definition of *city* developed by James Bird: " 'City' is taken to be a canonized form of center at the apex of a hierarchy," focusing on the sociopolitical rather than the economic implications of the term *hierarchy*. [15] Building on this definition, we need to explore further the terms *city* and *hierarchy* in such a way as to illuminate both the language of building and the language of sacrality. Only then can we turn to an interpretation of the maps in Ezekiel 40–48.

The richest contemporary theoretician and historian of the city is Paul Wheatley. In a stunning series of papers and monographs, he has elaborated a detailed, cross-cultural understanding of both the processes of urban genesis and the city's complex symbolic dimensions. [16]

In his early work *The Pivot of the Four Quarters*, while focusing on the ancient Chinese city, Wheatley proposes an account of the origin of the city based on a comparison of data from the "seven regions of primary urban generation": Mesopotamia, Egypt, the Indus Valley, the North China plain, Mesoamerica, the central Andes, and the Yoruba territories of southwestern Nigeria. In each of those cases, the city developed, as it were, "sui generis out of purely local conditions" (as opposed to by imitation or imposition through contact with other cultures or imperial expansion), and, thus, provides evidence for the processes of urban genesis. [17] Each illustrates the characteristics of urbanism, "a particular set of functionally integrated institutions devised . . . to mediate the transformation of relatively egalitarian, ascriptive, kin-structured groups into socially stratified, politically organized, territorially based societies." [18] On the basis of his comparisons, Wheatley states his historical thesis boldly:

> Whenever, in any of the seven regions of primary urban generation, we trace back the characteristic urban form to its beginnings we arrive not at a settlement that is dominated by commercial relations, a primordial market, or one that is focused on a citadel, an archetypal fortress,

but rather at a ceremonial complex. . . . Beginning as
little more than tribal shrines, in what may be regarded
as their classic phases, these centers were elaborated
into complexes of public ceremonial structures. . . .
Above all, they embodied the aspirations of brittle, pyra-
midal societies.[19]

After reviewing a number of factors frequently proposed by
scholars as central components in urban genesis (such as
environment, demography, technology), he concludes that,
though they all were concomitants, they were not independent causal agents. The process of urban genesis:

is seen to be sustained by the concurrent emergence of a
redistributive superordinate economy focused on the
ceremonial complex. Such a change not only implies the
generation of a centralizing power whose authority is
validated by formalized sanctions . . . but also presup-
poses the development of new social institutions. Indeed the questions it poses relate primarily to social differentiation, and it is this which, in formal terms, must
be regarded as the dependent variable when we seek to
elucidate the complex series of interrelated changes that
eventuated in the emergence of the ceremonial city.[20]

The primary social differentiation, in Wheatley's view, was the
emergence of specialized priests (as opposed to the later
kings),[21] and Wheatley sees religion as providing the ideological grounds for the hierarchical restructuring of society. The
ceremonial centers:

assumed the role of chief innovative foci for both the restructuring of society and the advance of those branches
of technology concerned with ritual display. They functioned as instruments for the dissemination through all
levels of society of beliefs which, in turn, enabled the
wielders of political power to justify their goals. . . . At
the same time the rituals and ceremonies celebrated at
the great cult centers would appear to have acted as mir-
rors to society at large, as reflectors of a sacrally sanc-
tioned social order, as inculcators of the attitudes and
values appropriate to that order. . . . In other words they
may be regarded as idealized structural models which,

> while giving ritual expression to the moral framework of
> social organization, defined the approved status rela-
> tionships between groups and between "social persons"
> (Radcliffe-Brown's term) within those groups.[22]

Although many of Wheatley's historical reconstructions
may be subject to question or to alternative interpretations,[23]
there are grounds for graver reservations with respect to theory. From our perspective, the most troublesome aspect of
Wheatley's early formulations in *Pivot* is his alternation between two, seemingly incompatible, theories of ritual: one
which is overly instrumental and functional; the other which
values too highly the ideology of the symbolism of the "center."[24] In part, this incompatibility is the result of Wheatley's
reliance on relatively unsophisticated works on religion in
contrast to the subtle and complex works of social theory that
form the background for his thought. There is simply no con-
test, for example, between the irresponsibly crude formulations of Robert Bellah in "Religious Evolution"[25] and the sophisticated models of multivariate evolutionary theory in the
works of Julian Steward and Robert McCormick Adams.[26]
This imbalance has, to a considerable degree, been rectified in
Wheatley's later work. Nevertheless, in *Pivot*, Wheatley has
provided us with a range of terminology and notions on
which we will continue to draw: the city as a "ceremonial center" with one of its chief crafts being the "technology of ritual
display"; the city as an "organizing principle"; and urbanism
as the "hierarchical patterning of society in its totality."

In his more recent writings, Wheatley has recognized both
the problems inherent in the functionalist bias of his earlier
works and the inadequacies of his formulations regarding ritual. In answer to the first, he has shifted to a model first
developed by Kent Flannery to explain the origins of the
state[27]—one not entirely free, however, of a functionalist bias;
in answer to the second, religion, he has drawn on the sophisticated work on ritual of Roy Rappaport.[28]

Flannery argues that the state (and Wheatley, *mutatis mutandis*, the city) can be best understood as a "living system"
organized around two principles: "segregation," the degree
of internal differentiation and specialization of its subsystems; and "centralization," the linkages between the subsys-

tems and the degree of highest order controls. Although the particular "socioenvironmental stresses" that select for the mechanisms which make these principles operational may vary, the mechanisms are common cross-culturally: "promotion," whereby an institution rises from its original position in the control hierarchy to a position at a higher level, either giving rise to a new institution or becoming less specific with respect to its purpose within a given system (that is, becoming more "self-serving" and general); and "linearization," a contrary mechanism for segregation, whereby a subsystem is repeatedly bypassed. Thus, a city may be conceived of as:

> a series of subsystems arranged hierarchically, from lowest and most specific to highest and most general. Each subsystem is regulated by a control apparatus whose job it is to keep all the variables in the subsystem within appropriate goal ranges. . . . On all levels the social control apparatus compares output values not merely with subsistence goals but with ideological values, the demands of deities and ancestral spirits, ethical and religious propositions—the human population's "cognized model" of the way the world is put together.[29]

There are, as well, three dysfunctional mechanisms: "usurpation," the elevation of a subsystem to preeminence, attending to its own goals rather than general ones (the opposite side of "promotion"); "meddling," the subjection to a higher order control of variables properly regulated by lower order subsystems; and "hypercoherence," the extreme of meddling, whereby there is overcentralization that deprives subsystems of their legitimate spheres of control.[30]

With respect to ritual, Wheatley remains overly instrumental, but with more complexity. He lifts out of Rappaport's multidimensional studies of ritual only the notion that ritual transforms the arbitrary conventions of any organized society into the necessary by reference to the "sacred," thus providing an easily internalized control mechanism. In Rappaport's pungent formulation: "Sanctity helps keep subsystems in their places."[31] But he has, in his most recent work, shown an appreciation of the sort of understanding of "ceremonial display" richly amplified by Clifford Geertz in his notion of the "theatre state"—although Wheatley has not found a way to integrate such an understanding with his instrumental bias.[32] In *Negara: The Theatre State in Nineteenth Century Bali*, Geertz enunciates his thesis:

> The expressive nature of the Balinese state was apparent throughout the whole of its known history, for it was always pointed not toward . . . government, which it pursued indifferently and hesitantly, but rather toward spectacle, toward ceremony, toward the public dramatization of the ruling obsessions of Balinese culture: social inequality and status pride. It was a theatre state in which the kings and princes were the impresarios, the priests the directors, and the peasants the supporting cast, stage crew, and audience. The stupendous [ceremonies] . . . were not means to political ends: they were the ends themselves, they were what the state was for. . . . Power served pomp, not pomp power. . . . The state cult was not a cult of the state. It was an argument, made over and over again in the insistent vocabulary of ritual, that worldly status has a cosmic base, that hierarchy is the governing principle of the universe. . . . [This is] the point that the state ceremonies made: Status is all.[33]

Throughout this discussion, the term "hierarchy" has been used as if it is synonymous with "differentiation," "social stratification," and "class." In part, this reflects Wheatley's own shifting terminology as he moves from the theoretical resources provided by Durkheim in *The Division of Labor* to the neo-Marxist formulations by such social theorists as Jonathan Friedman.[34] The issue is difficult, and there is no consensus.[35]

Nonetheless, a major advance toward clarifying these matters has been made by Louis Dumont in *Homo Hierarchicus*.[36] Dumont gives priority to hierarchy as "meaning," while viewing stratification as "mere external form," concluding, therefore, that hierarchy must be studied at the level of ideology.[37] Hierarchy, so understood, while expressed in a variety of segmentations, may be reduced, conceptually, to a structural opposition.[38] Dumont insists on a sharp distinction between systems of status and systems of power.[39] Status is founded on the absolute dichotomy of the pure and the impure, and is expressed as a relative hierarchy of degrees of purity and impurity, with the priest at its summit. It is, essentially, a sacer-

dotal system.[40] Power is dominance—a hierarchy of degrees
of legitimate force, with the king at its summit. It is, essentially, a juridical system.[41] The two systems exhibit a necessary
complimentarity. The king will always be impure with respect
to the priest (largely, though not exclusively, due to corpse
pollution); but the priest will be inferior to the king with respect to authority. The priest legitimates the power of the
king; the king supports, protects, and preserves the power of
the priests.[42]

In the first edition of *Homo Hierarchicus,* Dumont employed
the traditional, somewhat static, rank-oriented definition of
hierarchy as "the principle by which the elements of a whole
are ranked [by grades] in relation to the whole."[43] In the second edition, drawing in part on an article he wrote explor-
ing the notion of the dual as presented by the Durkheimian
school,[44] he provides a more complex formulation.

> I believe that hierarchy is not, essentially, a chain of su-
> perimposed commands, nor even a chain of beings of
> decreasing dignity, nor yet a taxonomic tree, but a rela-
> tion that can succinctly be called "the encompassing of
> the contrary". . . . This hierarchical relation is . . . that
> between a whole (or set) and an element of this whole
> (or set): the element belongs to the set and is in this
> sense consubstantial or identical with it; at the same
> time, the element is distinct from the set or stands in op-
> position to it.[45]

He then supplies the social concomitant. "One category (the
superior) includes the other (the inferior) which in turn ex-
cludes the first."[46] Thus:

> At the superior level there is unity; at the inferior level
> there is distinction, there is . . . complementariness or
> contradiction. Hierarchy consists in the combination of
> these two propositions concerning different levels. In hi-
> erarchy thus defined, complementariness or contradic-
> tion is contained in a unity of superior order. But as
> soon as we intermingle the two levels, we have a logical
> scandal, because there is identity and contradiction at
> the same time.[47]

There is one further theoretical assist that we might gain from Dumont, although here I am quite conscious of pressing him a bit further than he might want to go. There is no doubt, in Dumont, that the opposition pure/impure is to be associated with a hierarchy of status and the priestly function. It is less clear that Dumont would want to formulate (as I would) the distinction sacred/profane as a hierarchy of power to be associated with the royal function (although that seems to me to be the clear implication of the few statements in his work consecrated to that theme).[48] The former is the language of vulnerability to degradation; the latter, a language of dangerous access.

Drawing on what we have learned from Wheatley, Geertz, and Dumont, we may return to the text of Ezekiel. There are four homologous ideological maps in Ezekiel 40–48. The first map (Ezekiel 40.1–44.3) is a hierarchy of power built on the dichotomy sacred/profane. The second map (Ezekiel 44.4–31) is a hierarchy of status built on the dichotomy pure/impure. The third map (Ezekiel 45.1–8 and 47.13–48.35) is civic and territorial, and the fourth map (Ezekiel 46) is predominantly orientational. These last two appear to be isomorphic to the first map.[49]

From one point of view, the first map (Ezekiel 40.1–44.3) makes only one distinction, that between the sacred and the profane. "This is the *tora* of the temple [precinct]: the whole territory round about the top of the mountain is sacred" (Ezekiel 43.12). With respect to that which is down the mountain, or off the mountain (namely, the profane), the top of the mountain is the undifferentiated and oppositional sacred, a place of dangerous access.

From another point of view, focusing only on the top of the mountain, an analogous, though more graded, set of differentiae is established. At the center is the "most holy place" (Ezekiel 41.3–4)—it is restricted to YHWH, his "glory," and his angels—it is his "throne place," the "place of the soles of my [YHWH's] feet" (Ezekiel 43.7), the center of YHWH's royal function.

This is elaborated in a series of segmentations characteristic of sacred/profane hierarchies.[50] With respect to the temple mount, the land is profane; with respect to the temple, the temple mount is profane; with respect to the throne place, the temple is profane. The royal place is, at one and the same time, both the most inclusive category—"the place where I will dwell for all time *in the midst of Israel*" (Ezekiel 43.7)—and the most sharply distinguished and delineated. These distinctions are reenforced by their verticality. Despite the blueprint character of the first map, we should picture the hierarchy of places not as concentric circles on a flat plane but instead as altitude markers on a relief map. Each unit is built on a terrace, spatially higher than that which is profane in relation to it. Thus, there are seven steps up to the outer court (Ezekiel 40.22, 26); eight steps up to the inner court (Ezekiel 40.31, 34, 37); ten steps up to the vestibule of the temple proper (Ezekiel 40.49). As the dangerously powerful throne room is approached, the spatial vocabulary shifts to one of increased difficulty of access and increased focus, expressed through the narrowing width of entranceways rather than the language of verticality. The entrance to the vestibule is fourteen cubits wide (Ezekiel 40.48); that of the temple hall, ten cubits (Ezekiel 41.2); that of the forbidden throne room, only six cubits (Ezekiel 41.3). The pattern of steps and ascent has yielded to that of a funnel with increased need for caution.

Although it is tempting to pursue what Geertz has termed the distinctions of power "cast in a vocabulary of walls, gates, passageways, sheds and furniture,"[51] the architectural language is mirrored in the social. The various actors of the ritual drama in the temple exhibit clear spatial placement (see figure 1). They operate in different spheres of relative sacrality, ranked in relations of power. In close proximity to the throne room is the sphere of the Zadokite priests. They are the ones who are in charge of the altar; they alone may come near to YHWH to minister to him (Ezekiel 40.46); they are the ones who eat the "most sacred offerings" dedicated to YHWH (Ezekiel 42.13); if they leave their proper sphere of activity, they must change their garments (which have become charged with sacrality) so as not to endanger those of lower status (Ezekiel 42.14, cf. 44.19).

The next sphere of activity, moving outward, is that of the temple proper, the realm of the "priests who are in charge of the temple" (Ezekiel 40.45). As will be discussed below, whereas the Zadokite priests perform transactions with YHWH, the transactions of this latter group of priests are with

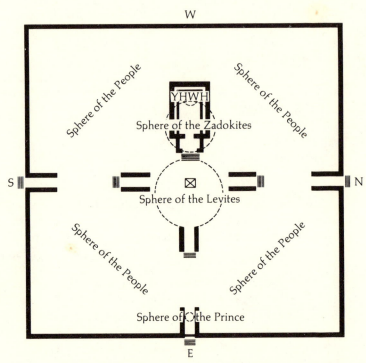

FIGURE 1. The Hierarchy of Power as Displayed in the Spheres of Activity of the Ritual Actors (Ezekiel 40.1–44.3).

the people. Finally, there is the outer limit, "the place where the people are" (Ezekiel 42.14).

From another vantage, the spheres of activity and degrees of relative sacrality are correlated in terms of centrality and adjacency (see figure 2). From a bird's-eye view of the temple precincts, there is a central spine, running east to west. This spine has eleven horizontal segments with three vertical differentiations. Of the horizontal, there are (1) the eastern steps, which lead up to (2) the outer court gate (Ezekiel 40.6); (3) the inner court stairs, which lead up to (4) the inner court gate (Ezekiel 40.32, 34); (5) the altar (Ezekiel 40.47); (6) the stairs (Ezekiel 40.49) that lead up to (7) the vestibule (Ezekiel 41.3–4); (10) a narrow band of restricted space (*gizrā*, Ezekiel 41.12–13); and, finally, (11) the obdurately vague construction designated only as the "building" (*binyan*, Ezekiel 41.12) at the

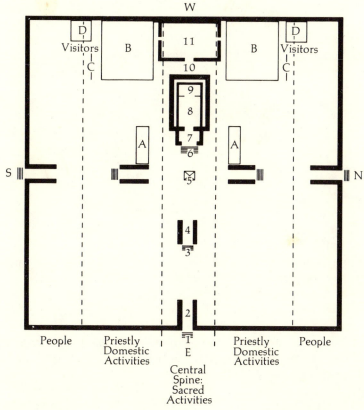

FIGURE 2. The Hierarchy of Power as Displayed in the Three Zones of Relative Sacrality (Ezekiel 40.1–44.3).

westernmost extremity of the spine. It is along this central spine or axis that all of the sacred transactions of the temple occur. In both legal and ritual terms, it is this axis that may be understood as the "god's house," centered on the throne room, marked off to the west by the "restricted space," to the north and south by the lateral "open space" (*munnah*, Ezekiel 41.9), and frontally by the funnel of entranceways and shifts in height described above.

The second zone, surrounding the spine and inhabited by the permanent priestly residents, is one of domestic activity transferred to a marked-off space of power. It contains their sleeping chambers (Ezekiel 40.44) and a set of "sacred chambers"—for dining, for changing their vestments, and for the deposit of gifts and offerings (Ezekiel 42.1, 4, 7–13)—marked off by a dividing wall from the outer court (Ezekiel 42.7).

A third zone appears to be interstitial (if modern scholars have understood it correctly).[52] It consists of a set of rooms at the westernmost extremities of the outer court which appear to be reserved for overnight visitors to the temple precincts (Ezekiel 40.17). The fourth hierarchical zone is the outer court, "the place where the people are" (Ezekiel 42.14).

Thus far, the first map (Ezekiel 40.1–44.3) represents a classic model of the hierarchy of power, arranged in terms of the sacred/profane, expressed in both a social and an architectural idiom. But there is more. The system appears to be perturbed by a conflict at the level of power. If the priest is clearly subordinate to the royal YHWH—the highest rank of priests ministers to him—what about the Israelitic king? This question would be especially acute within those Israelitic ideologies (like the Zion traditions) that concentrate all of the royal function in YHWH alone.

You will recall from the précis of Dumont that, whereas hierarchy of power places the priest as subordinate to the king, hierarchy of status (especially by focusing on corpse pollution) provides the theoretical grounds for the subordination of the king in terms of pure/impure. As if to answer this question, the first map abruptly breaks with its system of power and introduces the vocabulary of status and the idiom of pure/impure that will appear in the second map. Ezekiel 43.4–9 is the decisive passage.

In direct speech, YHWH charges that the kings, and through them the people of "the house of Israel," have polluted the

temple by their actions. In particular, they have caused pollution by burying dead kings[53] on the temple mount (thus intro-
ducing corpse pollution) and by building the royal palace adjacent to YHWH's palace (the temple), setting "their thresholds
beside my threshold, and their doorposts beside my doorposts, so that [only] a wall lay between me and them" (Ezekiel
43.7–8). The solution to the first problem is given in this passage: removal. "Let them keep . . . the dead bodies of their
kings far from me" (Ezekiel 43.9).

The second problem appears more intractable, but an ideological solution is offered in Ezekiel 44.1–3:

> /1/ Then [the angel] brought me back to the outer gate of
> the sanctuary which faces east, but it was shut. /2/ Then
> YHWH[54] said to me: This gate shall remain shut. It shall
> not be opened, and no one shall enter by it; for YHWH,
> the God of Israel, has entered by it, therefore it shall re-
> main shut. /3/ Only the prince, only he alone,[55] may sit in
> it in order to eat food before YHWH. He shall enter by
> way of the vestibule of the gate, and shall go out by the
> same way.

It would appear, at first glance, that the royal figure is being
given special status. He has access to the vestibule of the
outer, eastern gateway, which is reserved for YHWH alone (see
figure 1). No other human being has such access. Walther
Eichrodt, and other scholars, reading this passage in light of
the parallel[56] in Ezekiel 46.1–15 (which I would insist is a different map), has concluded, "The one person counted worthy
of treading on such a holy spot is the reigning prince of
Israel."[57] Jon Levenson goes even further, declaring "the nāśî
occupies center stage in the temple."[58] Surely not! This is to
overlook the orientation of Ezekiel's temple map. Because the
gate is barred, the "prince" does not enter from the aus-
picious, solar east toward which the temple faces (Ezekiel
43.1–5, for example), but from the dark west—the only one
of the four cardinal directions not to have a temple gate.
(Similarly, in the third civic map of Ezekiel 48, west is "the
least honored direction.")[59] The "prince" enters in a manner
counter to the royal path of YHWH. This is to suggest that the
"prince" is no king, that, at best, he is a mock king as in some
saturnalian role reversal. The putative special status of the
prince turns out to be both literally and figuratively "arsey-

turvey" with respect to YHWH's royalty. Furthermore, by limiting the prince's sphere of activity to the gatehouse of the outer gateway that opens onto the outer court, the king, rather than being "center stage," appears to be excluded, in this map, from the temple proper.[60] To invoke, anachronistically, the scheme of far later temple maps, the king's royal sphere with respect to YHWH and his royal temple sphere, is, at best, to be located in the "Court of the Gentiles," that is to say, in the public, civic space of the temple. The hierarchy of status has been put in place: the king's place is that of subordination to the priest; while the hierarchy of power is reaffirmed: with relation to YHWH's royal function, the priest is subordinate. Although the distinctions have not been worked out here in a manner so close to the Indic system as in 11Q Temple Scroll—where the high priest is the permanent resident of the temple, and the king, governed by priestly law, is largely confined to the function of military defense[61]—the dynamics of Dumont's models of the hierarchical systems have been observed.

The second map, Ezekiel 44.4–31, exhibits a hierarchy of status constructed around the idiom of pure/impure. The overall topic is well captured by the Revised Standard Version's free, paraphrastic recasting of the difficult Hebrew of verse 5. It is concerned with "those who may be admitted to the temple and all those who are to be excluded from the sanctuary."[62]

The foreigners, those "uncircumcised in heart and flesh"[63] are the utterly impure. They "defile" the temple and are to be excluded (Ezekiel 44.7, 9). What is of interest about this otherwise unexceptional classification is that it is presented as an innovation. Formerly, the text states, such foreigners were employed as servants within the sanctuary, they were "given charge of the service due to me [YHWH] in my sanctuary," and they were given "charge of my [YHWH's] sacred things" (Ezekiel 44.8). Nor is this all. In an exceedingly murky passage that has given rise to much scholarly speculation, it is declared that the Levites, because of their participation in idolatry, will take the place of the foreigners and assume their roles in the temple (Ezekiel 44.10–11). This is stunning in its systemic implications. If one takes the classic hierarchy of status as being (1) priests, (2) kings and warriors, (3) providers of the sacrifice, and (4) servants (with a fifth class for those outside of the system),[64] the foreigners have been reduced from class 4 to class 5, while the first priestly function has been split. The Zadokites remain in the first class; the Levites have been moved from the first to the fourth class! (We might compare the harshness of this degradation with the exchange of the king's position in that portion of the first map, Ezekiel 44.1–3, concerned with hierarchy of status: he has been degraded from the second to the third class.)

Within the temple precincts as described in the second map (leaving aside the foreigners who have been placed out of the system), there is an ascending hierarchy with respect to the purity of the ritual actors. At the lowest level are the people, concerning whom no ritual details are provided save that they shall be given "instructions concerning the difference between sacred and profane, and about the difference between pure and impure" (Ezekiel 44.23). Next come the Levites, who can pollute, but for whom no purity regulations are given (Ezekiel 44.10–14). At the summit stand the Zadokites, for whom detailed purity regulations are given as to dress and marriage rules, corpse and carrion avoidance (Ezekiel 44.15–31).[65]

This hierarchy may also be expressed in a spatial idiom (see figure 3). The people are confined to the outer court. The Levites range from the gates through the outer and inner courts (Ezekiel 44.11), but "they shall draw near to me [YHWH] no more to serve me as priests, nor come near to any of my sacred things, nor to the holy of holies" (Ezekiel 44.13). By contrast, the Zadokites have the greatest spatial range. They "enter" YHWH's space and "approach his table" (Ezekiel 44.15–16); they also "go out into the inner court of the people" (Ezekiel 44.19).

As the first map revealed a conflict with respect to the royal function at the level of power (between YHWH as king and the *nāśî*), so the second map reveals a conflict with respect to the priestly function at the level of status. The solution in both cases was fission and the demotion of one portion of the controverted function with (recalling Rappaport's formulation) a system of sanctity to keep subsystems in their place.

In the second map, using the terms employed at the beginning of this chapter, the Zadokites are the "encompassing"; the Levites, the "encompassed." From one perspective, the superior, there is the unitary priority of priesthood. From the subordinate perspective, there is the sharp distinction be-

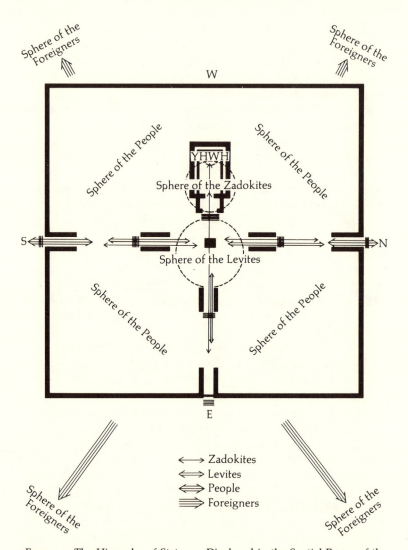

FIGURE 3. The Hierarchy of Status as Displayed in the Spatial Range of the Ritual Actors (Ezekiel 44.4–31).

tween "priests" and "servants" (Ezekiel 44.13). In Flannery's terms, the Zadokites have been "promoted" and the Levites, degraded, through a process of "linearization."

II

The first two maps of Ezekiel 40–48 are classic hierarchies, displayed in what was, in chapter 2, termed concentric systems, following Lévi-Strauss. The first displays the cartography of power, with yhwh as king at its apex; the second, the cartography of status, with the Zadokite priests at the summit. If this be accepted, a fair question becomes: Why, then, four maps? If, as has already been stated, the last two are, as they appear to be, isomorphic to the first, why the redundancy? It is a question that the approach we have taken will not allow us to answer on the level of the historical (by appealing to matters of redaction and the like); it is a question that can be answered only at the level of theory. And it is precisely the matter of theory that begins to suggest an answer. The first two maps are clear and relentless in their hierarchical principles, to such a degree that they exhibit what was earlier termed "hypocoherence." The social "realia" that affect the systematics (even in the abstract exilic situation in which the text is set) have been reduced to essentially empty categories. For example, the king has not been allowed to play his role as patron of the temple; the class, "the people," have been employed only to mark the outer limits of sanctity, their complex modes of engagement with pure/impure—that which drives both the sacrificial and the economic machinery of the temple—having been ignored; the city has been reduced to a residual category, swallowed up by the temple which is a "structure like a city." To put it another way, the bias has been overwhelmingly centripetal. There has been no account of countervailing forces. It is these matters that are addressed in the third and fourth maps, although always from the perspective of dominance.

In the third map (Ezekiel 45.1–8 and 47.13–48.35), a system of territorial distinctions and distributions is employed in which all elements—both those expressed and those suppressed in the previous maps—are given their topographical place. The map that is drawn no longer consists entirely of a center (like a black hole, constantly collapsing its periphery in on itself); instead, in the useful formulation of S. J. Tambiah, it exhibits a "galactic polity."[66]

In the first map, the land was compressed to a mountain; in the third map, while equally a matter of intellection rather than geography, the land is allowed to expand. From Hamath to Kadesh, from the Mediterranean to the Jordan River system, the land is given borders and boundaries to the north, to the east, to the south, and to the west (Ezekiel 47.15–20). What is more, this land is no longer the profane world of the undifferentiated people. It is now, in the fulfillment of a divine promise, the inheritance of the twelve tribes (Ezekiel 47.13, 14, 21) as well as their resident aliens (Ezekiel 47.22–23).

The division of the land is egalitarian with a superimposed hierarchy (see figure 4). From one perspective, the land is divided among the twelve tribes in equal allotments, one portion to each tribe, "each . . . as the other" (Ezekiel 47.14). But these are distributed in three segments: (1) a northern extremity, (2) a central area, and (3) a southern extremity. Both of the extremities are described in apparently neutral topographical order, from north to south; but their order of prestige is the reverse—running north from the center in the first segment, and south from the center in the third. Nor are the extremities equal. The northern extremity is divided, equally, among seven tribes; the southern, among five (Ezekiel 48.1–7, 23–29).

It is the central segment, as described in Ezekiel 48.8–22, that is of most interest, for it, too, has been expanded well beyond the temple that dominated the first two maps (see figure 5).

To begin with, there is a curious exchange at both the northern and the southern borders of the center—the two points of highest relative prestige among the twelve tribes. The royal southern tribe of Judah has been placed at the head of the northern tribal segment; the no less royal, though more ambiguously northern,[67] tribe of Benjamin has been placed at the head of the southern tribal segment. This inversion of long-standing sectional loyalties both recognizes the history of "real" political tensions and seeks to neutralize them. The distinction of north and south—one of the essential dualities

FIGURE 4. The Egalitarian Division of the Land (Ezekiel 45.1–8 + 47.13–48.35).

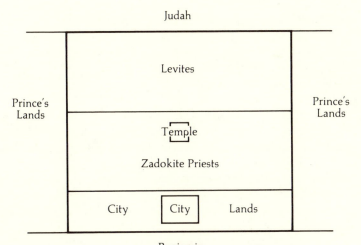

FIGURE 5. The Egalitarian Central Segment of the Land (Ezekiel 45.1–8 + 47.13–48.35).

of the monarchic temple period of Israelitic history—has been, at one and the same time, expressed and denied from the viewpoint of the powerful center.[68] In the language used to interpret the two differing maps of the Winnebago village in the previous chapter, the traditional concentric map has been replaced by a diametric one—a more symmetrical model deriving from the perspective of dominance.

The central segment comprises five components, each with its assigned portion: (1) the territory of the temple, (2) the territory of the Zadokite priests, (3) the territory of the Levites, (4) the territory of the "prince," and (5) the territory of the "city." Within this middle segment, the civic *and* the sacerdotal territories form the central spine on a north-south axis, with the territories of the prince flanking on either side (east and west). The territories of both priestly functions are equal (250 million square cubits each), and each one is twice as large as the area of the "city" (125 million square cubits; taken together, the total sacerdotal area is four times as large as the civic.

In the language of power, the entire sacerdotal area (the Zadokite and Levitical territories), not just the temple precincts, belongs to YHWH. It is a "sacred area," a consecrated area which you shall consecrate to YHWH," it is "holy to YHWH."[69] As we shall see, this is not, apparently, in total opposition to the "city," which is named (in the language of temple-presence) YHWH šāmāh, "YHWH is there" (Ezekiel 48.35); nevertheless, the text states, the city is "profane" (Ezekiel 48.15).

At the center of the central spine stands the temple and its precincts, "in the midst of the consecrated area," within the boundaries of the Zadokites but, in the northernmost portion, adjacent to the area of the Levites. The temple is centered with respect to the sacerdotal-and-the-civic; it is decentered with respect to the sacerdotal—recognizing the split in the priestly function—but placed to minimize the duality without losing it.[70]

The "city" (*hā'ir*) represents an innovation in the cartography of power. It appears in two guises. First, in Ezekiel 48.15–20, as something of a residual category. It is a "remainder," it is "profane." Like the temple's centrality with respect to the entire middle segment, the city occupies the center of the civic band. Like the temple, it is square and surrounded by a band of pasture land (although, compared to the temple precincts, it is considerably larger—more than seven times greater in area). It is to be a place of secular work and agricultural production, with a mixed population, drawing upon all of the tribes of Israel. Presented thus, it is a model of egalitarian social and civic space juxtaposed to an egalitarian model of sacerdotal space.

The second description of the "city" (Ezekiel 48.30–35), possessing a gate for each tribe and the pregnant name "YHWH is there," portends even more. The city is here depicted as a structure like a temple—the inverse of the description that began the first map. This is to suggest that there is a center of gravity within the civic, profane sphere that, to some degree, counterbalances the gravity of the temple within the holy realm.[71]

This unexpected importance given the civic realm is strengthened by the flanking domains of the prince (Ezekiel 48.21–22). Although, like the city, the prince's land is a "remainder," it is as well a part of a complex, though cryptic, system of reciprocity. As the parallel passage in Ezekiel 45.8 makes plain, the prince will have his lands; in return, he will give (or permit) the other lands to the people whom he will no longer oppress.

The third map (figure 5) is a map of power that utilizes the idiom of sacred/profane. It stands in striking contrast, however, to the first two maps because it provides more balance between the components and thus a less rigid hierarchical structure. Rather than asymmetry, there appears to be a measure of parallelism. Perhaps the key is in the quid quo pro with respect to the prince. In the first map, the king violated both the sanctity of the temple and the kingship of YHWH by an adhesion that was too close: "Only a wall lay between them and me" (Ezekiel 43.8). Here, in the third map, the temple is safely insulated. The Levitical and the civil zones separate the temple, to the north and south, from the royal houses of Judah and Benjamin. The pasture lands of the temple and the bulk of the territory of the Zadokite priests separate the temple from the flanking lands of the prince to the east and west. In the first map, the actions of the king represented, in terms of Wheatley's model, "meddling." In this third map, the varied systemic elements have kept their place, and, therefore, their varied and legitimate spheres of influence can be recognized and permitted space.[72]

If this is so, we should be able to predict on the basis of Wheatley's model that ritual will play a major role in these arrangements. For, according to his model, ritual, above all, prevents undue "promotion" and "meddling."[73] It is ritual that is the subject of the fourth and final map (Ezekiel 46), here expressed in the idiom of pure/impure. If, in the first map, the king and the people caused impurity and pollution by their improper intrusion into the temple's space, here, they play their proper roles. The people cannot move beyond the outer court; the king (allowed relative prestige) can come no further than the inner threshold of the inner gate (see figure 6). Both king and people have access to the temple on ritual occasions, but their entrances and exits, their movements through that space, are governed by strict rules of etiquette and decorum (Ezekiel 46.1–3, 8–10). Their presence in the sanctuary is solely for the transaction of proper business: the provision of offerings for the exemplary ritual of reciprocity—sacrifice (Ezekiel 46.2, 4–7, 11–15, cf. 45.10–25).

On the basis of this analysis of the last two maps, it is possible to hazard a conclusion. The third and fourth maps are not merely redundant, reenforcing the message of the first and second maps. Rather, they represent a rectification, a shift in focus possible only after the perspective gained from the first two maps has been internalized. As we have seen, the first two maps were hierarchical, insisting repeatedly on the absolute subordination to YHWH as king in a system of power, and to the Zadokite priests in a system of status. The temple served as a metonymy for the totality of the social domain of Israel, and the key distinctions inherent in the "house of Israel" were mapped in terms of its topography and architecture. Having gained such a hierarchical perspective, the third and fourth maps dissolved the metonymy and allowed the complexity of the chief components of the "house of Israel" to emerge in their reciprocal relations, one to the other, integrated into a total system. This system appears to have been more egalitarian, recognizing the integrity and legitimacy of each of the subsystems. But it is an egalitarianism possible only from the perspective of hierarchical domination by the highest order, with its attendant clarity as to the classification

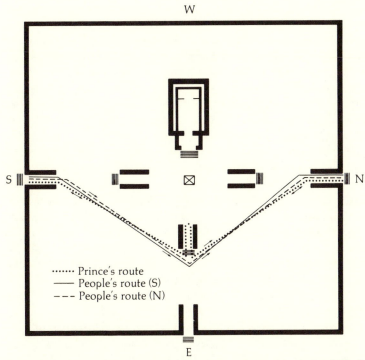

W

S   N

······ Prince's route
——— People's route (S)
– – – People's route (N)

E

FIGURE 6. The Rectified Movements of the Prince and the People (Ezekiel 46).

and ranking of subsystems achieved in the first two maps.
The first and second maps exhibit a "concentric" schema from
a (rhetorical) perspective of subordination; the third and
fourth maps display a "diametric" schema from the perspective of superordination.

III

It will be of some assistance in appreciating the intellectual
power of the strong systemic models provided in Ezekiel
40–48 with respect to place if they are compared, briefly, with
a far weaker cartography, that provided in *Aristeas* 83–121,[74] a
second century (B.C.) Jewish work.

In his description of Judea, the author of *Aristeas* provides
a picture of a well-ordered state, dominated by its capital city,

which, in turn, is dominated by its temple. But this domination is not expressed in terms of a systematics of hierarchy. There is no status, there are no degrees of purity or impurity, there is almost nothing by way of rank.[75] This may be attributable to the author's apparent lack of first-hand acquaintance with Jerusalem; to his imitation of hellenistic, utopian ethnographies; or to his self-conscious deparochialization of Jewish religious institutions.[76] Nevertheless, the contrast to what we have been considering in Ezekiel remains, and it should be removed from the status of an accidental idiosyncrasy and raised to the level of systematic thought. *Aristeas* reveals an understanding of Jerusalem, not as a primary part of a religious system, but rather as a part of a political order. Jerusalem, here, is exemplary civil space. Jerusalem is a cosmopolitan capital, though small by sophisticated Alexandrian standards.

In the map in *Aristeas*, the periphery of Judea is completely encircled by high mountains, which supply natural defenses, and surrounded by the river Jordan, which rises annually to irrigate the fields (*Aristeas*, 116, 118). The country is primarily agricultural (*Aristeas*, 112) and is arranged, checkerboard fashion, in equal-sized lots (*Aristeas*, 116). At its center, situated on a high mountain (*Aristeas*, 83), is a *polis*, described with extreme brevity—only the layout of its streets being thought worthy of comment (*Aristeas*, 105–6). At the center of the city, at its highest point, stands the temple (*Aristeas*, 84). No expense has been spared in its construction (*Aristeas*, 85). Its sewer system is especially noteworthy (*Aristeas*, 88–91).

Within the temple, sacrifices are carried out in absolute silence by some 700 well-ordered, highly industrious priests. There is no explanation why sacrifices are being performed; no language of clean/unclean; no suggestion of varying ranks of priests or regions of sanctity within the temple; no indication of any separation between priests and lay people; no suggestion that anyone is forbidden access to the temple or to any of its precincts (*Aristeas*, 92–95). Indeed, there is more of a sense of separation and more awe on the part of the author in gaining admission to the citadel—a matter of military security—than in entering the temple (*Aristeas*, 102–4). The high priest is introduced as a civil figure of sovereignty, rather than of sacerdotal purity (*Aristeas*, 96–99). His major function in the narrative is to discourse, in a learned, hellenistic fashion, on the *topos* concerning the ecological elements that determine the optimal size of cities (*Aristeas*, 112, cf. 107–11).

The importance of the contrast between Ezekiel 40–48 and *Aristeas* may be briefly stated here; it will be exposed fully in the fourth chapter. Ezekiel, by employing complex and rigorous systems of power and status with their attendant idioms of sacred/profane and pure/impure, established structures of relationships that were capable of being both replicated and rectified within the temple complex. Being systemic, they could also be replicated without. Even lacking a king or temple, or (as later) even without the realistic hope of a restored kingship or temple, the system of status could be transferred, even though that of power might have to be adjusted or abandoned. Whether it be expressed in the arrangement of the crops in a farmer's field (as in the wisdom poem of Isaiah 28.23–29) or in the complex exfoliation of Mishnah, the hierarchical relations of status do not require centralization in the temple. The system can be decentered. The capital/countryside, center/periphery model employed in *Aristeas* cannot. The map enshrined in the text could not survive the final destruction of the temple or the political disenfranchisement of Jerusalem. The model in *Aristeas* is flawed in principle— unlike hierarchy, it is indeterminate at the fringes.[77] But of greater gravity, it is inextricably tied to the accidents and fortunes of geopolitical history. It is not systemic, hence it is neither necessary nor replicable. It is historical; hence, unrepeatable. It is this last characteristic that raises the question of comparison to the understandings of place in Christian traditions concerning Jerusalem. It is to that subject that we turn in the next chapter.

FOUR

TO REPLACE

From cities of brick to cities in books to cities on maps is a path of increasing conceptualization. A map seems the type of the conceptual object, yet the interesting thing is the grotesquely token foot it keeps in the world of the physical, having the unreality without the far-fetched appropriateness of the edibles in communion, being a picture to the degree that the sacrament is a meal.

Robert Harbison

I

In 1968, when Clifford Geertz first formulated three interrelated notions that, combined, made up a distinctive "world view"—the "Doctrine of the Exemplary Center," the "Doctrine of Graded Spirituality," and the "Doctrine of the Theatre State"—he had in mind the vast edifices of Indic Java.[1] If one were to seek a western parallel, surely one of the first to come to mind would be that uniquely Christian site, Constantinople. For Constantinople was designed as far more than a new royal capital; it was deliberately crafted, over time, as a stage for the distinctive drama of the early Byzantine liturgy[2] and for the later complex elaboration of imperial-Christian ritual.[3]

The creation of a new ritual site is always an intriguing process. For, from the standpoint of ritual, novelty may result in a functional gain, but, just as often, in an ideological loss. If the former allows the freedom to innovate, the latter may result in a lack of resonance. In terminology borrowed from linguistics, novelty may give clarity to elaborate syntagmatic relations at the cost of impoverishing associative relations.[4]

The complexity of relations between old and new is not just an issue to be raised from afar. It was central to the early Christian enterprise. It was a constitutive part of the traditions of the foundation of Constantinople itself: Constantine as the "new sun";[5] Constantinople as the "new" or "second Rome"—just as later Byzantine and Carolingian emperors would be called "new Constantines," and Aachen, and, later, Moscow, would be called the true "new Rome"—or the "other" or "new Jerusalem."[6] Buried in this chain of mimetic titles is an even older association, that of Constantinople as the "new Troy,"[7] so that, in later tradition, the old and the new symbols of mythic victory—the Palladium and a relic of the Cross—would be described as being joined together in the column and statue of Constantine in the Forum.[8] The ritual of *locatio*, Constantine tracing out the boundaries of the city with a spear, resonates with ancient Roman tradition, but testifies, at the same time, to a self-consciousness that, for all the old city of Byzantium, this was a new foundation.[9]

The advantages of a new foundation were more than symbolic. Unlike Rome, where Constantine placed his new Lateran basilica in a remote location, at the very edge of the city, so as not to offend non-Christian sensibilities and perturb hallowed archaic traditions, in Constantinople, Constantine could place his church at the very center of the city, integrally connected to both royal and civic space.[10] Indeed, we do well to remember that, like the Aranda we considered in the first chapter, before Constantine the Christians may be said not to have built. To be sure, there were the refurbished (and often disguised) *domūs ecclesiae*, but it was, in effect, the foundation of Constantinople that allowed experimentation in the development of a new Christian architectural idiom in the period from Constantine to Justinian.[11]

The same freedom of utter novelty was not available in Constantinian Jerusalem, and it is the relationship between new and old in that venerable city that concerns us here. This is to ask, at the outset, a historical question. For this reason, the approach is necessarily different from the more structural inquiries of the previous chapter.

The particular place on which we shall focus is that known in eastern Christian and Muslim discourse as "The Resurrection" (*Anastasis*; in Muslim literature, after the Crusades, by a wicked pun, the church of the Resurrection [*al-Qiyâma*] is termed *al-Qumâma*, the "heap of dung").[12] In western Christian literature, it bears the fabled name, "the Holy Sepulchre"—made famous by the Crusaders' rallying cry, "*ad Sepulchrum Domini*," "[take up the way] to the Holy Sepulchre."[13]

Surprisingly, the location of the grave of Jesus and the site of Christ's resurrection is indeterminate in Synoptic tradition. John supplies only the barest details: It is close to Golgotha (John 19.41), near to the city (John 19.20), in other words, outside the walls.[14] This last detail has resulted in a lengthy controversy over the precise extent of the so-called second wall of Jerusalem, a controversy that, fortunately, need not detain us.[15] In later amplifications of the Passion Narrative (for example, the Gospel of Peter, the Acts of Pilate), no further traditions as to location are preserved.

It is reasonable to presume that there were early Christian traditions concerning the location of *ho topos*, "the place" par excellence, and that some form of veneration would have occurred. But there is no clear evidence to this effect until the time of Constantine. While there are shadowy reports of second and third century Christian pilgrimages to Jerusalem to see the "holy places" (chiefly those associated with the Hebrew Bible),[16] there is no mention of any tradition with respect to the location of this central event within the Christian myth.[17] (It might be noted that the term "holy places" is the common one, and by no means confined to Palestine. The term "holy land" [*terra sancta*] does not come into use in

Christian discourse until the twelfth century, although the notion of Jerusalem as the "holy city" [civitas sancta] is older, though most usually used in an eschatological context.[18])

The issue of the site, when it was finally raised in the fourth century, appears in a setting quite distant from pious memorials or pilgrimages. It appears in the political context of a church council called into being by imperial patronage—the Council of Nicaea. That is to say, in the distinctions of the previous chapter, it was first raised in the idiom of power, prestige, and sanctity. This is not unexpected. Within systems of status, grave sites (no matter how special) will always give rise to the question of corpse pollution. Thus, the uneasiness with which religious traditions with a clear notion of status, with a developed idiom of pure/impure (such as Judaism and Islam), have approached the issue of the veneration of tombs and relics. By contrast, within systems of power and force, possession of the *sancta* of the mighty and illustrious dead conferred prestige. Hence, the distinction noted by Peter Brown:

> The joining of the ecclesiastical hierarchy of western Europe to the tombs of the dead set the medieval Catholic church apart from its Byzantine and Near Eastern neighbors—Christian, Jewish and Muslim. In western Europe, the power of the bishop tended to coalesce with the power of the shrine. Elsewhere, the shrine tended to go its own way. The great Christian shrines of the eastern Mediterranean and pilgrimage sites of the eastern Mediterranean and the Near East—even Jerusalem—were never mobilized, as they came to be in the West, to form the basis of lasting ecclesiastical power structures.[19]

This may be illustrated by the anonymous non-Christian Palestinian attacks on Constantine's building of the memorial of the Holy Sepulchre: There are those "who in the blindness of their souls are ignorant of matters divine [and] hold the deed a joke and frankly ridiculous, believing that for so great a sovereign to bother himself with memorials to human corpses and tombs is unfitting and demeaning."[20]

There is little doubt that the chief figure in pressing the special cause of the "holy places" was Macarius, bishop of Jerusalem, distinguished as an early opponent of Arius (in a letter by Arius, in which Eusebius of Caesarea is listed as a possible ally).[21] For this reason, he held a particularly strong position at Nicaea. "Macarius was in an attacking position; Eusebius of Caesarea was on the defensive."[22] Despite the strong imperial support for Eusebius, Macarius won the day in the struggle for prestige in Palestine between Caesarea and Jerusalem. In the well-known seventh canon of Nicaea, "because of custom and ancient tradition" special status is conferred on Jerusalem while, apparently, preserving the civil power of Caesarea as metropolis.[23] It is difficult not to believe that the possession of the *locus* of Jesus's final deeds of salvation played some role in this decision, as, in a later period, the establishment of an independent patriarchate of Jerusalem at the council of Chalcedon, a result of the intense political activity of Juvenal,[24] the Church of the Holy Sepulchre, the *Anastasis*, serves as a synonym for Jerusalem and its powers: "The most holy Juvenal . . . or rather, the most holy Anastasis of Christ shall have [power over] the three Palestines."[25]

Whatever the content of his representations to the emperor, the result appears to have been a set of instructions to Macarius to seek out and restore the "holy places."

It is here that the Christian legend concerning the site of the tomb and resurrection of Jesus begins. Our major witness is Eusebius, whose account has gone through several versions. Although there is endless controversy over the veracity of Eusebius, especially in the *Vita Constantini*,[26] the fact that at least one of the versions was dedicated to (and probably delivered before) Constantine is sufficient for our purposes. It insures the ideological probity of Eusebius's account, and that is our central concern.[27]

The earliest Eusebian references, written in the period surrounding the dedication of the Constantinian church at the site of the tomb (September 335), speak only of the significance of the site: It is the "witness to the resurrection," the "scene of the great struggle," the place of the "saving sign," a "memorial full of eternal significance," a "trophy of [his] victory over death."[28] The full account of both the discovery of the site and the construction of the memorial is given later, in the *Vita Constantini* 3.25–40[29]—a work Eusebius began immediately after the death of Constantine (May 337) and left unfinished at his own death (May 339), posthumously published later that year by Acacius, his successor as bishop of Caesarea.

Indeed, the bulk of the second half of Book 3 (3.25–58) might be subtitled, "On Sacred Places," treating: (1) the site and church of the grave and resurrection (*Vita Constantini* 3.25–40); (2) Helena and the churches at Bethlehem and the Mount of Olives (*Vita Constantini* 3.41–47); (3) Constantine's church constructions in Constantinople and other cities *Vita Constantini* 3.48–50); (4) Eutropia and the church at Mambre (*Vita Constantini* 3.51–53); and (5) the destruction, by Constantine's orders, of pagan shrines (*Vita Constantini* 3.54–58). The grave site and memorial has pride of place, but it must be seen in the context of the vast church building and patronage program of Constantine. These complex and costly endeavors not only precipitated an economic boom in Palestine (comparable to our own Alaskan pipeline construction), but also were a tangible sign of Constantine's new order. What could not be accomplished in Rome (because of counterpressures), what lacked resonance in Constantinople (due to novelty), was here brought to fruition. Constantine created, for the first time, a Christian "Holy Land," laid palimpsest-like over the old, and interacting with it in complex ways, having for its central foci a series of imperial-dynastic churches. It was a venture made possible at least as much by the Hadrianic "erasure" of elements of the past as it was by the discovery of new modes of Christian topographical significance. In this process, what Constantine accomplished with power and wealth was advanced by rhetors like Eusebius who built a "Holy Land" with words.[30]

To summarize Eusebius's account: Constantine, under divine guidance, addressed himself to constructing a building at the site of the resurrection in Jerusalem. (No indication is given as to what traditions were available to determine the place.) "He deemed it necessary to bring to light . . . the blessed place . . . so that all might be able to see and venerate it" (*Vita Constantini* 3.25). There was a problem, however. The "place" was buried under rubble and dirt. From our vantage point, we would understand this to have been the result of a landfill project undertaken to provide the foundation for the vast Hadrianic urban renewal project of Aelia Capitolina. Eusebius perceives it differently. The entire "race of demons," through the instrumentality of "impious men" and "atheists," sought to place in "darkness" and "oblivion" that spot marked

by the "light of the angel who had descended from heaven"
(Matthew 28.3). This they accomplished by "piling up dirt
brought to this place from elsewhere" and by covering the
packed earthfill with paving stones (*Vita Constantini* 3.26).

Note Eusebius's interpretative frame. He intends us to
understand these actions, not as part of an overall civil engi-
neering project (regardless of Hadrian's putative motivations),
but as a premeditated, demonic attack taken against this one
particular *topos*. The razing of Jerusalem was undertaken neither in response to the Revolt nor, as Christian apologists
maintain, in punishment for the Crucifixion—it was to conceal the site of Jesus's tomb and resurrection.

The language Eusebius uses in this introductory narrative
is the archaic imperial language of cosmogonic myth. (Indeed, a bit later in the text, Constantine is made to say that the
place has been holy *ex archēs* [*Vita Constantini* 3.30].) It was a
place once marked by light; demonic forces plunged the light
into darkness; now the place, once more, through the agency
of the king, has been restored to light. This is the fundamental royal cosmogony—the revival or renewal of the cosmos
after a period of disorder or chaos (a symbolism continued to
the present day in Easter traditions with Jesus as king, in the
Roman paschal candle of Holy Saturday and, above all, in the
"Easter Fire" at the Church of the Holy Sepulchre).[31]

After this mythic passage, Eusebius shifts his language to
the idiom of the pure/impure, that is, from a royal to a sacerdotal schema. For, he reports, after covering the site, the demons, working through men, built a temple and altar to Aphrodite, a "licentious demon," above the place of the tomb. On
her "profane" altar were offered "polluted sacrifices." The
place became one of "abominations." Constantine, again acting under divine instruction, ordered a "*katharsis*" of these
"impurities" and "pollutions." Aphrodite's temple and altar
were pulled down (*Vita Constantini* 3.26). And more was required. The stones and timbers that had made up the temple
were "carted far out into the countryside," and the ground
underneath the temple was dug up "to a considerable depth"
and likewise carted away (*Vita Constantini* 3.27).

This conjoining of a royal-cosmogonic victory and a royal-
sacerdotal purification is a recurrent pattern in the Constantinian ideology as elaborated by Eusebius. It occurs as a generic,
theoretical pattern in the course of the complex comparison of

Constantine and the Logos in *De laudibus Constantini* 2.1–3.1 (especially 2.3; 2.5 and 3.1). It would appear to be a part of Constantine's self-understanding as well. This is most marked in the language adopted to interpret Constantine's victory over Licinius. On the one hand, it was described as the battle of king versus chaos-monster, as revealed in the narrative summary where Licinius is termed *drakōn* (*Vita Constantini* 2.46), in the SPES PVBLIC coins showing the *labarum* piercing a serpent, and in the similar device painted on a tablet at the entrance to Constantine's palace: a *drakōn* underneath the feet of Constantine and his sons, pierced with a lance (*Vita Constantini* 3.3).[32] On the other hand, the defeat of Licinius could be described, not in the royal language of victory, but in the idiom of pure/impure: it was a *katharsis*, a purifying of the realm from an agent of demonic pollution (*Historia ecclesiastica* 10.9.9; *Vita Constantini* 2.19). Indeed, the pattern as depicted with respect to Licinius has three parts that exactly parallel the pattern of the discovery of the tomb: the cosmic victory, the purgation, and instructions to build churches (*Vita Constantini* 2.46).

To continue with Eusebius's narrative, now of the discovery of the tomb. Eusebius returns to the language of myth, here correlating the generic myth of a renewed creation as the emergence from chaotic-demonic darkness with the specifically Christian myth of the resurrection. It was not so much a discovery as an act of self-display. After removing the polluted earth, "the most holy place which had witnessed the resurrection of the Savior came into view—beyond all our hopes." The grave itself was resurrected.

> The cave, the holy of holies, was, in a manner so similar to that of our Savior, restored to life in that, after lying buried in darkness, it again emerged into the light [*Vita Constantini* 3.28].[33]

There can be no question as to the accuracy of the identification. In the phrase used by William James, the tomb appeared as a "self-authenticating cheque."

Within a century, a new myth would be supplied, one which, in the East, overshadowed the discovery of the site[34]— the legend of the discovery of the Cross.[35]

It is not necessary, here, to rehearse fully the complex development of this legend as it began to embellish the narrative of discovery (the *inventio crucis*) as opposed to reports of relics of the wood of the Cross (the *lignum crucis*). The earliest report of the latter appears around 350;[36] the earliest version of the former, between 390 and 395.[37]

What is of interest to us is that the legend of the invention of the Cross began to interact with the Eusebian version of the discovery of the site. This is a process that began with Rufinus (c. 403), the continuator of Eusebius's *Historia ecclesiastica*, who spent some twenty years residing in Jerusalem. The crosses of Jesus and the two thieves are to be found underneath the Aphrodite temple, which Helena orders destroyed. To determine which of the crosses was that of Jesus, it is tested by curing a gravely ill woman. It is Helena who orders a basilica to be built on the spot commemorating the discovery of the site of the Cross's concealment.[38] In 403, Paulinus of Nola adds the detail that the Cross was tested, not by curing a dying woman, but by resurrecting a dead man.[39]

With this last item, the basic dossier is complete. The later church historians (Socrates, Sozomen, Theodoret) will complete the process, setting the discovery of the site of the tomb within the context of Helena's discovery of the Cross. The Eusebian sequence—(1) discovery of the site of the tomb and Constantine's building; (2) Helena's construction of churches at Bethlehem and the Mount of Olives—has been disturbed, in these later accounts, by adding a prefatory account of Helena: (1) Helena's discovery of the Cross; (2) discovery of the site of the tomb and Constantine's building; (3) Helena's construction of churches at Bethlehem and the Mount of Olives.[40] Helena discovers the Cross and tests it; she then clears the site of the tomb and constructs a church. It is the presence of the Cross and its power to resurrect, rather than the resurrection of the tomb itself, that guarantees the authenticity of the site in these later traditions.

To return to Eusebius's narrative. Constantine, having been represented as playing the mythic-heroic role of king and the cleansing role of priest, now reverts to the more usual role of king in relation to temple. He becomes its chief patron, devoting large sums of money to the construction and adornment of the new church building at the site of the tomb (*Vita Constantini* 3.29 and 40).[41]

Fortunately, it is possible for us to abstain from discussing Eusebius's description of the Constantinian building (*Vita Constantini* 3.34–39).[42] It is fraught with difficulties and ambiguities. Although the recent textual researches of E. Wistrand[43] and the archaeological explorations by V. Corbo[44] have clarified much, there remain many uncertainties. Nonetheless, in this chapter, we are once again concerned not with architectural realities, but with the understanding of ritual place. On this matter, Eusebius provides only one additional detail. The building, built on a site described as the "holy of holies," one that was "holy from the beginning" (*Vita Constantini* 3.28, 30) is to be the new temple of the new Christian Jerusalem. It is a "new Jerusalem, face to face with the old," that "second new Jerusalem spoken of by the prophets" (*Vita Constantini* 3.33).

Eusebius has here invited us to compare the Constantinian foundation with the temple in Jerusalem (as later Byzantine tradition will compare Hagia Sophia in Constantinople with the Temple, alleging that Justinian cried out, at the dedication, "Solomon, I have outdone you").[45] We should accept the invitation.

II

There is nothing inherent in the location of the Temple in Jerusalem. Its location was simply where it happened to be built. There are other shrines, often rivals to Jerusalem, for which aetiological traditions have been transmitted. Bethel is the most obvious example, both for its name and for its identification with a significant event in the legend of a patriarch (Genesis 28.10–22; 35.1–8), a narrative that expresses, in passing, several of the central ideological features of Near Eastern temples. How different the case with Jerusalem. The major narratives present the portrait of the Temple being built as a royal prerogative at a place of royal choosing. Its power over the populace, and with respect to its rival shrines, was maintained or reduced by the *imperium*. There is no biblical aetiology for the location of Jerusalem's temple, except for the brief, late, post-exilic accounts in 1 Chronicles 22.1 and 2 Chronicles 3.1.[46]

To put this another way, the Temple in Jerusalem was the

focus of a complex, self-referential system. It could, in principle, have been built anywhere else and still have been the same. It required no rationale beyond the obvious one that, once having been declared a temple and accepted as such (by YHWH, king, priests, and people), it became a place of clarification—most particularly of the hierarchical rules and roles of sacred/profane, pure/impure. In an apparent paradox, its arbitrariness, its unmotivated character, guaranteed its ordering role. There was nothing to distract from the system.

Later Jewish traditions will develop a complex mythology of the Temple site and its "Stone of Foundation" ('*eben šĕtîyâ*), beginning with creation.[47]

1. It is the place where the waters of the "Deep" were blocked off on the first day of creation;
2. it is the source of the first light of creation;
3. the Temple site was the first place in the world; hence, it is the "center" of the world;
4. it is the place from which the dust was gathered to create Adam;
5. it is the location of Adam's first sacrifice;
6. it is the site of Adam's grave;
7. it is the place where Cain and Abel offered sacrifice and, hence, the location of Abel's murder;
8. the Flood was caused by lifting the Temple's Foundation Stone and releasing the waters of the Deep;
9. the Temple site was where Noah first sacrificed after the Flood.
10. Abraham was circumcised at the Temple place;
11. the Temple site was the location of Melchizedek's altar;
12. the Temple was the site of the altar prepared for Isaac's sacrifice in the narrative of the Akedah;
13. Jacob's Bethel vision occurred at the site of the future Temple;
14. the Foundation Stone was the rock from which Moses drew water;
15. YHWH stood on the Temple site to recall the plagues;[48]

and so forth. Indeed, in one narrative, the Stone itself testifies to its significance in direct speech to David while he is digging the foundations of the Temple (b. *Sukkah* 53a–b and parallels)—thus guaranteeing that the Temple was built at the "right" place. (Many of these events appear to have been correlated temporally as well as spatially; they are held to have occurred on the eve of Passover.)[49] These same identifications are retained in Islamic traditions concerning the Dome of the Rock.[50] In Christian discourse, they have been transferred to Golgotha.[51] Here, the Temple is no longer arbitrary; it has been invested with thick temporal significance. For just this reason, it no longer functions as a systemic entity, but only as an object of pious fantasy.

Aristeas tells us (and there are no grounds in the biblical accounts of the cult to deny his claim) that the Temple in Jerusalem was a silent cult. "Complete silence prevails, so that one may suppose that no person was present in the place" (*Aristeas*, 95).[52] Translated into our terms: within the Temple, all was system from which nothing could distract. The actions within the Temple consisted of a series of hierarchical and hieratic transactions concerning pure/impure. This is, above all, a matter of difference. The ritual elements in the Temple functioned much as do phonemes within Roman Jakobson's linguistic theory, as "purely differential and contentless signs" forming a system "composed of elements which are signifiers and yet, at the same time, signify nothing."[53] That is to say, despite ingenius attempts, there is no possibility of decoding the meaning of the causes of impurity—they signify sheer difference. Nor is there any relationship of equivalence between the modes of purification and the forms of impurity—they signify sheer change in status, or, again, sheer difference. In the language adopted by Claude Lévi-Strauss from Jakobson to interpret totemism, pure/impure in the Temple ritual is "based on the postulate of a homology between two systems of differences," where the relationship is between the relation of difference, not the terms themselves:

$$1 \neq 2 \neq 3 \ldots \neq n$$
$$\mid \quad \mid \qquad \mid$$
$$1 \neq 2 \neq 3 \ldots \neq n.$$

"The system would be profoundly altered if . . . the entire system of homologies were transferred from relations to terms:"[54]

$$1 \neq 2 \neq 3 \ldots \neq n$$
$$\mid \quad \mid \quad \mid \qquad \mid$$
$$1 \neq 2 \neq 3 \ldots \neq n.$$

Within the Temple, as characteristic of a sacerdotal hierarchy employing the idiom pure/impure, relations of difference, and their ritual expression and manipulation, are everything. Within its arbitrarily demarcated boundaries, each transaction was the focus of all transactions; each transaction was capable of endless formal replication. In short, the Temple was a synchronic structure. The place could be replicated in a system of differences transferred to another realm or locale (for example, Mishnah). For it is not the terms but the relations that mattered.

The Christian understanding of place must be juxtaposed to that of the Temple. A Constantinople could be arbitrary, hence, highly systematized—but what of Jerusalem or Galilee? The Church of the Holy Sepulchre (unlike the Temple) could not have been built anywhere else and still be the same. Its *locus* had to correspond fully to the *topos* of the gospel narratives. It is tied, inextricably, to sacred biography and history. It is its locative specificity and thick associative content, rather than its arbitrariness, that guarantees the site's power and religious function. There cannot be two ways about it. For all the commonsense charm of the formulation, it cannot be, as Dean A. P. Stanley would have it, that the Church of the Holy Sepulchre is: "the most sacred of all the Holy Places; in comparison of which, if genuine, all the rest sink into insignificance; the interest of which, even if not genuine, stands absolutely alone in the world."[55] For the latter option would render the site a mere historical or folkloristic curiosity. The Church of the Holy Sepulchre requires relations of equivalence, indeed, of identity; there is no room in its systemic articulation for homologies, let alone for relations of difference.

In the Christian Jerusalem of the fourth century, gesture and story could be brought together in a unique fashion. Any homiletician of modest accomplishment and learning could develop the typology: "After these things you were led to the holy pool of divine baptism, as Christ was carried from the Cross to the Sepulchre," but no one, except a Cyril *in* Jerusalem, could then add, "from the Cross to the Sepulchre which is before our eyes."[56] In Jerusalem, story, ritual, and place could be one.

It was possible to attempt various modes of symbolic replication, substituting relations of equivalence for those of identity, exchanging parts for wholes. In the first instance, one could attempt to reproduce the Holy Sepulchre elsewhere; in the second, to export it.

The processes of reproduction could be carried out in the most literal sense: the use of the *Anastasis* as a model to be replicated in church construction or in the building of large, scaled models of the shrine to be placed as side chapels or in close association with Christian churches.[57] With less concern for verisimilitude, small constructions of wood or fabric could be fashioned and placed on or before the altars of European churches as representations of the Holy Sepulchre. These would serve as the objects of the forty-hour Easter vigil[58] or as focal points for the extraliturgical, dramatic practices of the *Depositio*, the *Elevatio*, and the *Visitatio Sepulchri*.[59]

The equivalence of terms (not relations) could be carried directly into the medieval liturgical manuals, especially in connection with the rituals for Good Friday and Holy Saturday. Although there might be a representation of the Sepulchre on the altar,[60] most frequently, in European medieval practice, it was the altar itself that was directly addressed as "sepulchre" during ceremonial moments such as the "little elevation."[61] The same mode of address could be directed to the baptismal font.[62] Alternatively, the host (as the body of Christ) in the *Missa praesanctificatorum* was reserved in a receptacle termed the *sepulchrum*—a symbolism not without controversy.[63] Perhaps the most familiar form of equivalence, as well as the most recent, is the widespread practice of the "stations of the Cross," developed from the Crusaders' experience of the Holy Land as interpreted in the tableaux they constructed of the sites they had visited (called "Little Jerusalems"),[64] and judged (at least since Innocent XII in 1694) to be the analogue of a pilgrimage to Palestine.[65]

The substitution of *pars pro toto*, in this case, the exportation of the Holy Sepulchre, is more familiar through various types of relics. In addition to pieces of the site itself—small portions of earth and chips of the rock of the tomb that were carried off by pious pilgrims and that sometimes appear in inventories of relics—[66] there was wide distribution of the relics of the wood of the Cross. It is a phenomenon that begins in the fourth century, grows precipitously in the tenth, and peaks in the thirteenth.[67] The result of this process is that

there is far more of the putative Cross to be found outside
Jerusalem than within.[68]

But neither replication nor exportation will solve the problem. For all its complex typology, Aix-la-Chapelle (Aachen) is
not, nor will it ever be, the Church of the Holy Sepulchre.[69]
The problem was created by ritual in Jerusalem; its solution
would have to come through ritual in Jerusalem.

We often fail to appreciate what a decisive impact the fourth
century creation of Christian Jerusalem had on Christian ritual. As F. L. Cross puts it:

> In earlier times [before the fourth century] Christian
> worship had been supra-historical in its relationship to
> the Lord's humanity. There was the one annual feast of
> Easter (the Passover), and this festival had commemo-
> rated simultaneously the Incarnation, the Redemption,
> the Resurrection, and the Ascension, that is, the whole
> range of God's redemptive activity for mankind. But the
> effect of the interest in the historic aspects of Christ's life
> was to bring about a differentiation. A whole cycle of
> separate feasts from Christmas to Ascension Day gradu-
> ally came into being and led to the creation of the Chris-
> tian Year. . . . The interest in the Lord's earthly life which
> contact with the sacred sites aroused gave a wholly new
> orientation to the liturgy.[70]

To translate the above into a less theological and Christo-
centric vocabulary, while retaining the important historical
point: Christian ritual, once brought into contact in the fourth
century with the *loca sancta* of Palestine, turned from the vertical dimension of the associative to the linear dimension of
the syntagmatic, to an emphasis on narrative and temporal relations. This process of turning has been preserved, like a fly
in amber, in one of the most precious of pilgrimage documents, the *Pilgrimage of Egeria*.[71]

There is much about this text that remains a mystery. The
sole manuscript (*Codex Arentinus* VI.3, from the eleventh century) is damaged—estimates vary, from one-half to two-thirds
is missing. We are not certain as to the name of the author,
although Egeria has emerged as the most plausible possibility.
We do not know where her journey originated, although
southwestern Spain (Galacia) appears most likely possibility.

And we are not certain as to her religious status. In recent years, there has been a convergence of scholarly opinion as to dates. Although not without challenges, the probability is high that the "three years" she spent in Jerusalem were between 381 and 384.[72] If this be the case, the *Pilgrimage* is the second oldest report we possess for Christian Jerusalem, and one that is uncommonly rich. The earliest, that of the anonymous Bordeaux Pilgrim (333) is in the form of an *itinerarium* with relatively few extended comments.[73]

The first part of the text, the itinerary (*Egeria* 1–23), begins in the middle of her travels to Sinai and takes her to Jerusalem. As expected, this part is dominated by *loci:* "This is the place where . . ." some scriptural "event" occurred; "this is the place according to scriptures . . ."; or "this is the place called" by scripture. It is a device that dominates pilgrim texts, the scripture as a *Guide bleu.*[74] There is the clear notion of a link between a particular passage in the text and the place before which she stands. The text expresses this almost by way of a pun between finding a geographical *locus* mentioned in scripture and finding the written *locus* in scripture for the appropriate reading.[75] The *loci* of text and topography become one; expressed in language of the *aptus locus* (*Egeria* 4.4) and the *pertinens ad rem* (*Egeria* 10.7). Indeed, there is an incipient liturgical pattern to Egeria's experience of a place: she arrives at a place noteworthy in scripture; a prayer is said; this is followed by a reading of the biblical passage "proper" to the place (given her itinerary, usually from the Hebrew Bible, and usually from the Pentateuch); then a psalm "appropriate" to the place is recited; and the proceedings conclude with a final prayer (*Egeria* 4.3; 10.4–7; 11.3; 12.3; 14.1; 15.4; 20.3; 21.1).[76]

In visits to the more recent Christian memorials, the same general pattern is followed with appropriate lectionary substitutions. Thus, passages concerning St. Thomas were read at his church in Edessa; "the complete acts of St. Thecla" at her church of Isauria, outside Seleucia (*Egeria* 19.2; 23.5).

In this manner, story and text, liturgical action, and a unique place are brought together in relations of equivalence. One example may serve for the rest.

> He [the bishop of Carrhae, formerly Harran] immediately took us to the church which was outside of the

city, [built] on the very spot where the house of Abraham had stood. According to the holy bishop, it was
built of the same stones and on the same foundations.
After we had entered the church, a prayer was said and
the proper passage from Genesis was read; then one
Psalm, and a second prayer; the bishop then blessed us,
and we went outside. Then he kindly agreed to guide us
to the well from which the holy woman, Rebecca, used
to draw water [*Egeria* 20.3].[77]

In this first, itinerary section, for all its arduous travel,
matters proceed, narratively, at a rather leisurely pace: the
finding of this or that *locus*, being endlessly shown "all the
places I was always seeking out following the scriptures"
(*Egeria* 1.1; 5.12; 6.13; *et passim*). In part, this is because the
sites themselves are rather thinly scattered. The only place
where there is a density of significance is the valley at the base
of Mount Sinai (for which we have only a partial description).
Here, significance becomes *de trop*, and the pilgrim becomes
"overloaded."

And so we were shown everything written in the holy
books of Moses that was done there in that valley. . . . It
was too much, however, to write each one down individually, because so many details could not be retained
(*Egeria* 5.8).

In the previous eight sentences, the verbal construction,
"they showed . . ." (*ostenderunt*) occurs eight times (*Egeria*
5.5–8). If this is the case for a Christian standing at Sinai, how
much more so for one in Jerusalem! For there would be a plen-
titude of significance that, if allowed to remain unchecked,
would simply result in static, in a failure of signification and
communication.

It is at this point that formal, liturgical ordering takes hold,
establishing a hierarchy of significance that focuses the de-
vout attention, chiefly achieved by adding a temporal dimension to the locative experience. The pilgrim is free to be at
whatever place he or she wishes to see, at whatever time; the
celebrant must be at a fixed place, at a fixed time, to perform
or participate in a fixed act that focuses the intended significance of this conjunction.

Hence, to move from the first part of Egeria's report to the second, from her travels around Syria-Mesopotamia to her participation in and description of the liturgical practices of Jersualem (*Egeria* 24–49), is to move from the leisurely to the highly determined, from the spatial to the temporal mode. All is done *per ordinem*, in a prescribed manner; everything is *consuetudinem*, what is customary.[78] The concern for "appropriateness" continues, but no longer, as for Egeria as pilgrim in the first section, in terms of appropriate to the place (*aptus locus*); for Egeria as celebrant in the second section, the interest is in what is appropriate to the day (*apta diei*, *Egeria* 25.11; 35.4 [twice]) or, with respect to the special situation of Jerusalem, appropriate to the day and place (*apta diei et loco*, Egeria 32.1; 35.2; 35.4; 39.5; 40.1 [twice]; 42; 43.5 [twice]; 47.5).

Although it may be a function of what has been preserved (the text breaks off in the middle of her description of the Feast of the Dedication of the Constantinian construction of the Holy Sepulchre), there is no sight-seeing in Egeria's Jerusalem narrative. It consists entirely of a record of prescribed movements among ten liturgical centers in Jerusalem and its environs (see figures 7 and 8, below). Nor does the pilgrim choose the appropriate passage in scripture; rather, there is a prescribed set of lections that are read to the congregation.[79]

Since the pioneering researches of Anton Baumstark, it has been well established that, due in no small part to pilgrimage, the indigenous liturgy of Jerusalem had a decisive role in the development of liturgical practices in both the East and the West,[80] especially as they developed from concentration on the eucharistic celebration and Easter to a fully elaborated Christian year. Much of what we know about the indigenous liturgy of Jerusalem is based on *Egeria*, on the writings of Cyril of Jerusalem (or, perhaps, those of his successor John of Jerusalem),[81] as well as on what can be reconstructed from other, later rites (most especially the Old Armenian, Old Georgian, Old Palestinian Melkite, and Old Iberian).[82]

What is most characteristic of the indigenous Jerusalem liturgy is its stational character (see figures 7 and 8). That is to say, all the liturgical action is not concentrated in a single building (an artifact of the archaic Christian "house church"), but rather is spread throughout all of the major churches in the region—the celebrants moving from one to another locale

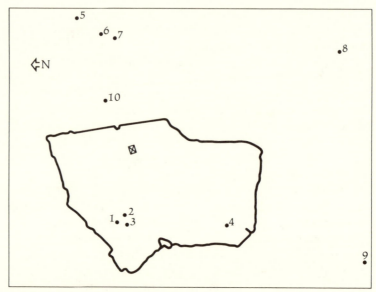

FIGURE 7. Map of the Central Liturgical Sites in Christian Jerusalem in the Fourth Century (not to scale).

1–3. Holy Sepulchre   6. Imbomon
  1. Anastasis (tomb)   7. Eleona
  2. Golgotha "At the Cross"   8. Lazarium at Bethany (not to scale)
  3. Martyrium "on Golgotha"   9. Nativity at Bethlehem (not to scale)
  4. Sion   10. Gethsemane
  5. Mount of Olives   ⊠ Ruins of Temple

at various parts of the day to perform different ceremonial functions. The bishop moves with the congregation, presiding at each church in turn.[83] This is worship as pilgrimage. It reflects the movement of a secure Christianity from an essentially private mode of worship to an overwhelmingly public and civic one of parade and procession. It is a system that (outside of Jerusalem) eventually would yield to parish churches as centers of liturgical activity, and to the concomitant distinction between "high" and "low" masses. (The earliest evidence for this is the Frankish Council of Vaison in 529, but this appears exceptional).[84]

From our perspective, what is important about this development is that it brought about the overlaying of a temporal system and a spatial system. In fact, the intercalation was more complex than that, for two different temporal systems were fused: an essentially ahistorical system of salvation (the archaic rituals for the Lord's Day, the Pascha, and Pentecost) with a historical system of commemoration, memorialization, and recollection (the Christian year, from Epiphany to Easter; the Saint's Days). It was not Rome but Jerusalem that crafted this double innovation.[85] In addition to the structure of the Christian year, the most dramatic and long-lasting effect of the Jerusalem innovation was on scripture as heard in the church, the adoption of an eclogadic lectionary, the reading of passages appropriate to the time, as opposed to the more familiar *lectio continua*, which marked a sharp difference from the practices of both earlier Christianity and Judaism.[86] In Egeria's words:

> What I admire and value most is that all of the hymns and antiphons and readings they have [in Jerusalem], and all the prayers the bishop says, are always relevant

LITURGICAL TIME	CHURCH LOCALE
Daily Service	1/2
Sunday	3/1
Wednesday and Friday	4
Epiphany Octave	9(?)/1/3/1
1	3/1/[9]
2	3 [9]
3	3 [9]
4	7 [9]
5	8 [9]
6	4 [9]
7	1 [9]
8	2 [9]
40th Day	1
Lent	
Sunday	1/2/3/1/2
Monday	1/1
Tuesday	1/1
Wednesday	1/4/1/2
Thursday	1/1
Friday	1/4/1/2 (7th week: 4/1/2)

FIGURE 8. Chart of the Stations for the Christian Liturgy in Jerusalem in the Fourth Century. (The numbers indicate the churches as located in figure 7. Brackets denote a conjectured conclusion of the service as the indicated church.)

> to the day which is being observed and to the place in
> which they are used. They never fail to be appropriate
> [*Egeria* 47.5].

As this last passage indicates, in Jerusalem the coexistence of
apta diei et loco could be maintained. Indeed, it was deliberately crafted at every turn. The celebrant was moved from
place to place—but in a sequence determined by temporal relations not topographical contiguities (see figures 7 and 8).
Thus, while the highest concentration of liturgical activity was
focused on the complex of the Holy Sepulchre, a day such as
Pentecost involved movement between eight locations. This
latter, even the indefatigable Egeria admits, produced "the
greatest strain on the people" (*Egeria* 43.1, cf. 43.9).[87]

Outside Jerusalem, the relationship had to be sundered.
While the *locus* was left behind, the system of "days" and the
correlation of the *loci* of scripture to those days could be maintained. Through a concentration on the associative dimensions of place together with the syntagmatic dimensions of
narrative, a system was formulated that could be replicated
away from the place. In this case, unlike the Temple, it was
not arbitrariness, but temporality, that guaranteed replicabil-
ity. With few exceptions,[88] the hymns, prayers, scripture les-
sons, and gestures tied to particular places in the indigenous
Jerusalem liturgy could be expropriated and exported. The sequence of time, the story, the festal calendar, have allowed a
supersession of place. It is the *apta diei* that will be endlessly
replicable, rather than the *aptus locus*.

Although some theological studies of the Christian liturgy
have sensed the import of this revolutionary separation (for
example, Dom Gregory Dix's model of the "sanctification of
time"),[89] the theoretical grounds for understanding the systemic implications of this shift were first laid by a Polish member of the Durkheimian school in his doctoral dissertation
prepared for Henri Hubert: Stefan Czarnowski and his study
of the Irish cult of St. Patrick.[90] Czarnowski argues that, in the
processes of forming a national community, the celebrations
of those heros whose feast days are marked out in time, rather
than being distributed in different places, supply the unifying
occasions.[91] It is through structures of temporality, as ritu-

alized, that the divisiveness and particularity of space are overcome.

The structured temporality of the liturgy accomplished for Christianity in its relationship to the *loca sancta* what the Jewish hierarchical distinctions accomplished with respect to Jerusalem and its Temple. Both structures—being structures and, hence, replicable—could become independent of place. They could become independent structures of thought, creativity, and human action for which the events in Jerusalem of 70 or 135, of 614 or 1244, were, strictly speaking, irrelevant. These structures undertook different (in important ways, opposing) forms in Judaism and Christianity. For the one, Mishnah; for the other, the liturgical year. Each of these two enduring monuments, perhaps, deserves to be titled the true "new Jerusalem."

FIVE

TO TAKE PLACE

Nothing shall have taken place but place.

Stéphane Mallarmé

I

Between 1724 and 1725, Conyers Middleton, D.D., English divine and recently appointed University Librarian at Cambridge, undertook a journey to Italy, most especially, to Rome. It was a curious sort of a trip, one that might be described as a reverse pilgrimage. For Middleton insists that he went to Rome, not out of "any Motive of Devotion":

My Zeal was not that of visiting the Holy Thresholds of the Apostles or kissing the Feet of their Successor: I knew that their Ecclesiastical Antiquiaries were mostly fabulous or legendary; supported by Fictions

and Impostures, too gross to employ the Attention of a Man
of Sense.[1]

Rather than wishing to gaze at "ridiculous Fictions of this
Kind," Middleton hoped to encounter the "genuine Remains
and venerable Reliques of Pagan Rome; the authentick Monuments of Antiquity." He keenly anticipated his "Joy at viewing
the very Place and Scene of these important [ancient] Events
. . . treading on that ground . . . [where the] Great Heroes of
Antiquity had been personally engaged."[2] He thrilled at the
thought of standing before "those very Walles where Cicero
and his Friends had held their Philosophical Disputations."[3]
Some 1300 years after Egeria, this Christian pilgrim was about
to undertake an opposite sort of journey, filled with the same
emotions at encountering the associative conjunction of textual and topographical *loci*, but now in terms of the "very Place
and Scene" of a pre-Christian, non-Christian "Pagan" past.

Unlike Egeria, Middleton was not delighted by the contemporary ceremonial world he encountered. He was annoyed,
troubled, and, finally, repelled by it. It presented itself to him
as static, interfering in his communion with the antique past.

Middleton had vowed, before traveling to Rome, "to lose as
little Time as possible in taking notice of the Fopperies and
ridiculous Ceremonies of the present Religion of the Place."
But this would not prove possible. "I soon found myself mis-
taken; for the whole Form and outward Dress of their Worship seemed so grossly idolatrous and extravagent."[4] To his
surprise, although he was not unaware of other authors who
had claimed the same,[5] "all these Ceremonies appeared plainly
to have been copied from the Ritual of Primitive Paganism."[6]
His beloved past was alive in contemporary Roman Catholic
ritual, but distorted, as in a fun-house mirror. He scoffs at
the priest who presides "with many ridiculous Motions and
Crossings."[7] He observes votive objects that belong "in the
Cabinets of the Curious."[8] In what might appear to us to be
all but a grotesque parody of the sort of locative enthusiasm
typified by figures like Egeria, he observes that some Catholic
ceremonies "called to his Mind" a passage in a classical text,
where "the same Ceremony was described, as transacted in
the same Form and Manner, and in the same Place . . . where
I now saw it before my eyes."[9] The rituals were performed in

"the same Temples, at the same Altars, sometimes [before] the same Images, and always with the same Ceremonies."[10] He compares, often at considerable length, parallels in eleven ceremonial categories,[11] all of which he has been "a Witness to myself."[12]

What had occurred, Middleton believes, was a process of linguistic sleight of hand. He returns to this theme insistently. The present ritual activities are but "verbal Translations of the old Originals of Heathenism."[13] "By a Change only of Name they have found the means to return to the Thing."[14] They have "changed the Name rather than the Object of their Worship."[15] But what stands revealed after the disguise has been penetrated is not the cool rationalism of his beloved Cicero (a quote from whose *De natura deorum* prefaces the work),[16] but the "superstitious man" caricatured by Theophrastus. There was, as the title of his published diatribe states, "an Exact Conformity between Popery and Paganism."

Middleton was far from an original thinker. In many respects, this makes him a more precious witness, for it allows us to perceive what is typical and characteristic in his work. He is an already late representative of a change in the Christian imagination at least as profound and far-reaching as that of the fourth century, considered in the previous chapter. It is a change that made possible, for the first time, the western imagination of religion (as opposed to religions) and gave rise to those three classic works which stand at the origin of our present academic enterprise: John Spencer's *De legibus Hebraeorum et earum rationibus* (1685); David Hume's dissertation *The Natural History of Religion* (written between 1749 and 1751, published in 1757); and Charles de Brosses's *Du Culte des Dieux fétiches, ou Parallèle de l'ancienne Religion de l'Egypte avec la Religion actuelle de Nigritie* (1760). It is an enterprise that was influenced as much by the novelties of exploration as by the polemics of theological disputation: an affair, jointly, of humanists, reformers, and philosophes. It marked the study of religion as, essentially, a Protestant exercise, a heritage that continues to haunt theorists of religion even to the present day.

Claude Lévi-Strauss has written: "Anthropology is the science of culture as seen from the outside," that "anthropology, whenever it is practiced by members of the culture it endeavors to study, loses its specific nature and becomes rather akin to archaeology, history and philology." [17] He makes an important point. And so it is well, from time to time, for those concerned with aspects of western civilization to learn about generalities concerning the West that are made from the outside—an endeavor in reverse anthropology. The particular work I have in mind is that by J. P. Singh Uberoi, a professor of sociology at the University of Delhi.

Uberoi is part of a lengthy tradition of those both within and outside the West who identify its unique characteristics with the enterprise of (modern) science. Likewise, he stands within a dominant intellectual tradition (from Max Weber through Robert K. Merton) in locating the source of modern western science in relation to the Protestant tradition. Where he differs is in where he places the generating issue. Writing from the perspective of what he terms an Indian "semaisiological world-view" (a tradition he traces back to Pāṇini), he insists that the decisive moment was the debate over "the question of liturgy, i.e. the mode of presence of divinity in Christian ritual," [18] and that it was Zwingli who established the crucial distinction that was to give rise to a distinctive western world view.

> Zwingli insisted that in the utterance "This is my body" (*Hoc est corpus meum*) the existential word "is" (*est*) was to be understood, not in a real, literal and corporeal sense, but only in a symbolical, historical or social sense (*significat, symbolum est* or *figura est*). . . . Dualism or double monism was fixed in the world-view and the life-world of the modern age, which was thereby ushered in. . . . By stating the issue and forcing it in terms of dualism, or more properly double monism, Zwingli had discovered or invented the modern concept of time in which every event was either spiritual and mental or corporeal and material but no event was or could be both at once. . . . Spirit, word and sign had finally parted company for man at Marburg in 1529; and myth or ritual . . . was no longer literally *and* symbolically real and true. . . . Zwingli was the chief architect of the new schism and . . . Europe and the world followed Zwingli in the event. Zwingli, the reformer of Zurich, was in his system of thought the first philosopher . . . of the modern world. [19]

Matters were, of course, more complex than Uberoi's analysis suggests, as the history of eucharistic controversies makes
plain,[20] but there is no doubt that he has focused attention on
a major revolution in thought: ritual is not "real"; rather, it is a
matter of "signification" for Zwingli,[21] or of "metonymy" for
Theodore Beza.[22] A wedge was decisively driven between
symbol and reality; there was no necessary connection between them.

There was an implication in this position, already faced in
disputation by Beza: Does such an understanding of eucharistic presence imply that ritual is "something ineffectual, as if
a thing were represented to us by a picture or a *mere* memorial
or figure?"[23] Beza's answer was clearly negative, but to no
avail. Despite what may have been the intentions of the Reformers, a new language was brought into being with respect
to ritual. Rather than some rituals being "idolatrous," that is,
false, one could speak of all rituals as being "only" or "merely
symbolic." Thus, the position of Zwingli and others could be
described in a 1585 polemic as being that of "the Symbolists,
Figurists, and Significatists who are of [the] opinion that the
Faithfull at the Lord's Supper doe receive nothing but naked
and bare Signes."[24] Ritual could be perceived as a matter of
surface rather than depth; of outward representation rather
than inward transformation. It was a matter of "bare ceremo-
niousnesse" (1583); "it is onlie a ceremonie" (1693), a "mere
ceremony" (1759).

As such, ritual was to be classed with superstition (shal-
low, unreasoning action) or with habit (a customary, repetitive, thoughtless action). "Let vs not come to y^r. Chirche by
vse & custome as the Oxe to his Stalle" (1526). Although this
language might be directed by Protestant authors against
"Jewish" or "Pharasaic ritualism,"[25] its polemic object was, in
fact, always Roman Catholicism. It was Catholicism that could
be described as having "Rytes superstycyouse" (1538), "a
vayne supersticious ceremoniall Masse" (1545), "superstious-
ness of Beades" (1548), "papistical superstitions" (1547); the
host was an example of "supersticious worshippyng" (1561),
of "paganick rites and foolish observances" (1573).

It is this controversy literature concerning what will be
termed "pagano-papism" (a term apparently introduced into
English by John Corbet in 1667)[26] out of which Middleton

came. Of greater significance to our topic, it is this same (often ugly) controversy literature that decisively established the valences of ritual as expressed in theories of religion up to our own time. It was a literature that sometimes took the form of learned treatises (Pierre Mussard, *Les conformitez des cérémonies modernes avec les anciennes* [1667] was, perhaps, the most influential example of the genre);[27] but it could be fulminated against in versified sermons:

> *And what are Ceremonies? are all vaine? are all*
> *superstitious?*
> *God forbid.*
> *Many are tolerable. A few necessary.*
> *Most are ridiculous. And some abominable.*[28]

or ridiculed in bald-faced doggerel:

> *Natural Religion was easy first and plain,*
> *Tales made it Mystery, Offrings made it Gain;*
> *Sacrifices and Shows were at length prepar'd,*
> *The Priests ate Roast-meat and the People star'd.*[29]

No matter what the format, the matter and message remained the same. In Erasmus's blunt formulation, "To place the whole of religion in external ceremonies is sublime stupidity."[30]

I insist on this point, in part, because the usual histories of the study of religion conceal it. They speak as if the correlation of myth and ritual was commonplace, as if the major task of rectification was to disabuse the notion that myths were false or that they were lies. Not so! The history of the imagination of the categories myth and ritual was sharply divergent. To say myth was false was to recognize it as having content; to declare ritual to be "empty" was to deny the same.

The study of myth was conceived, from the beginning, as the study of belief, an enterprise of a "hermeneutic of recovery" in that the study welcomes the foreign if only to show, by some allegorizing or rationalizing procedure, that it is, in fact, the "same." The *logos spermatikos* turned out to be fecund beyond the wildest erotic fantasies of the old Church Fathers. Utilizing the same methods the Fathers had employed on the Greco-Roman fables, the sages of the Enlightenment insisted that in even the most "savage corruptions" one could find "signs of truth." It was only a matter of decoding, of decipherment.[31] It was an enterprise of recovering "remnants," "remainders," "reminders," "seeds," "sparks," "traces," and "footprints."[32] It was a rare figure, such as the always-provocative Charles de Brosses, who would protest on behalf of both the "primitive" and the "ancient" that "their religion is never allegorical."[33] For most, the study of myth was an exercise in cultural appropriation.

How different the attitudes at the beginnings of the study of ritual! It is a difference signaled by the earliest instance of the English use of the word reported by the *Oxford English Dictionary:* "contayning no manner of Doctrine . . . but onely certayn ritual Decrees to no purpose" (1570). Here, there is no question of beliefs, no problem of the endless subtlety of words, but rather, nonsense. Ritual, lacking speech, resisted decipherment. The "other," with respect to ritual, remained sheerly "other"—there could be no penetration behind the masks, no getting beneath the gestures. The study of ritual was born as an exercise in the "hermeneutic of suspicion," an explanatory endeavor designed to explain away. That which was "other" remained obdurately so and, hence, was perceived to be bereft of all value. The "other" displayed in ritual could not be appropriated as could myth and was therefore shown the reverse face of imperialism: subjection or, more likely, extirpation.

The Protestant insistence on the "emptiness" of ritual has had a number of additional consequences that persist. Perhaps the most significant affects the mode of the academic presentation of rituals. If exegesis has been held to be the proper mode for studying the linguistically rich myths, then description becomes the proper mode for the linguistically impoverished rituals. The scholar can be "hot" with respect to his or her interpretation of myth, while remaining more or less "cool" with regard to ritual—except for certain selective and highly condensed moments, such as in examining sacrifice.

On the other hand, attempts could be made, especially in the beginning of this century, to "save the phenomenon." Most prominent has been the largely failed enterprise of providing ritual with a verbal text, the conjoining of myth to ritual, with the former serving as a libretto for the latter. Almost as common, in some circles, has been the imposition of a Romantic (and equally Protestant) theory of origination on ritual. Its first instance, it was declared, was some awe-filled, spontaneous, dramatic moment of "seizure" that subsequently became "depleted" by repetition.[34] Common to both these attempts, however, is the insistence that ritual once had meaning, but has, somehow, lost it—through historical processes of becoming separated from its text (so that ritual becomes a mere "survival"), or through routinizing processes of impoverishment.

More recently, especially in contemporary American theory, there has been an attempt to invert the valences. Priority is given to the categories of action and experience at the expense of rationality and language. It is as if the Faustian proposal were accepted, substituting "in the beginning was the deed" for "in the beginning was the word." In such proposals, the old dualistic problems return, merely in reversed guise.

I shall want more to argue forcefully against such attempts to "restore" ritual than to quarrel with the older formulations of its emptiness. Though I reject the evaluation, I find a shrewd recognition of a characteristic of ritual in the Reformation formulations. That is to say, I shall use their initial perception concerning ritual to argue a quite different conclusion in terms of the test cases we have considered in the previous chapters. What is required is a rectification of the old theory of the emptiness of ritual, not its outright rejection; a repositioning of the theory that will take its start from thinking about ritual itself and, only then, go on to consider hybrid forms such as myth/ritual.

II

Ritual is, first and foremost, a mode of paying attention. It is a process for marking interest. It is the recognition of this fundamental characteristic of ritual that most sharply distinguishes our understanding from that of the Reformers, with their all too easy equation of ritual with blind and thoughtless habit. It is this characteristic, as well, that explains the role of place as a fundamental component of ritual: place directs attention.

Such a preliminary understanding of ritual and its relation

to place is best illustrated by the case of built ritual environments—most especially, crafted constructions such as temples. When one enters a temple, one enters marked-off space (the usual example, the Greek *temenos*, derived from *temno*, "to cut") in which, at least in principle, nothing is accidental; everything, at least potentially, demands attention. The temple serves as a focusing lens, establishing the possibility of significance by directing attention, by requiring the perception of difference. Within the temple, the ordinary (which to any outside eye or ear remains wholly ordinary) becomes significant, becomes "sacred," simply by being there. A ritual object or action becomes sacred by having attention focused on it in a highly marked way. From such a point of view, there is nothing that is inherently sacred or profane. These are not substantive categories, but rather situational ones. Sacrality is, above all, a category of emplacement.[35]

This understanding of emplacement is insistently testified to by ancient stories and debates concerning ritual. It is present in the defense of the status of the Song of Songs attributed to Akiva, that "he who sings it like a secular song or pronounces a verse in a banquet house . . . brings evil into the world" (b. *Sanhedrin* 101a; cf. Tosefta *Sanhedrin* 12.10 and parallels). The issue, here, is not the content of this collection of erotic ditties, but their place. When chanted in the Temple (or its surrogate), they are, perforce, sacred; when chanted in a tavern, they are not. It is not their symbolism or their meaning that is determinitive; the songs are sacred or profane sheerly by virtue of their location. A sacred text is one that is used in a sacred place—nothing more is required.

The same point recurs in other traditions. As a part of the extensive Egyptian section in book 2 of his *Histories*, Herodotus narrates the tale of Amasis. Amasis was a "mere private person" who was elevated to king but despised because of his "ordinary" origins. He had a golden footpan in which he and his guests used to wash their feet. This was melted down and remolded into the statue of a god, which was then reverenced by the people. Amasis called a public assembly and drew the parallel as to:

> how the image had been made of the footpan, in which they formerly had been used to washing their feet and to

deposit all manner of dirt, yet now it was greatly reverenced. And truly it has gone with me [Amasis] as with
the footpan. If I were formerly a private citizen, I have
now come to be your king, and therefore I bid you to do
honor and reverence to me.[36]

This is a sophisticated story concerning the arbitrariness of
place and of placement and replacement. It comes out of the
complex ideology of archaic kingship that foreshadows the
kinds of distinctions later, western political thought will make
between the king as divine with respect to office and human
with respect to person. For example, in the twelfth century
Christian writing attributed to the Norman Anonymous:

We thus have to recognize in the king a twin person. . . .
One through which, by the condition of nature, he con-
formed with other men; another through which, by the
eminence of [his] deification and by the power of the
sacrament [of consecration], he excelled all others. Concerning one personality he was, by nature, an individual
man; concerning his other personality, he was, by grace,
a *Christus*, that is a God-man (*Deus-homo*).[37]

Note in this text that sacrality is conferred "by virtue of the
sacrament." We do well to remember that long before "the Sacred" appeared in discourse as a substantive (a usage that
does not antedate Durkheim),[38] it was primarily employed in
verbal forms, most especially with the sense of making an individual a king or bishop (as in the obsolete English verbs *to
sacrate* or *to sacre*), or in adjectival forms denoting the result of
the process of sacration.[39] Ritual is not an expression of or a
response to "the Sacred"; rather, something or someone is
made sacred by ritual (the primary sense of *sacrificium*).

In the examples just given, divine and human, sacred and
profane, are transitive categories; they serve as maps and la-
bels, not substances; they are distinctions of office, indices of
difference. The same point is made in the *topos* found inde-
pendently in both Israelitic and Latin literatures of the car-
penter who fashions a sacred object out of one part of a log
and a common household utensil out of the other.[40] Or the reverse, the melting down of a statue of a deity in order to fashion a commonplace vessel: Tertullian scoffs, "Saturn into a

cooking pot; Minerva into a washbasin."[41] Although such exempla are frequently used in antiritualistic polemics (especially against so-called idolatry),[42] this should not be allowed
to obscure their witness. The *sacra* are sacred solely because
they are used in a sacred place; there is no inherent difference
between a sacred vessel and an ordinary one.

In theoretical terms, this understanding of sacrality is most
congruent with that of Durkheim, who is largely responsible
for the widespread use, in religious studies, of the nominative
"the Sacred." The linchpin of Durkheim's argument, in *Elementary Forms*, occurs in a few pages of book 2, chapter 1, section 3.[43] The issue is the *tjurunga* and its markings.

> In themselves, the tjurunga are objects of wood and
> stone, like all others; they are distinguished from pro-
> fane things of the same kind by only one particularity:
> this is that the totemic mark is drawn or engraved on
> them. Thus it is this mark, and this mark alone, which
> confers on them their sacred character.[44]

It is the nature of these "marks" that most interests Durkheim
and provides him with his key argument. The marks are non-
representational, that is to say, not natural. Hence, they are to
be derived from social rather than sensory experience. This
latter is Durkheim's persistent claim, and here he comes close
to developing an adequate linguistic model that would have
decisively advanced his work. Although the Australians are
capable of depicting natural objects with reasonable accuracy
(in, for example, their rock paintings), they do not do so when
marking their *tjurungas*. These marks:

> consist essentially of geometric designs . . . having only
> a conventional meaning. The connection between the
> sign and the things signified [*entre la figure et la chose fi-
> gurée*] is so indirect and remote that it cannot be seen ex-
> cept when it is pointed out. Only the members of the
> clan can say what meaning is attached to such and such
> combinations of lines. . . . The meaning of the figures
> thus obtained is so arbitrary that a single design may
> have two different meanings for the men of two different
> totems.[45]

Unfortunately, Durkheim did not further develop this linguistic analogy for the sacred, turning instead to the unnecessarily mystifying notion of *mana*, and the social covariation of the alternation of ceremonial and ordinary life, to explain the duality sacred/profane.[46] It remained for Claude Lévi-Strauss to develop the linguistic analogy with respect to even *mana* itself.

Lévi-Strauss takes up the Durkheimian agenda in the context of writing on Marcel Mauss, Durkheim's closest collaborator.[47]

> Conceptions of the *mana* type are so frequent and so widespread that we should ask ourselves if we are not in the presence of a universal and permanent form of thought which, far from being characteristic of only certain civilizations or alleged "stages" of thought . . . will function in a certain situation of the mind in the face of things, one which must appear each time that this situation is given.[48]

To elucidate this "situation," Lévi-Strauss calls attention to the "exceedingly profound remark" of Father Thevanet with respect to the Algonquin (as quoted by Mauss), that *manitou* "particularly refers to all beings which still have no common name, which are not familiar."[49] After giving a set of ethnographic examples, Lévi-Strauss draws the striking conclusion:

> Always and everywhere, notions of this [*mana*-]type intervene, somewhat as algebraic symbols, to represent a value of indeterminate signification, in itself empty of meaning and therefore susceptible to the reception of any meaning whatsoever. Thus [*mana's*] unique function is to make good a discrepancy between the signifier and the signified, or more precisely, to signal the fact that in this circumstance, on this occasion, or in this one of its manifestations, a relationship of inadequacy is established between the signified and the signifier to the detriment of the anterior relation of complimentarity.[50]

Thus, for Lévi-Strauss's argument, the notion of *mana* does not pertain to the realm of "reality" but rather to that of thought; it marks discontinuity rather than continuity by representing, with precision, floating or undecided signification (*signifiant flottant*).[51] *Mana* is neither an ontological nor a substantive category; it is a linguistic one. It has a "semantic function."[52] It possesses a *valeur symbolique zéro*. It is a mark of major difference, like the zero, signifying nothing, devoid of meaning in itself, but filled with differential significance when joined to another number (as in the decimal system). It allows thought to continue despite discontinuity.[53] "It is the function of notions of the *mana*-type to oppose themselves to the absence of signification without allowing, by themselves, any particular signification."[54] In the language of typography, Lévi-Strauss's notion of *mana* might be thought of as an italicizing device; in the language of ritual books, it serves as a rubric. It signals significance without contributing signification.

It is this latter characteristic that most resembles ritual, and it is exemplified by the practices of the Temple in Jerusalem. In chapter 4, where the Temple was compared with the Church of the Holy Sepulchre, the Temple ritual was described in language congruent with that adopted here. The Temple in Jerusalem was the focus of a complex, self-referential system. Its arbitrariness guaranteed its ordering role. Within the Temple, all was system from which nothing could distract. The actions in the Temple consisted of a series of hierarchical and hieratic transactions concerning pure/impure, sacred/profane. These are, above all, matters of difference. The ritual elements in the Temple, it was claimed, functioned much as do phonemes in Roman Jakobson's linguistic theories: as "purely differential and contentless signs" forming a system "composed of elements which are signifiers and yet, at the same time, signify nothing." That is to say, despite ingenius attempts, there is no possibility of decoding the meaning of the causes of impurity—they signify sheer difference. Nor is there any relationship of equivalence between the modes of purification and the forms of impurity—they signify sheer change in status, sheer difference. Within its arbitrarily demarcated boundaries, each transaction was the focus of all transactions; each transaction was capable of endless formal replication. For it is not the terms but the relations that mattered.[55]

Admittedly, there are documentary problems with this description. There are no surviving ritual books from the Israelitic period. What is preserved in the Hebrew Bible is a set of brief descriptions gathered together for other than ritual purposes. Not a single Temple ritual in the Hebrew Bible is capable of being performed fully on the basis of the information contained therein. There are, no doubt, particular historical reasons for this,[56] but the fact remains: in their present form, the largely Priestly documents have already reduced the rituals of the Temple from performances to systems—primarily by mapping modes of emplacement. As we have seen, these maps allow a prescission from place. They could be thought about in abstract topographies; they could be transported to another place; they could be extended to other sorts of social space; they could become sheerly intellectual systems.

In each of these, there is no break with the dynamics of ritual itself. Ritual is, above all, an assertion of difference. Elsewhere, interpreting a set of rituals far removed from Jerusalem, I have written that, among other things, ritual represents the creation of a controlled environment where the variables (the accidents) of ordinary life may be displaced precisely because they are felt to be so overwhelmingly present and powerful. Ritual is a means of performing the way things ought to be in conscious tension to the way things are. Ritual relies for its power on the fact that it is concerned with quite ordinary activities placed within an extraordinary setting, that what it describes and displays is, in principle, possible for every occurrence of these acts. But it also relies for its power on the perceived fact that, in actuality, such possibilities cannot be realized. There is a "gnostic" dimension to ritual. It provides the means for demonstrating that we know what ought to have been done, what ought to have taken place. Nonetheless, by the very fact that it is ritual action rather than everyday action, ritual demonstrates that we know "what is the case." Ritual thus provides an occasion for reflection on and rationalization of the fact that what ought to have been done was not, what ought to have taken place did not. From such a perspective, ritual is not best understood as congruent with something else—a magical imitation of desired ends, a translation of emotions, a symbolic acting out of ideas, a dramatization of a text, or the like. Ritual gains force where incongruency is perceived and thought about.[57] This view accords well with a recent description of Indic sacrificial ritual:

> [The ritual] has nothing to say about the world, its concerns and conflicts. It proposes, on the contrary, a separate, self-contained world ruled exclusively by the compr~hensive and exhaustive order of the ritual. It has no meaning outside of its self-contained system of rules to connect it with the mundane order. . . . The ritual is *ardṛṣṭārtha*, without visible purpose or meaning other than the realization of its perfect order, be it only for the duration of the ritual and within the narrow compass of the ritual enclosure. . . . The ritual holds out to man the prospect of a transcendent world he creates himself on condition that he submits to the total rule of the ritual injunction. But at the same time, the open gap between the transcendent order of the ritual and the mundane ambivalence of conflict and interest is all the more obvious.[58]

Ritual is a relationship of difference between "nows"—the now of everyday life and the now of ritual place; the simultaneity, but not the coexistence, of "here" and "there." Here (in the world) blood is a major source of impurity; there (in ritual space) blood removes impurity. Here (in the world) water is the central agent by which impurity is transmitted; there (in ritual) washing with water carries away impurity. Neither the blood nor the water has changed; what has changed is their location. This absolute discrepancy invites thought, but cannot be thought away. One is invited to think of the potentialities of the one "now" in terms of the other; but the one cannot become the other. Ritual precises ambiguities; it neither overcomes nor relaxes them.

Ritual, concerned primarily with difference, is, necessarily, an affair of the relative. It exhibits, in all its forms, what Arnold van Gennep terms the "pivoting of the sacred."[59] As such, ritual is systemic hierarchy par excellence. In ritual, the differences can be extreme, or they can be reduced to microdistinctions—but they can never be overthrown. The system can never come to rest. This accounts for the definitive characteristics of ritual as described by its two most profound students: Freud and Lévi-Strauss, the former in his brief essay

Zwangshandlungen und Religionsübungen, the latter in the exas-
perating and controversial "Finale" to *L'homme nu.*

As is well known, Freud, in his first essay on religion, proposed an analogy between "what are called obsessive acts in
neurotics and those of ritual observances." The connection
was to be found in the notion of "obsession," in the compul-
sion to do certain repetitive things and to abstain from others.
The things done and the things not done are ordinary, everyday activities that are elaborated and made "rhythmic" by ad-
ditions and repetitions. Obsessive acts in both individuals
and religious rituals are described by Freud as exhibiting an
overwhelming concern for:

> little preoccupations, performances, restrictions and ar-
> rangements in certain activities of everyday life which
> have to be carried out always in the same or in a methodi-
> cally varied way . . . elaborated by petty modifications
> . . . [and] little details . . . [accompanied by the] ten-
> dency to displacement . . . [which] turns apparently
> trivial matters into those of great and urgent import.

In this early essay, the defining characteristic of ritual is "con-
scientiousness [toward] details."

> The ceremonial appears to be only an exaggeration of an
> ordinary and justifiable orderliness, but the remarkable
> conscientiousness with which it is carried out . . . gives
> the ceremonial the character of a sacred rite.[60]

Lévi-Strauss, starting from the analysis of quite different
sorts of data, comes to an analogous conclusion. He asks the
question that confronts any theorist of ritual: How are the actions in ritual to be distinguished from their close counterparts in everyday life? His answer (like Freud's) is by way of a
characterization. "In all cases, ritual makes constant use of
two procedures: parcelling out [*morcellement*] and repetition."
It is the first procedure that is of most interest to us. Parcelling
out is defined as that activity in which:

> within classes of objects and types of gesture, ritual
> makes infinite distinctions and ascribes discriminatory
> values to the slightest shade of difference. It has no con-

cern for the general, but on the contrary goes into great detail about the varieties and sub-varieties in all the taxonomic categories.[61]

Parcelling out is the same procedure that Lévi-Strauss elsewhere describes as the processes of "microadjustment" (*micropéréquation*), which are the central concern and chief characteristic of ritual.[62]

If ritual is concerned with the elaboration of relative difference that is never overcome, myth begins with absolute duality (for our purposes best expressed as the duality of "then" and "now"); its mode is not that of simultaneity, but rather of transformation. In myth, through the devices of narrative and the manipulation of temporal relations, the one becomes the other—often after much conflict and a complex repertoire of relations.

If the Temple ritual may be taken as exemplary of ritual itself, what of the conjoining of myth to ritual with respect to place as we saw in the case of the Aranda (in the first chapter) and the post-Constantinian Christian experience of Palestine (in the fourth)? Typically, these combinations focus neither on the simultaneous modes of difference characteristic of ritual nor on the serial modes of conflict and transformation characteristic of myth. The issue is not diverse forms of differentation but rather of coexistence. Such conjoined instances of myth/ritual are not so much invitations to reflectivity as invitations to reflexivity: an elaboration of memory.

Although the Aranda myths appear to be loose, paratactic constructions, connected only by "then . . . then . . . then . . .," they presuppose an absolute duality between "then" and "now," between the time of the Dreaming and the present.[63] At the juncture between the two are the mediating processes of transformation described in chapter 1. In the words used there, the transformation of the ancestor is an event that bars, forever, direct access to his particular person. Yet through this very process of metamorphosis, through being displaced from his "self" and being emplaced in an "other"—in an object, person, or mark—the ancestor achieves permanence. He becomes forever accessible, primarily through modes of memorialization.[64] Here, myth/ritual loses ritual's definitive character of sheer differentiation.

Matters, especially those bearing on temporal relations, are, in fact, more complex. Ancestral time—"their" time, "then," the time of the Dreaming—is characterized by a sort of perpetual motion as the ancestors freely transform the featureless landscape (as often by accident as by design) into its present configuration. All is fluidity, all is process and change; everything is indeterminate, everything is exponential, and, to that degree, might be termed historical. Our time—the "now," what *we* might identify as the historical present—is, in fact, characterized by a sort of atemporality from the point of view of the myths. In an inversion of ancestral times, "now" all is determinate and constant; the fluidity of the ancestors has established the forms of the present. The ancestral motion has been permanently frozen in stabile memorials. It is not the ancestor, but, paradoxically, his movement, his act of transformation, that remains forever fixed and accessible. In this system, movement is what is most at rest.

How is this paradoxical inversion systemically accomplished? Nancy Munn provides part of the answer when she writes that, since the transformations were effected in Dreamtime, but remain visible forever, "they condense within themselves the two forms of temporality"—what we have termed the "then" and the "now"—"and are thus freed from specific historical location." [65] More precisely, the prescission from temporal location results in spatial location. In W. E. H. Stanner's formulation, "a time sequence . . . is transposed into a spatial sequence." [66]

In what way does this sense of place differ from that already described as characteristic of pure ritual? All the qualities of attention are present in this form of myth/ritual—all but the arbitrarily demarcated boundaries. Any place can, in principle, be a focus of ancestral presence. Indeed, while some places are forgotten, other places may be newly discovered.

> Change, in Aboriginal religion, can take place through the discovery of sacred objects left by the Dreamtime beings. . . . This is often effected through dreams: thus, Aborigines claim that they have met spirit beings in dreams who have described the whereabouts of objects left behind by the beings of the Dreaming. The implication of this is that the "deposit of revelation" is not defi-

nitely completed or closed for Aboriginals since traces of the Dreamtime heroes may still be brought to light.[67]

The repertoire is not fixed but remains open. Anything, any place, can potentially become the object of attention; the details of any object or place can be infinitely elaborated in the myth. It is a notion of difference so universalized in its potential that difference disappears. To cite Stanner: "Anything that is symmetrically patterned attracts notice, and the same is true of marked asymetry."[68]

Such a mode of myth/ritual resists the economy of signification, the exercise of the strategy of choice, that is characteristic of ritual.[69] The only economy occurs not with respect to ritual categories but with respect to social ones. Each *tjurunga* is owned by either an individual or a clan—indeed, such ownership is one of the very few forms of personal property recognized by the Aranda.[70] Rather than Lévi-Strauss's concept of "parcelling out" with respect to ritual elements, we find Stanner's use of the same term to describe the social process. "The effect . . . is to parcel out, on a kind of distributive plan, all the non-human entities made or recognized by the ancestors."[71]

A different set of dynamics appears to be at work in the case of the Christian conjoining of myth to ritual with respect to a quite particular, indeed, a unique, place. The Christian practice appears, in many respects, to be the inverse of the Aranda.

As was argued in chapter 4, the early Christian ritual was atemporal and paradigmatic. It was contact with the *loca sancta* of now-Christian Palestine in the fourth century that transformed Christian ritual into a celebration of the historical and syntagmatic as well as, in Palestine, the topographic. As we saw, the historical and syntagmatic was continued apart from Palestine and was, through structures of temporality, the means of overcoming the topographic.

Unlike the Aranda, whose mythology was largely developed through encounters with their land, the fourth century Christians came to Palestine with preexisting lists of loci to be located in the land—onomastika and other concordance materials to both Israelitic and Christian mythic, scriptural traditions. They came, as well, with rituals that had been devel-

oped apart from the land, rituals in which topography played
no role. The full Christian myth (the life and deeds of Jesus
and their connection with a Christian reading of Israelitic narrative), which had previously played but little part in Christian ritual, was now freely projected onto the land. In the for-
mative fourth century, it was the myth—the conjunction of
the *locus* in the text with the topographical *locus*—that provided both the meaning of the place and the principles of ritual economy. It was the myth that generated the places which
became the objects of memorialization. The ritual was extended to take account of this projection—employing, within
Palestine, both spatial and temporal coordinates.

As the nontransferable stational liturgy evolved in Jerusalem, it could be exported (as we saw in the fourth chapter)
only by inverting the Aranda model. That is to say, a spatial
sequence was transposed into a temporal one—the newly invented Christian year.

Within Palestine, especially within Christian Jerusalem,
other sets of transformations can be observed. Some were the
creations of Constantinian and early post-Constantinian
times; others were Byzantine; others, the creations of the
Latin Kingdom of Jerusalem in the eleventh and twelfth centuries, following the Crusades when Christian Jerusalem was
reinvented. Regardless of the date, these transformations
have a single feature in common: the expansion of the lists, of
the repertoire of *topoi* through new narrative.

The most familiar and striking example has already been
discussed: the *inventio Crucis* associated with Helena. There is
little doubt that, in the East, this narrative rapidly came to
overshadow that of the discovery of the Tomb. Or, to put it another way, a contemporary Christian experience displaced the
archaic. What was joined together in the West under a single
name, the Church of the Holy Sepulchre, was, in Eastern
sources, carefully distinguished: the *Anastasis* as the site of
the Tomb; the *Martyrium* (with its sense of contemporary witness) as the site of the Crucifixion and the place of the discovery of the Cross. These differing spatial arrangements were
replicated on the temporal plane. In the West, both the discovery of the tomb and the discovery of the Cross were celebrated
on a single day (September 17; later, May 3). In the East, there
were two separate celebrations—closely linked, as were the

two churches—but nevertheless distinct: September 13 for
the discovery of the Tomb; September 14 for the discovery of
the Cross.[72]

Later, in a process described by Anton Baumstark as the
development of "concomitant feasts," that is, "feasts immediately following some other feast of higher rank of which
they are a kind of echo," a third feast was superimposed on
these significant dates, that of the Exaltation of the Cross.[73]
This feast represents a second, contemporary overlay placed
on the archaic myth. It commemorates the restoration of the
relic of the Cross in 627 by Heraclius after it had been removed by the armies of the Sassanian king, Khosrau II.[74] Although the event commemorated is more closely tied to the
Helena myth of the discovery of the Cross, later Christian tradition made of the "second" recovery a replication of Constantine's victories and recovery of the site of the Tomb. Khosrau
was equated with Lucifer. Demonic forces had, once again,
gained possession of a central Christian sign, and once again
it was liberated by a pious Christian emperor.[75]

If the Helena myth may be understood as a secondary elaboration out of contemporary Christian experience, to it, at the
level of narrative, was added a tertiary elaboration of pre-
history: the legend of the wood of the Cross (the Rood Tree).[76]
The wood was passed down from Adam, at length becoming
an element in Solomon's Temple, before ultimately being fashioned into the Cross. In both the *inventio Crucis* associated
with Helena and the prehistoric legend of the *origo Crucis,* the
temporal narrative has all but replaced the spatial memorial.

The processes of both condensation and concomitant du-
plication characteristic of Jerusalemite tradition continued.[77]
The Church of the Holy Sepulchre became an immense trea-
sury of relics that conferred even greater density on this holy
site.[78] The activities in the narrative of the Passion were further divided, new *topoi* were invented and connected to the
Church: the Stone of Unction; the "prison" where Jesus
awaited crucifixion.[79]

For the bulk of Christendom, however, especially in the
West, such matters became increasingly irrelevant. Through
schism and conquest, Jerusalem was lost to Christian experience and became, increasingly, an object of fantasy. If Jerusalem were to be accessible, it was to be gained through partici-

pation in a temporal arrangement of events, not a spatial one. It was through narrative, through an orderly progression through the Christian year, by encountering the *loci* of appropriate Scripture, and not by means of procession and pilgrimage, that memorialization occurred.

For this reason, our consideration of the Christian myth/ ritual must end, not with the brief recovery of the place by the Crusaders, or with the beginnings of the complex negotiations for rights of access to the place between varieties of Christians and the Muslims, or with the intricate arrangements of article 62 of the Congress of Berlin (1878), which froze the status quo with respect to the Church of the Holy Sepulchre (and the other holy places) and which persists, in its bizarre patchwork, even to this day. Rather, we may make a halt in a distant land, in Paris, in 1535. For there, bringing to conclusion a project begun in a small village thirty miles from Barcelona twelve years earlier, and possibly influenced by a one-month pilgrimage to Jerusalem,[80] Ignatius of Loyola completed his classic manual of devotion, *The Spiritual Exercises.* There, as the first set of exercises for the third week of retreat, he commends, for the contemplation at midnight, meditation on the events of the Passion of Christ spread out over seven days.[81] In each of these, the individual is asked, first, to "call to mind the narrative of the event" and, second, to make a "mental representation of the place."[82] Here, all has been transferred to inner space. All that remains of Jerusalem is an image, the narrative, and a temporal sequence.

Abbreviations

CCSL
Corpus Christianorum, Series Latina
(Turnholt, 1953–).

GCS
*Die griechischen christlichen
Schriftsteller der ersten drei
Jahrhundert* (Berlin, 1897–).

Migne, *PG*
J.-P. Migne, *Patrologiae cursus
completus, Series Graeca* (Paris,
1857–66).

Migne, *PL*
J.-P. Migne, *Patrologiae cursus
completus, Series Latina* (Paris,
1841–55).

SC
Sources chrétiennes (Paris, 1941–).

NOTES

Preface

1. J. Z. Smith, *Imagining Religion: From Babylon to Jonestown* (Chicago, 1982), xi.
2. C. Lévi-Strauss, *La pensée sauvage* (Paris, 1962), 17 (English translation, *The Savage Mind* [Chicago, 1966], 10). Note that the source from which Lévi-Strauss quotes the "native thinker"— A. C. Fletcher, "The Hako: A Pawnee Ceremony," in *Twenty-Second Annual Report of the Bureau of American Ethnology* (Washington, D.C., 1904), 2: 34—actually has a somewhat different implication. In Fletcher's report, it is the ritualist who sets apart a place for the sacred, not, as in Lévi-Strauss, being in place which confers sacrality. "The first act of a man must be to set apart a place that can be made sacred and holy, that can be consecrated to Tira'wa . . . a place where a man can put his sacred articles, those articles which enable him to approach the powers. . . . We are now to set aside a place where we shall put the sacred articles. . . . The sacred fire must come in a place set aside for it. All sacred things must have their place. Kataharu is the place set aside for the sacred fire, where it can

121

come and bring good to man." Regardless of its ethnographic accuracy, Lévi-Strauss's statement is extremely provocative on the level of theory. See, further, J. Z. Smith, *Map Is Not Territory: Studies in the History of Religions* (Leiden, 1978), 148 and n. 5.

3. See my remarks on Neusner as a comparativist in Smith, *Imagining Religion*, 33–35.

4. J. Neusner, *Judaism: The Evidence of the Mishnah* (Chicago, 1981), 282, cf. 228–29.

One

1. M. Eliade, *The Sacred and the Profane* (New York, 1959), 32–33. This work was first published in German translation, *Das Heilige und das Profane* (Munich, 1957). The English translation was prepared from the first French edition, *Le Sacré et le profane* (Paris, 1965). A second French edition has appeared; see note 6, below.

2. M. Eliade, *Australian Religions* (Ithaca, 1973); 51–53. The passage quoted occurs on p. 53. Compare Eliade's earlier summary in *The Sacred and the Profane;* p. 34: "Life is not possible without an opening toward the transcendent; in other words, human beings cannot live in chaos. Once contact with the transcendent is lost, existence in the world ceases to be possible—and the Achilpa let themselves die." Contained within these statements is Eliade's always implicit definition of religion. See Eliade, "Structures and Changes in the History of Religions," in *City Invincible*, ed. C. H. Kraeling and R. McC. Adams (Chicago, 1960), 366, and the discussion of this passage in J. Z. Smith, *Map Is Not Territory* (Leiden, 1978), 91–95.

3. Eliade's formulation of the ideology of the "sacred center," primarily developed in relation to Near Eastern temples, owes much to the researches of the Pan-Babylonian School. See J. Z. Smith, "Mythos und Geschichte," in *Alcheringa oder die beginnende Zeit*, ed. H.-P. Duerr (Frankfurt am Main, 1983), 29–48, esp. 35–41.

In developing this ideology, which is central to Eliade's thought, one notion has been crucial—his understanding of the title *Dur-an-ki* (bond of heaven and earth), applied in cuneiform texts to the Babylonian temples. (See, among others, Eliade, *The Sacred and the Profane*, p. 41. The consistently cited source is the Pan-Babylonian work of A. Jeremias, *Handbuch der altorientalischen Geisteskultur*, 2nd ed. [Berlin-Leipzig, 1929], 113). This is, most likely, a misunderstanding of the title. *Dur-an-ki* refers to the "scar" or "navel" left when heaven and earth were separated by force in the creation myths. That is to say, *Dur-an-ki* is a term that emphasizes disjunction rather than conjunction. See T. Jacobsen, *Towards the Image of Tammuz* (Cambridge, Mass., 1970), 112–13; Smith, *Map Is Not Territory*, 98–99 and n. 50.

4. Compare the similar interpretation of the Tjilpa myth by E. de Martino, "Angoscia territoriale e riscatto culturale nel mito achilpa delle origini," *Studi e materiali di storia delle religioni* 23 (1951–52): 51–66, reprinted in idem, *Il mondo magico,* 2d ed. (Turin, 1958), 261–76.

5. For the relation of the symbolism of chaos and creation to the Temple in Jerusalem, see Smith, *Map Is Not Territory,* 104–28. For a sadly typical example of the apologetic distortion of the effect of the Temple's destruction, see S. G. F. Brandon, *The Fall of Jerusalem and the Christian Church* (London, 1951), 167, who writes that the destruction of the Temple "had a paralysing affect on the life of the Jewish people, and from it they only slowly recovered and settled into an essentially maimed existence, with their cherished religion bereft of much of its raison d'etre."

6. M. Eliade, *Le sacré et le profane,* 2d ed. (Paris, 1967), 31; idem, *Australian Religions,* 52 (emphasis added); idem, *Occultism, Witchcraft, and Contemporary Fashions* (Chicago, 1976), 20.

7. B. Spencer and F. J. Gillen, *The Native Tribes of Central Australia* (London, 1899), 388–444 (the episode of the broken pole occurs on pp. 414–15); idem, *The Arunta* (London, 1927), 1:355–90 (the episode of the broken pole occurs on pp. 387–88).

In most respects, *Arunta* may be treated as a revised edition of *Native Tribes* (*Arunta* 1:x). There are no narrative variations in the episode of the broken pole. There are, however, two major differences in the setting of the overall narrative sequence. First, in *Native Tribes,* the narrative is described as part of a putative generic Aranda mythology (pp. 387 *et passim*); an impossibility in a group that emphasizes "ownership" of particular myths and rites by specific "totemic" groups. See T. G. H. Strehlow, "Tjurunja Ownership," *Aranda Traditions,* (Melbourne, 1947; reprint, New York, 1968), 84–172; K. Maddock, *The Australian Aborigine* (Harmondsworth, 1974), 36–44. In *Arunta,* on the other hand, the narrative of the ancestral wanderings is identified as a specifically Achilpa (Tjilpa) tradition. Second, as will be detailed below, the figure of Numbakulla and his creative activities appears only in *Arunta.*

It should be noted that the specific occasion at which Spencer and Gillen collected the Tjilpa myths, an Injkura festival at Alice Springs in 1896, was "a serious breach" in tribal ritual etiquette, according to native informants. See Strehlow, *Aranda Traditions,* 109–10.

8. Spencer and Gillen, *Arunta* 1:356.

9. See the moving paragraphs on the "secret life of the Aborigine" in A. P. Elkin, *The Australian Aborigines,* 3d ed. (Garden City, 1964), 168–71. On A. W. Howitt and the issue of "secrecy," see Smith, "Mythos und Geschichte," 33–35.

10. Spencer and Gillen, *Arunta* 1:x. This new information dates from 1926 (*Arunta* 1:373 n. 1).

11. T. G. H. Strehlow, *Aranda Phonetics and Grammar* (Sydney, 1944), 22; idem, "Personal Monototemism in a Polytotemic Community," in *Festschrift Ad. E. Jensen* (Munich, 1964), 2:727. Contrast these with Spencer and Gillen, *Arunta*, 1:356, in which Numbakulla "was the great original *Inkanta Alchera Numbakulla*," a term they translate as meaning the one who "arose out of nothing" (see the better translation of this phrase and its probable origin in note 15, below).

Matters are more complex. In chapter 12 of *Arunta* (esp. 1:307–18), Numbakulla consistently appears in the plural. It is only in chapter 13 of *Arunta* (esp. 1:355–61), where the cosmogonic myth is narrated, that he appears as singular. This change in number was caught by R. Pettazzoni, *Miti e leggende* (Turin, 1948), 1:434, who, quite properly, printed only the plural form (see *Miti e leggende* 1:434–38 = *Arunta* 1:307–18).

A generic, plural interpretation of Numbakulla is strengthened by the note in *Arunta* (1:355 n. 1) that Numbakulla is the "equivalent of Ungambikula," mentioned briefly in *Native Tribes*, 388–90. In the latter work, the *Ungambikula* is clearly a collective term and not the name of an individual superordinate ancestor.

For the singular Numbakulla as a possible instance of Christian-Aranda syncretism, see note 15, below.

12. See the comments on a similar Southern Aranda myth of the Ntjikantja ancestors in Strehlow, *Aranda Traditions*, 78.

13. Strehlow, "Personal Monototemism," 2:729.

14. Strehlow, *Aranda Traditions*, 139–53 (passage quoted, p. 140); idem, "Personal Monototemism," 2:728–29.

15. See T. G. H. Strehlow, "Geography and the Totemic Landscape in Central Australia," in *Australian Aboriginal Anthropology*, ed. R. M. Berndt (Nedlands, 1970), 138–39 n. 25. He writes, among the Aranda "each set of the multitudinous earth-born totemic ancestors exercised their power only in relatively small geographically delimited areas; and . . . sky dwellers . . . exerted no influence whatever. . . . The only myth to the contrary is that concocted for Sir Baldwin Spencer's consumption by the Alice Springs police tracker Charlie Cooper. It is ironic that Spencer . . . was taken in by Charlie Cooper so completely that he wrote the whole of the Chapter XIII in *The Arunta* [the chapter that contains the myth of Numbakulla summarized by Eliade] on this subject . . . Unfortunately, the very name given to Spencer's Supreme Being shows that his informant had syncretized Aboriginal beliefs with the new doctrines of the Hermannsburg missionaries: for 'Injkara Altkira Njambakala' was merely the Hermannsburg translation of a common title given to the Christian God: it means 'Lord God Eternal'."

For a more complex interpretation of such pious frauds in the context of nineteenth century native-Christian syncretisms, see Smith, *Imagining Religion* (Chicago, 1982), 66–89.

16. Spencer and Gillen, *Native Tribes*, 388–402. The more traditional nature of this version is suggested by the closely parallel myth from a different Aranda group collected by C. Strehlow, *Die Aranda und Loritja Stämme in Zentral-Australien* (Frankfurt am Main, 1907–20), 1:3–6.

17. The material on sacred poles was already gathered together in a synthetic passage by É. Durkheim, *Les formes élémentaires de la vie religieuse* (Paris, 1912; I cite the 6th ed. Paris, 1979), 174–77. The most useful recent general discussion is in R. M. Berndt and C. H. Berndt, *The World of the First Australians* (London, 1964), 370–71, 376–77, and 501 s.v. "poles and posts."

In *Arunta*, Spencer and Gillen distinguish two major types of sacred poles. First is the *kauawa-awa* (sc. *kauaua*), which figures in the myth of Numbakulla (*Arunta* 1:288 n. 1, 357, 360); in the myths of the ancestral Tjilpa wanderings (1:364, 366, 376, 382–85, 387–88); as well as on the final day of the *engwura* (sc. *injkura*) festival (1:245, 286, 288, 293–98, and figs. 107, 111). The second is the *nurtunja* (sc. *tnatantja* or *tnatanja*), which appears frequently in the myths of the ancestral Tjilpa wanderings (1:359, 364, 375–76, 379–83, 386–90) as well as in other myths (e.g., 1:170–71, 270–72); in the subincision ceremony (1:208–9); and throughout the *injkura* (1:236–39, 245–46, 269–71, 276, 285–86, 288, and figs. 65–67, 71, 77, 81–82, 104–5). See, further, the splendid color photographs in *Arunta* 2: plate I (items 20–24) and the discussion in *Arunta* 2:564–66.

Although Spencer and Gillen distinguish two types of sacred poles, in fact, the *kauaua* (Northern Aranda), *tinjara* (Western Aranda), and *tnatantja* (Southern Aranda) are local terms for the same sacred object. See C. Strehlow, *Die Aranda und Loritja Stämme* 2:23 n. 2; T. G. H. Strehlow, *Aranda Phonetics and Grammar*, 19–20; idem, *Aranda Traditions*, 77.

18. The following discussion questions the presumption—crucial for Eliade's interpretation of the myth—that the broken *kauaua* is homologous to the *kauaua* ascended by Numbakulla.

19. (1) The myth states that the *kauaua* was fashioned by Numbakulla. Spencer and Gillen do not report that it was fashioned from a gum tree, only that its ritual "representation" at the *injkura* was so made (*Arunta* 1:357). As will be noted below, there is no evidence in Spencer-Gillen that the *kauaua* at the *injkura* is understood to be a representation of Numbakulla's pole. Eliade has conflated the mythic pole and the pole used in ritual.

(2) The myth states that the *kauaua* was smeared with blood to make it easier for Numbakulla to climb. The blood's slippery qualities made it impossible for the Tjilpa ancestor to follow him. Eliade does

not specifically note the otiose detail, "Numbakulla drew the pole up after him and was never seen again" (*Arunta* 1:360).

(3) That the pole is a "cosmic axis" is Eliade's characteristic interpretation of any pole. It is nowhere suggested in the myth or in native interpretation. (A similar understanding is offered by Martino, *Il mondo magico*, 267–69, 273).

(4) There is no doubt that a variety of poles play roles in Aranda ceremonial (see note 17, above). This is especially the case among the Northern Aranda, and most especially among the Tjilpa. Although some of the poles have distinct traditions associated with them (T. G. H. Strehlow, *Aranda Traditions*, 106), I can find no evidence that the poles in the Tjilpa wandering-ancestor myths or the poles in the various Tjilpa (or other Aranda) ceremonies are in any way identified with "the pole" of Numbakulla. In part, this is because the connection of the narrative of Numbakulla's pole with the wandering-myth is an artifact of modern scholarship. The connection is not made by the Tjilpa.

It is the case that Spencer and Gillen attempt a linguistic distinction: the *Kauwa-auwa*, they claim, is the name for Numbakulla's pole and the name for the pole used in the *injkura* ceremony; *kauaua*, they claim, is the term used for a "smaller pole used in lesser ceremonies." They go on: "The pole used during this [*injkura*] ceremony . . . represented that used by Numbakulla" (*Arunta* 1:288 n. 1). This is contradicted, however, by a detail in their presentation of the myth. Numbakulla declares to the Tjilpa ancestor, before ascending the pole, "*Unta Engwura Kauaua kurka atchikka*" ("You use a small Kauaua at the Engwura") (*Arunta* 1:360). There is thus no support for this linguistic distinction (see note 17, above).

(5) The poles carried by the ancestors are nowhere identified with Numbakulla's pole. Some ancestral groups are represented in the myths as carrying poles or other ritual objects (*Arunta* 1:364, 376, 382, *et passim*); others do not.

(6) It is a thorough misreading of the text to claim that the ancestors got their direction from the pole. It is the other way around. "A sacred pole was always erected and made to lean in the direction in which they intended to travel" (*Arunta* 1:382).

(7) The pole is broken by accident; (8) the Tjilpa ancestors die. But that these two events are causally related is not clear. That (7) is the cause of (8) is reenforced by (9), the notion that the breaking of the pole is a catastrophic, all-but-apocalyptic event. This, in turn, depends on Eliade's misreading of the pole as a "cosmic axis" (3). If this be rejected (as, indeed, it must), the rest no longer follows with any necessity.

(8) The breaking of the pole is *not* the reason for the ancestors' death as given in the myth; rather, it is their embarrassment that their

pole is no longer as splendid as that of their host-group: "their *kauaua* in its broken state was inferior to many of those which the Unjiamba people had so they did not erect it, but, lying down together, died where they lay" (*Arunta* 1:388). It is loss of status rather than loss of orientation to the sacred that is the apparent cause of death. (See, further, item [9], below.)

(9) The breaking of the pole is nowhere interpreted as an apocalyptic event, as Eliade would have it. There are several other myths of ancestral times in which broken poles are connected with ancestral deaths (e.g., the Ragia Aranda myth in *Arunta* 1:270–71 and fig. 92). More usually, the breaking or theft of poles is connected with intergroup rivalry. As T. G. H. Strehlow reports: "In the *tjilpa* myths a common theme is the theft of the high *tnatantja* pole . . . by a stranger. . . . Sometimes the wandering *tjilpa* men insulted the local ancestors . . . and broke down their *tnatantja* poles" (*Aranda Traditions*, 18, 155). Indeed, there are Tjilpa traditions suggesting that the breaking of a pole in ancestral times could be understood as a creative act, even though the loss or theft of the pole is lamented (see the complex Kerenbennja myth in *Aranda Traditions*, 24–25). Finally, it should be noted that the pulling up or destruction of the *kauaua* is the final act of the *injkura* ceremony. There is no hint, in the ritual descriptions, that this in any way is understood as a dramatic "reversion to chaos." Compare the descriptions of this incident in *Arunta* 1:298 with *Aranda Traditions*, 77–78, cf. 14, 111, and figs. 7 and 9).

20. This characteristic of Australian myths has often been commented on. See Spencer and Gillen, *Arunta* 1:88–98. The most elegant example is in C. P. Mountford, *Ayers Rock* (Honolulu, 1965), 31–154.

21. Incident 5: Spencer and Gillen, *Arunta* 1:375. I have numbered as a separate "incident" each change in locale in the long narrative in *Arunta* 1:355–90.

22. Incident 32: ibid., 1:381.

23. For example, ibid., 1:375, 376 (twice), 381.

24. Incident 8: ibid., 1:375.

25. Incident 63: ibid., 1:386.

26. T. G. H. Strehlow, *Aranda Traditions*, 153–54.

27. See the excellent brief description in G. Róheim, *The Eternal Ones of the Dream* (New York, 1945), 1.

28. Spencer and Gillen, *Native Tribes*, 414–15; idem, *Arunta* 1:388.

29. For example, incident 20, Spencer and Gillen, *Arunta* 1:377. The motif of the ancestors being "tired" appears in incidents 32 (1:381), 35 (1:381), 46 (1:383), and 66 (1:386). In incident 46, the Tjilpa men are too tired to carry their *kauaua*, they drag it on the ground behind them, and they are drowned. (Compare the similar incident in T. G. H. Strehlow, *Aranda Traditions*, 89).

30. This double structure of event-memorial recurs in other mythic incidents involving broken or stolen poles. In one, the event is memorialized in "a special rounded stone which projects from the ground . . . for a height of three feet" (Spencer and Gillen, *Arunta* 1:270–71). In another, a broken portion of the pole "is still standing in the form of a blood-wood tree" (T. G. H. Strehlow, *Aranda Traditions*, 24–25).

31. (1) Incident 78, that of the broken pole, once severed from its dubious connection to the equally questionable mythic incident of Numbakulla and his pole, appears unexceptionable. It is an "accident" in the ancestral period that leads to a transformative event, the appearance of the tall stone that "represents" that *kauaua*—a feature found in other myths (see note 30, above). Indeed, such "accidents" are not uncommon. They are a frequent element in the plot of ancestral narrative. For example, within the Tjilpa cycle, incident 30 tells how a small *tjurunga* was accidentally lost when the string binding the bundle in which it was carried broke. From this lost *tjurunga* "arose a Purula man named Ultanchika, whose descendent *now* lives in Alice Springs" (Spencer and Gillen, *Arunta* 1:380, emphasis added). Even the most "casual" ancestral act can become a transformative event. In incident 74, the ancestors briefly rest their *kauaua* on the ground before erecting it. "A steep, high bank . . . arose to mark the exact spot" where it rested (*Arunta* 1:387).

(2) Incident 79, that of the death of the third group of Tjilpa ancestors, is more complex. But it, too, contains narrative elements that recur in the Tjilpa ancestral cycle. The motif that the ancestors were tired turns up at several points (see note 29, above), as does the motif that the ancestors were embarrassed by the condition of their *kauaua* in comparison with more splendid ones owned by another group. Compare incidents 34 (*Arunta* 1:381), 45 (1:383), and T. G. H. Strehlow, *Aranda Traditions*, 153.

(3) More work needs to be done on the narrative frame of incident 79, the contact of the Tjilpa migratory ancestral horde with another indigenous group. This is a widespread theme in the Tjilpa myths. "Sometimes the wandering *tjilpa* men insulted the local ancestors, or stole their *tjurunja* and broke down their *tnatantja* poles; at other times they rested in peace and concord at the side of common campfires and induced the local *tjilpa* contingents to join their ranks" (*Aranda Traditions*, 155).

In incident 79, the indigenous Aranda group is identified as N'tjuiamba men and women—indeed, the place where the death occurs is called "the place of the N'tjuiamba men." Encounters between the Tjilpa and the N'tjuiamba are frequent in the Spencer-Gillen mythic cycle: incidents 25 (*Arunta* 1:379), 26 (1:380), 31 (1:380), 37 (1:382), 39 (1:382), 40 (1:382), 41 (1:382), 70 (1:386–87), 78 (1:388), cf. 84 (1:389). The majority of these encounters are peaceful. Only one (incident 70)—when the Tjilpa attempt to steal a large *tnatantja* from a N'tjuiamba ancestor by force—is clearly hostile.

Among the above-listed encounters between the Tjilpa and the N'tjuiamba, incident 26 is of most interest. Here, the Tjilpa ancestors "journeyed to Urthipata, a swamp on the Emily plain, journeying, as they went northwards, close by but not actually along, the tracks of the Unjiamba women who were travelling in the opposite direction" (*Arunta* 1:380). This appears to be a reference to the Northern Aranda cycle of the "Two N'tjuiamba Women," which is paraphrased in exceedingly brief form in Spencer-Gillen (*Arunta* 1:74–75, 338). The cycle concerns two N'tjuiamba ancestresses who "sprung up" at Ungwuranunga, traveled south some 200 miles to Neri-iwa, and died. At two places along the way, they broke their *tnatantja* into pieces and traveled underground, reassembling the *tnatantja* when they reemerged. Urthipata was the site of their second reemergence and reassembling of the pole. The site of the second disassembling of the pole was Ooraminna, the same locale as in the Tjilpa incident 25. Here, the Tjilpa "saw a number of Unjiamba women who had originated there, and also the two Unjiamba women who had come from Engurnanunga" (*Arunta* 1:379). The reference to the "Unjiamba Women" must be to the two figures in the N'tjuiamba myth, as Enjurnanunga was the camp preceding Ooraminna on their itinerary. The Tjilpa performed ritual introcision on the two women. This myth of separate hordes of male and female ancestors with crossing paths appears to be a specifically Northern Aranda tradition. See T. G. H. Strehlow, *Aranda Traditions,* 92, and I. M. White, "Sexual Conquest and Submission in the Myths of Central Australia," in *Australian Aboriginal Mythology,* ed. L. P. Hiatt (Canberra, 1975), 127. Spencer-Gillen are in error in saying the paths of the Tjilpa ancestors and the "Two N'tjuiamba Women" never crossed (*Arunta* 1:238).

At Ooraminna, the site of the second disassembling of the pole, there is a brief (five-minute) contemporary Tjilpa ritual that commemorates the "Two N'tjuiamba Women." A *tnatantja* is erected, after some four hours have been spent on its decoration, and hung with six *tjurunga*—five of which belong to the N'tjuiamba. The pole is danced with, bent over the heads of some of the men, then laid down. Bits of fluff from the *tnatantja* are then placed on the stomachs of some of the men, and the pole is dismantled (*Arunta* 1:234–39). This mix of a Tjilpa ceremony commemorating a N'tjuiamba mythic event using N'tjuiamba *tjurungas* may be due to the peculiar, non-traditional, syncretic character of the 1896 Alice Springs festival (see T. G. H. Strehlow, *Aranda Traditions,* 109–10; idem, "Personal Monototemism," 735; idem, "Totemic Landscape," 129–30), but there may be grounds for the observation by Spencer and Gillen that "it is a remarkable fact that in one way or another the Achilpa and Unjiamba totems seem to be connected" (*Arunta* 1:239). This connection may provide additional context for the broken *kauaua* incident.

The Tjilpa myth of the accidental breaking of the pole appears to be an inversion of the deliberate breaking of the pole in the myth of the "Two N'tjuiamba Women." This is a hypothesis that may well repay further research.

32. Eliade, *Australian Religions*, 53.

33. The distinction between the cosmogonic mythologem and the ancestral mythologem has been explored by Eliade in one of his most important essays, "Cosmogonic Myth and Sacred History," *Religious Studies* 2 (1967): 171–83, reprinted in Eliade, *The Quest* (Chicago, 1969), 72–87, esp. 84–86. Eliade has failed to make this distinction in his treatment of the Tjilpa myth. He has far too easily assimilated his understanding of the *kauaua* to the complex of pole-ladder-celestial ascent traditions he brought together in a masterful fashion in *Shamanism* (New York, 1964), 125–44, 259–87, *et passim.* These shamanic traditions depend on the mythologem of a celestial "High God" rather than terrestrial ancestors. Hence, Eliade's eagerness to assimilate the Tjilpa myth to such a celestial pattern.

34. I prefer the term "objectification" to that of "reincarnation" used by T. G. H. Stehlow and others (e.g., *Aranda Traditions*, 86–96).

35. Róheim, *Eternal Ones of the Dream*, 211, 213.

36. See the various accounts in Spencer and Gillen, *Arunta* 1:8–11, 62–98, *et passim*; O. Pink, "Spirit Ancestors in a Northern Aranda Horde Country," *Oceania* 4 (1933): 176–86; idem, "The Landowners in a Northern Division of the Aranda Tribe," *Oceania* 6 (1936): 275–322; T. G. H. Strehlow, *Aranda Traditions*, 139–50 *et passim*; idem, "Culture, Social Structure and Environment in Aboriginal Central Australia," in *Aboriginal Man in Australia*, R. M. Berndt and C. H. Berndt (Sydney, 1965), 121–45; T. G. H. Strehlow, "Geography and Totemic Landscape in Central Australia," in *Australian Aboriginal Anthropology*, ed. R. M. Berndt (Nedlands, 1970), 92–140.

The notion of the Australian "horde" has been sharply challenged in recent research. See, especially, L. R. Hiatt, "Local Organization among the Australian Aborigines," *Oceania* 32 (1962): 267–86; idem, "The Lost Horde," *Oceania* 37 (1966): 81–92. See also the excellent review of the state of the question in J. Birdsell et al., "Local Group Composition among the Australian Aborigines: A Critique of the Evidence from Fieldwork Conducted Since 1930," *Current Anthropology* 11 (1970): 115–42 (120–21 focuses on the Aranda).

37. N. Munn, "The Transformation of Subjects into Objects in Walbiri and Pitjantjatjara Myth," in *Australian Aboriginal Anthropology*, ed. Berndt, 141–63 (passages quoted, 142–44).

38. See the discussion of these terms with reference to Spencer

and Gillen's and Strehlow's treatment of the Aranda in R. Merz, *Die numinose Mischgestalt: Methodenkritische Untersuchungen zu tiermensch-lichen Erscheinungen Altägyptens der Eiszeit und der Aranda in Australien* (Berlin, 1978), 162–64.

39. T. G. H. Strehlow, *Aranda Traditions*, 28–30.

40. Ibid., 126.

41. While I abstain from the theoretical framework (see Smith, *Imagining Religion*, 96–101), A. E. Jensen, *Myth and Cult Among Primitive Peoples* (Chicago, 1963), 201, cf. 173, has a series of pregnant formulations on the relationship between forgetfulness and "sacrilege."

42. M. Eliade, *Patterns in Comparative Religion* (New York, 1958), 316. Compare the same formulation in idem, *The Myth of the Eternal Return* (New York, 1954), 12. The theme is one of Eliade's earliest pre-occupations, first fully developed in his *Cosmologie si alchimie babilo-niana* (Bucharest, 1937), 26–50. It is most fully developed in his *Patterns*, 367–87; *The Sacred and the Profane*, 20–65; *Images and Symbols* (New York, 1969), 27–56; and "Centre du monde, temple, maison," in *Le symbolisme cosmique des monuments religieux*, ed. G. Tucci (Paris, 1957), 57–82, in the series Serie Orientale Roma, 14.

43. Eliade, *Images and Symbols*, 39.

44. Eliade, *Shamanism*, 259–87 et passim.

45. Eliade, *The Sacred and the Profane*, 32–33; idem, *Zalmoxis: The Vanishing God* (Chicago, 1972), 186. The same use of the Tjilpa inci-dent of the broken pole, with Eliade as its source, can be found in S. D. Gill, *Beyond "The Primitive": The Religion of Nonliterate Peoples* (Englewood Cliffs, N.J., 1982), 19–22, 27.

46. Spencer and Gillen, *Arunta* 1:14–15. See the brief, gener-alized description of the lean-to in C. S. Coon, *The Hunting Peoples* (Harmondsworth, 1976), 49–50. I do not mean to suggest that any mode of human habitation—be it cave or lean-to—is devoid of con-ceptual or symbolic significance (see A. Leroi-Gourhan, *Le geste et la parole* [Paris, 1964–65], 2:139–40), only that there is a specific horizon associated with building that is presupposed by the "Center" pattern and that is most likely not present in these modes of habitation.

47. See note 20, above.

48. Spencer and Gillen, *Arunta* 1:103.

49. See the description of the *eretitja* platform in T. G. H. Streh-low, *Aranda Traditions*, 114–15. This seems to accord with what Spen-cer and Gillen term the *tanuda* platform in *Arunta* 1:110, 227, 229, cf. fig. 68 facing p. 230.

50. W. Dampier, *Voyages and Descriptions*, 1st ed. (London, 1699), in *Dampier's Voyages*, J. Masefield, ed. (London, 1906), 1:453.

51. Spencer and Gillen, *Arunta* 1:vii.

52. See, among others, the brief summary in A. Jeremias, *Das Alte Testament im Lichte des Alten Orients*, 2d ed. (Leipzig, 1906), 49:

"As microcosmos, every country had a mountain which is the throne of the divinity and the location of paradise, a *Weltmittelpunkt*, a navel or omphalos . . . [which is] similar to the maternal link binding together the terrestrial and celestial worlds . . . an entrance to the underworld, and so on." Compare the more elaborate descriptions in P. Jensen, *Die Kosmologie der Babylonier* (Strassbourg, 1890), 195–201 *et passim*; B. Meissner, *Babylonien und Assyrien* (Heidelberg, 1925), 107–11.

53. For the sharp distinctions drawn by the Pan-Babylonians between ancient Near Eastern ideology and the anthropological "primitives," as well as the relationship between the Pan-Babylonian theories and Eliade's œuvre, see Smith, *Imagining Religion*, 26–29; idem, "Mythos und Geschichte," 35–42.

54. R. J. Clifford, *The Cosmic Mountain in Canaan and the Old Testament* (Cambridge, Mass., 1972), 2, in the series Harvard Semitic Monographs, 4.

55. See the review of the most important terms in ibid., 10–13.

56. See note 3, above. *Dur-an-ki* is not the only such temple title. See the list of temple names from Sumer in ibid., 15–16, n. 12, and from Babylonia in ibid., 15 n. 12, and in K.-H. Golzio, *Der Tempel im alten Mesopotamian und seine Parallelen in Indien* (Leiden, 1983), 58–59, in the series Beihefte der Zeitschrift für Religions- und Geistesgeschichte, 25. It is impossible when considering this language, which is not confined to temples, not to entertain the thought that it may well be a hyperbolic way of saying one's temple is very large. See W. G. Lambert, *Babylonian Wisdom Literature* (Oxford, 1960), 327, and Clifford, *The Cosmic Mountain*, 21. After all, the same sort of language is used in the praise texts of the ancient Mesopotamian kings. No matter how great or how small the extent of their individual kingdoms, they are almost always acclaimed as universal sovereigns (as are their patron deities). On the latter point, see the shrewd remarks of M. Smith, "The Common Theology of the Ancient Near East," *Journal of Biblical Literature* 71 (1952): 138–39.

57. Strehlow, "Personal Monototemism," 727–28.

58. See the rich discussion in N. Munn, *Walbiri Iconography: Graphic Representation and Cultural Symbolism in a Central Australiam Society* (Ithaca, 1973), 119–82.

59. See the early discussion of this formula in H. Grapow, "Die Welt vor der Schöpfung," *Zeitschrift für ägyptische Sprache und Altertumskunde* 67 (1931), 34–38, and the substantial review of its appearance in ancient Near Eastern materials in C. Westermann, *Genesis 1–11: A Commentary* (Minneapolis, 1984), 43–46.

60. Cited from a bilingual tablet from Sippar, as translated in A. Heidel, *The Babylonian Genesis*, 2d ed. (Chicago, 1951), 62, lines 1–9). Compare the translation in P. Garelli and M. Leibovici, "La naissance

du monde selon Akkad," in *La naissance du monde* (Paris, 1959), 145, in the series Sources orientales, 1.

61. See, among others, the Seleucid Babylonian text in J. B. Pritchard, ed., *Ancient Near Eastern Texts Relating to the Old Testament*, 2d ed. (Princeton, 1955), 341, lines 25–29.

62. For the *Enuma elish*, I have drawn on both the translation by Heidel, *Babylonian Genesis*, and that by E. A. Speiser in *Ancient Near Eastern Texts*, ed. Pritchard, 60–72.

63. B. Landsberger and J. V. Kinnier Wilson, "The Fifth Tablet of Enūma eliš," *Journal of Near Eastern Studies* 20 (1961): 154–79. See also the translation by A. K. Grayson in *The Ancient Near East: Supplementary Texts and Pictures Relating to the Old Testament*, ed. J. B. Pritchard (Princeton, 1969), 65–67.

64. See, W. L. Moran, "A New Fragment of *DIN.TIR.KI* = *Bābilu* and *Enūma elis* vi. 61–66," in *Studia Biblica et Orientalia* (Rome, 1959), 257–65, in the series Analecta Biblica, 16.

65. Although its proposed pattern is questionable, the classic article in this regard is that by A. S. Kapelrud, "Temple Building, A Task for Gods and Kings," *Orientalia*, n.s. 32 (1963): 56–62, reprinted in idem, *God and His Friends in the Old Testament* (Oslo, 1979), 184–90. Kapelrud builds on the work of J. Obermann, *Ugaritic Mythology* (New Haven, 1948), 1–7, 14–20, 83–87. For a searching critique of Kapelrud's pattern, see S. Rummel, "Narrative Structures in the Ugaritic Texts," in *Ras Shamra Parallels*, ed. S. Rummel (Rome, 1981), 3:277–84, in the series Analecta Orientalia, 51.

66. Text and translation in G. A. Barton, *The Royal Inscriptions of Sumer and Akkad* (New Haven, 1929), 204–55.

67. E. Isaac, "The Act and the Covenant: The Impact of Religion on the Landscape," *Landscape* 11 (1961–62): 12–17.

68. Compare Wheatley's attempt to reformulate Isaac's proposal in P. Wheatley, *The Pivot of the Four Quarters: A Preliminary Enquiry into the Origins and Character of the Ancient Chinese City* (Chicago, 1971), 416–17.

69. M. Heidegger, "Bauen, Wohnen, Denken," *Vorträge und Aufsätze* (Pfullingen, 1954), 145–62; for the English translation, see A. Hofstadter, *Martin Heidegger: Poetry, Language, Thought* (New York, 1971), 145–61.

70. Recall that, in some sense, animals build. See the thoughtful essay by H. Hediger, "How Animals Live," in *Animals and Plants in Historical Perspective*, ed. J. Klaits and B. Klaits (New York, 1974), 21–35.

71. See J. Pokorny, *Indogermanisches etymologisches Wörterbuch* (Bern, 1959–69), 146–50, s.v. *bheu*. Pokorny relates *bheu* ("to be, to exist, to grow"), in zero-grade form **bhu*, to both the Germanic **buthla*, giving both "building" and "house," and to the Greek, *phu-*

ein, "to bring forth," "to make grow." This is continued in modern German *bauen*, "to build" and "to cultivate."

72. Ibid., 1029–31. *Construere*, "to heap together," "to build," is an extended form of *struere*, *ster*, built on the zero-grade form **stru*, "activity" (cf. Latin, *industria*).

73. Ibid., 11–12. Edifice (*aedēs*) is from the root **aidh*, "to burn," in suffixed form **aidh-i*, "hearth and home."

74. Ibid., 1131. *Oikos* is from **ueik*, "clan," in suffixed O-grade form **woik-o*. Compare the discussion in E. Benveniste, *Le vocabulaire des institutions indo-européennes* (Paris, 1969), 1:294–98 *et passim*.

75. See, especially, the classic description in S. Kramrisch, *The Hindu Temple* (Calcutta, 1946), 1:126–28 *et passim*. I am aware that the complexity of the Hindu temple and of its mythology and ideology goes far beyond this simple characterization. Nevertheless, for heuristic purposes, I venture the comparison. The Indic temple and the Tjilpa notions bear comparison in other respects—especially on the plurality of "places"—but this would take us far from our theme. See, further, Golzio, *Der Tempel*, 116–34.

76. Kramrisch, *The Hindu Temple* 1:67–78.

77. K. 722 in L. Waterman, *Royal Correspondence of the Assyrian Empire* (Ann Arbor, 1930–36), 2:122–25 (no. 805), cf. 4:256. I follow the revised translation in A. L. Oppenheim, *Letters from Mesopotamia* (Chicago, 1967), 160–61.

Two

1. S. Freud, "A Disturbance of Memory on the Acropolis," in *Character and Culture*, P. Rieff, ed. (New York, 1963), 313, in the series The Collected Papers of Sigmund Freud, 9.

2. E. Jones, *The Life and Work of Sigmund Freud* (New York, 1955), 2:23 n. l.

3. For an early history of the excavations, see A. Bötticher, *Die Akropolis von Athen* (Berlin, 1888). The state of knowledge at the time of Freud's visit is best illustrated by the first edition of W. Judeich's classic work, *Topographie von Athen* (München, 1905), in the series Handbuch der klassischen Altertumswissenschaft, 3.2.2.

4. S. Freud, *Civilization and Its Discontents* (London, 1930), 17–18.

5. See both the translation of Jensen's novella and Freud's analysis in P. Rieff, ed., *Sigmund Freud: Delusion and Dream and Other Essays* (Boston, 1956), 25–118, 147–235. The crucial point in the analysis, dealing with the spatio temporal juxtaposition, is on p. 81.

6. The *locus classicus* is Aristotle, *De memoria*, 450a–b. See the translation and valuable commentary by R. Sorabji, *Aristotle: On Memory* (London, 1972). For a concise, modern statement of the issue, see D. Locke, *Memory* (Garden City, 1971): 1–4 *et passim*.

7. J. Locke, *An Essay Concerning Human Understanding*, 1st ed. (1690), book 2, chap. 10.2, in *An Essay Concerning Human Understanding by John Locke*, ed. A. C. Fraser (New York, 1959), 1:192. The figure is at least as old as Cicero's account of Simonides in *De oratore* 2.86.351–54, and is, perhaps, most familiar from Augustine, *Confessions* 10.8.

8. T. Reid, *Essays on the Intellectual Powers of Man*, 1st ed. (1785), essay 3, in *The Works of Thomas Reid*, 6th ed., ed. W. Hamilton (Edinburgh, 1863), 355.

9. F. Yates, *The Art of Memory* (Chicago, 1966).

10. I. Kant, *Kritik der reinen Vernunft*, 2d ed. (Riga, 1787), 42, in N. K. Smith, *Immanuel Kant's Critique of Pure Reason* (London, 1956), 71.

11. See, M. Jammer, *Concepts of Space* (Cambridge, Mass., 1957), 93–137.

12. See, among others, J. A. May, *Kant's Concept of Geography and Its Relation to Recent Geographical Thought* (Toronto, 1970), in the series University of Toronto Department of Geography Research Publications, 4.

13. Ibid., 3–4.

14. The classic work within religious studies remains the uncompleted study by H. Nissen, *Orientation: Studien zur Geschichte der Religion* (Berlin, 1906–10), 1–3. See the brief overview and selective bibliography in A. di Nola, "Orientazione," in *Enciclopedia degli religioni* (Florence, 1970), 4:1258–62.

15. I. Kant, "Von dem ersten Grunde des Unterschiedes der Gegenden im Raume" (1768), in *Kants gesammelte Schriften* (Berlin, 1902–66), 2:375–84; translated in J. Handyside, *Kant's Inaugural Dissertation and Early Writings on Space* (Chicago, 1929), 19–29. Cf. Kant, "Was heiszt: Sich im Denken orientiren" (1786), in *Gesammelte Schriften* 8:131–47.

16. Kant, *Gesammelte Schriften* 2:377–78; Handyside, *Kant's Inaugural Dissertation*, 20.

17. Controversy has centered around the issue of enantiomorphism and its demonstrative capacity for absolute space. For an overview within the Kantian corpus, see N. K. Smith, *A Commentary on Kant's Critique of Pure Reason* (New York, 1962), 161–66. For the recent philosophic controversy over Kant's claim, see J. Bennett, "The Difference between Right and Left," *American Philosophical Quarterly* 7 (1970): 175–91; J. Earman, "Kant, Incongruous Counterparts, and the Nature of Space and Space-Time," *Ratio* 13 (1971): 1–18; P. Remnant, "Incongruent Counterparts and Absolute Space," *Mind*, n.s. 72 (1963): 393–99; G. Nerlich, "Heads, Knees, and Absolute Space," *Journal of Philosophy* 70 (1973): 337–51; L. Sklar, "Incongruous Counterparts, Intrinsic Features and the Substantivity of Space," *Journal of Philosophy* 71 (1974): 277–90. The topic has been the subject of an

important monograph by J. V. Buroker, *Space and Incongruence: The Origins of Kant's Idealism* (Dordrecht, 1981), in the series Synthese Historical Library, Texts and Studies in the History of Logic and Philosophy, 21. A quite different, but extremely telling, criticism is brought forth by H. Weyl, *Philosophy of Mathematics and Natural Science* (Princeton, 1949), 84; cf. idem, *Symmetry* (Princeton, 1952), 16–38.

18. Kant, *Gesammelte Schriften* 2:378; Handyside, *Kant's Inaugural Dissertation*, 21.

19. Kant, *Gesammelte Schriften* 2:379–80; Handyside, *Kant's Inaugural Dissertation*, 23.

20. Compare the materials collected by H. Schröder, "Nord-Süd-Ost-West," *Germanisch-Romanisch Monatschrift* 17 (1929): 421–27, esp. 425–26.

21. Ad Hoc Committee on Geography of the National Academy of Sciences, *The Science of Geography* (Washington, D.C., 1965), 7. One is tempted to compare the classic formulation by P. Vidal de la Blache in his essay, "Des caractères distinctifs de la géographie," *Annales de Géographie* 22 (1913): 298, that "la géographie est la science des lieux," but note the special sense of terms such as *lieux* and *milieu* within the Vidalian project. See A. Buttimer, *Society and Milieu in the French Geographic Tradition* (Chicago, 1971), in the series Association of American Geographers Monograph Series, 6.

The Committee's formulation ought not to be taken to imply the geographers have come to definitional clarity on the issue of place. See the judgment in D. Parkes and N. Thrift, *Times, Spaces and Places: A Chronogeographic Perspective* (Chichester, 1980), 22: "Just what place is seems to be in more doubt amongst students of geography than [in] the population at large." Compare the impatient exclamation in E. Gibson, "Understanding the Subjective Meaning of Places," in *Humanistic Geography: Prospects and Problems*, ed. D. Ley and M. S. Samuels (Chicago, 1978), 138: "Let us not waste time debating the definition of *place*."

22. For a general orientation to humanistic geography, see D. R. Deskins, G. Kish, J. D. Nystuen and G. Olsson, eds., *Geographic Humanism: Analysis and Social Action* (Ann Arbor, 1977), in the series University of Michigan Department of Geography Publications, 17; and Ley and Samuels, eds., *Humanistic Geography.*

23. See B. J. L. Berry and A. Pred, *Central Place Studies: A Bibliography of Theory and Applications* (Philadelphia, 1961), in the series Regional Sciences Research Institute, Bibliography Series, 1.

24. E. Gibson, "Understanding the Subjective Meaning of Places," 138.

25. Y.-F. Tuan, *Space and Place: The Perspectives of Experience* (Minneapolis, 1977), 6.

26. Ibid., 29.

27. Ibid., 73.

28. Ibid., 199. Compare his further definitions on pp. 4, 72, 138, 144, 173, 179, 198.

29. W. Goyen, *The House of Breath*, reprint ed. (New York, 1975), 42.

30. I have borrowed this phrase, that home is where "un grand nombre de nos souvenirs sont logés," from G. Bachelard, *La poétique de l'espace*, 5th ed. (Paris, 1967), 27.

31. Ibid., 24.

32. C. C. Trowbridge, "Fundamental Methods of Orientation and Imaginary Maps," *Science* 38 (1913): 888–97; K. Lynch, *The Image of the City* (Cambridge, Mass., 1960); P. Gould and R. White, *Mental Maps* (Harmondsworth, 1974). See, further, R. M. Downs and D. Stea, *Maps in Minds: Reflections on Cognitive Mapping* (New York, 1977). For reviews of perceptual geography, see R. A. Hart and G. T. Moore, "The Development of Spatial Cognition: A Review," in *Image and Environment: Cognitive Mapping and Spatial Behavior*, ed. R. M. Downs and D. Stea (Chicago, 1973), 246–88, and D. Stea and J. T. Meyer, "Geography and the Mind: An Exploration of Perceptual Geography," *American Behavioral Scientist* 22 (1978): 59–77. For the variety of perceptual studies of specific cities, see the review article by R. W. Kates, "Human Perception of the Environment," *International Social Science Journal* 22 (1970): 648–60, esp. the valuable comparative chart on pp. 654–55.

33. A. Gussow, *A Sense of Place* (San Francisco, 1971), 27.

34. An issue not innocent of philosophical implications, though these shall not be developed here.

35. G. Steiner, *After Babel: Aspects of Language and Translation* (New York, 1975), 28.

36. D. E. Sopher, "The Landscape of Home: Myth, Experience, Social Meaning," in *The Interpretation of Ordinary Landscapes: Geographical Essays*, ed. D. W. Meinig (Oxford, 1979), 130–31. See Sopher's further development of this critique in his essay, "The Structuring of Space in Place Names and in Words for Space," in *Humanistic Geography*, ed. Ley and Samuels, 262–64, and compare, K. Birket-Smith, *The Paths of Culture* (Madison, 1965), 199–200.

37. For this theme, representing somewhat different perspectives, of humanistic geographers, see E. Relph, *Place and Placelessness* (London, 1976), and A. Buttimer and D. Seamon, eds., *The Human Experience of Space and Place* (Newe York, 1978). There is a shrewd discussion in A. A. Moles and E. Rohmer, *Psychologie de l'espace* (Tournai, 1972), 7–10, on the discrepancy between an individual's felt perception of his home as "center" and his knowledge that this perception is not shared by his community.

38. C. J. Glacken, *Traces on the Rhodian Shore: Nature and Culture in*

Western Thought from Ancient Times to the End of the Eighteenth Century (Berkeley, 1967).

39. I. Kant, *Physische Erdbeschreibung*, 1st ed. (1802), in Kant, *Gesammelte Schriften* 9:159–63. I have quoted the translation by R. Hartshorne, *The Nature of Geography*, 2d ed. (Washington, D.C., 1946), 134–35, a monographic reprint of *Annals of the Association of American Geographers* 29 (1939): 173–658 as this is the source of most of the references to Kant's text in the geographical literature. A slightly improved translation may be found in May, *Kant's Concept of Geography*, 259–61.

40. See, E. Cassirer, *The Problem of Knowledge* (New Haven, 1950), 118–28.

41. Compare the formulations in D. Harvey, *Explanation in Geography* (London, 1969), 70–71.

42. R. Hartshorne, *The Nature of Geography*, 372–73.

43. Ibid., 374.

44. I have borrowed this syllogism from a critique of Hartshorne by F. K. Schaefer, "Exceptionalism in Geography: A Methodological Examination," *Annals of the Association of American Geographers* 43 (1953): 238.

45. Hartshorne, *The Nature of Geography*, 432.

46. Ibid., 393.

47. Ibid., 396.

48. See, in general, H. Rickert, *Die Heidelberger Tradition und Kants Kritizismus* (Berlin, 1934).

49. A. Hettner, "Das System der Wissenschaften," *Preussische Jahrbücher* 122 (1905): 251–77, esp. 254–59. Cf. idem, *Die Geographie, ihre Geschichte, ihr Wesen und ihre Methoden* (Breslau, 1927), 221–24.

50. Hartshorne, *The Nature of Geography*, 379. Cf. idem, "Exceptionalism in Geography Reexamined," *Annals of the Association of American Geographers* 45 (1955): 205–44; idem, "The Concept of Geography as a Science of Space from Kant and Humboldt to Hettner," *Annals* 48 (1958): 97–108; idem, *Perspective on the Nature of Geography* (Chicago, 1959), esp. 149.

51. H. Rickert, *Kulturwissenschaft und Naturwissenschaft*, 5th ed. (Tübingen, 1921), 63. An almost identical formulation appears in idem, *Die Grenzen der naturwissenschaftlichen Begriffsbildung* (Tübingen, 1902), 255. Compare W. Windelband's major address, "Geschichte und Naturwissenschaften" (1894), in Windelband, *Präluden: Aufsätze und Reden zur Einführung in die Philosophie*, 5th ed. (Tübingen, 1914), 2:136–60.

This concern for method rather than object of study, and the insistence that any object may properly be considered from both a nomothetic and an idiographic point of view, distinguishes the approach of the Heidelberg school from that associated with Wilhelm Dilthey, who focused attention on the distinction of object in distinguishing between the *Naturwissenschaften* and the *Geisteswissenschaften*. See E. Cassirer, *The Logic of the Humanities* (New Haven, 1960), 86–91; H. White, *Metahistory: The Historical Imagination in Nineteenth-Century Europe* (Baltimore, 1973), 381–83.

52. Although the exceptionalists, such as Hartshorne, argue, when they are being careful, that geography is an "integrated dualism" (for example, Hartshorne, *The Nature of Geography*, 456–59, cf. 382–84), their overriding concern has been for the idiographic accepting, in principle, the sharp distinction between the individual and universal covering laws. I am less concerned with the explanatory issue (magnificently discussed by C. G. Hempel, *Aspects of Scientific Explanation* [New York, 1965], 231–44, which has generated an enormous literature within the philosophy of history) than I am with the implications of this dualism for the comparative and the taxonomic. For the beginnings of an important discussion on taxonomic and comparative criteria, see two essays by D. Grigg: "The Logic of Regional Systems," *Annals of the Association of American Geographers* 55 (1965): 465–91, and "Regions, Models, Classes," in *Models in Geography*, ed. R. J. Charley and P. Haggett (London, 1967), 461–509.

53. E. A. Ackerman, *Geography as a Fundamental Research Discipline* (Chicago, 1958), 15–16, in the series University of Chicago, Department of Geography Research Papers, 53.

54. N. L. Wilson, "Space, Time, and Individuals," *Journal of Philosophy* 52 (1955): 593.

55. D. Harvey, *Explanation in Geography*, 215–17.

56. Hettner, *Die Geographie*, 217; idem, "Die Begriff der Ganzheit in der Geographie," *Geographische Zeitschrift* 40 (1934): 143–44.

57. On this point, see W. W. Bunge, Jr., "Theoretical Geography," typescript, (University of Washington, 1960), 13–20, esp. 16 n. 1: "Hartshorne confuses unique with individual case. Individual case implies generality, not uniqueness." (Bunge's work has apparently been published, in 1966, in Lund Studies in Geography, Series C, no. 1, *non vidi*.)

In view of the importance given to the Durkheimian enterprise below, it is instructive to see the same arguments made with respect to uniqueness of locale and to comparison by F. Simiand in his review of five regionalist monographs in *Année sociologique* 11 (1910): 723–32. Although not unrelated, Simiand's critique should be distinguished from the attacks of Durkheim on Vidal and of Halbwachs on Ratzel. See V. Berdoulay, "The Vidal-Durkheim Debate," in Ley and Samuel, eds., *Humanistic Geography*, 77–90; R. Chartier, "Science sociale et découpage régional: Note sur deux débats, 1820–1920," *Actes de la recherche en sciences sociales* 35 (1980): 27–36; P. Besnard, "The Epistemological Polemic: François Simiand," in *The Sociological Do-*

main: The Durkheimians and the Founding of French Sociology, ed. P. Besnard (Cambridge, Eng., 1983), esp. 252–56; J. E. Craig, "Sociology and Related Disciplines Between the Wars: Maurice Halbwachs and the Imperialism of the Durkheimians," in *The Sociological Domain*, ed. Besnard, 269–71.

58. A. J. Toynbee, *A Study of History* (Oxford, 1961–64), 12:11.

59. I have taken the phrase from B. Schwartz, *Vertical Classification: A Study in Structuralism and the Sociology of Knowledge* (Chicago, 1981), 11. It is ultimately a play on Feuerbach's claim to have "turned speculative philosophy upside down" (M. Lange, ed., *Feuerbach: Kleine philosophische Schriften* [Leipzig, 1950], 56), as carried over into Marxist discourse (see, for example, *Karl Marx and Fredrick Engels: Collected Works* [New York, 1975–], 5:36). It should be noted that Schwartz by no means intends a compliment. He later refers to the Durkheimian reversal as "some trick" and an act of "intellectual jujitsu" (*Vertical Classification*, 182).

60. E. Durkheim, "L'individualisme et les intellectuals," *Revue bleue*, ser. 4, 10 (1898): 12n. English translation by S. Lukes and J. Lukes, "Individualism and the Intellectuals," *Political Studies* 17 (1969): 28n. For the historical context, see S. Lukes, *Émile Durkheim: His Life and Works* (New York, 1972), 332–49. See, further, the analysis by J. Neyer, "Individualism and Socialism in Durkheim," in *Émile Durkheim: 1858–1917*, ed. K. H. Wolff (Columbus, 1960), 35–40.

61. É. Durkheim and M. Mauss, "De quelques formes primitives de classification: Contribution à l'étude des représentations collectives," *Année sociologique* 6 (1901–2): 1–72; reprinted in V. Karady, *Marcel Mauss: Œuvres* (Paris, 1969), 2:13–89; English translation by R. Needham, *Primitive Classification by Émile Durkheim and Marcel Mauss* (Chicago, 1963).

62. Durkheim and Mauss, "De quelques formes," 2, 6 (= *Mauss: Œuvres* 2:14, 18); *Primitive Classification*, 4, 8.

63. Durkheim and Mauss, "De quelques formes," 6 (= *Mauss: Œuvres* 2:14); *Primitive Classification*, 9.

64. Durkheim and Mauss, "De quelques formes," 7–65 (= *Mauss: Œuvres* 2:19–82); *Primitive Classification*, 10–80.

65. Durkheim and Mauss, "De quelques formes," 66, cf. n. 225 (= *Mauss: Œuvres* 2:82, cf. n. 225); *Primitive Classification*, 81, cf. n. 1.

66. Durkheim and Mauss, "De quelques formes," 67 (= *Mauss: Œuvres* 2:83); *Primitive Classification*, 82–83.

67. Durkheim and Mauss, "De quelques formes," 68 (= *Mauss: Œuvres* 2:84); *Primitive Classification*, 83–84.

68. Durkheim and Mauss, "De quelques formes," 70 (= *Mauss: Œuvres* 2:86–7); *Primitive Classification*, 86.

69. Durkheim and Mauss, "De quelques formes," 72 (= *Mauss: Œuvres* 2:88); *Primitive Classification*, 88.

70. Needham, "Introduction," *Primitive Classification*, xxix.

71. Durkheim and Mauss, "De quelques formes," 67 (= *Mauss: Œuvres* 2:83); *Primitive Classification*, 82 (emphasis added).

72. Durkheim and Mauss, "De quelques formes," 8 (in the original, the entire sentence is in italics), 55 (= *Mauss: Œuvres* 2:20, 70); *Primitive Classification*, 11, 66 (emphasis added).

73. Needham, "Introduction," *Primitive Classification*, xxxvii.

74. É. Durkheim, *Les formes élémentaires de la vie religieuse*, 1st ed. (Paris, 1912). I cite the 6th ed. (Paris, 1979). English translation by J. W. Swain, *The Elementary Forms of the Religious Life* (London, 1915; reprint, New York, 1965).

75. H. Alpert, *Émile Durkheim and His Sociology* (New York, 1939), 55.

76. For a brief account, see S. Lukes, *Émile Durkheim*, 54–57.

77. Durkheim and Mauss, "De quelques formes," 5 (= *Mauss: Œuvres* 2:17); *Primitive Classification*, 7.

78. Durkheim and Mauss, "De quelques formes," 70 (= *Mauss: Œuvres* 2:86); *Primitive Classification*, 86.

79. For example, Durkheim and Mauss, "De quelques formes," 7 (= *Mauss: Œuvres* 2:19–20); *Primitive Classification*, 10.

80. For example, Durkheim, *Les formes élémentaires*, 17; *Elementary Forms*, 25. As Durkheim acknowledges in a footnote, this particular formulation owes much to the essay by R. Hertz, "La prééminence de la main droite: Étude sur la polarité religieuse," *Revue philosophique* 68 (1909): 553–80; English translation by R. Needham, "The Pre-eminence of the Right Hand: A Study in Religious Polarity," in *Right & Left: Essays on Dual Symbolic Classification*, ed. R. Needham (Chicago, 1973), 3–31.

81. Durkheim, *Les formes élémentaires*, 50–58; *Elementary Forms*, 52–57.

82. Durkheim, *Les formes élémentaires*, 55; *Elementary Forms*, 55.

83. Durkheim, *Les formes élémentaires*, 58; *Elementary Forms*, 57 (emphasis added).

84. Durkheim, *Les formes élémentaires*, 313; *Elementary Forms*, 250.

85. This theme of temporal alternation was developed at length by Durkheim's two closest associates: Hubert and Mauss. See H. Hubert, "Étude sommaire de la représentation du temps dans la religion et la magie," *Annuaire de l'École Pratique des Hautes Études, Section des sciences religieuses* (1905): 1–39; reprinted in H. Hubert and M. Mauss, *Mélanges d'histoire des religions*, 2d ed. (Paris, 1929), 189–229, in the series Travaux de l'Année sociologique. Mauss also summarized Hubert's work in *Année sociologique* 10 (1907): 302–5. Mauss's work is of even more direct relevance. See M. Mauss and H. Beuchat, "Essai sur les variations saisonnières des sociétés Eskimos," *Année sociologique* 9 (1906): 39–132. We shall return to the relationship of temporal to spatial patterns below, in chapter 4.

86. Durkheim and Mauss, "De quelques formes," 11, 16, 27–32

(= *Mauss: Œuvres* 2:23, 28–29, 41–46); *Primitive Classification*, 14, 20, 34–38.

87. Durkheim, *Les formes élémentaires*, 326; *Elementary Forms*, 260–61.

88. G. Dumézil, "Préface," to his *Mythe et épopée* (Paris, 1968–73), 1:15. Cf. idem, *L'ideologie tripartite des Indo-Européens* (Brussels, 1958), 17–18, 90–92, *et passim*, in the series Collection Latomus, 31. J.-C. Riviere, *Georges Dumézil à la découverte des Indo-Européens* (Paris, 1979), 21–24, has been most clear in stating this ideological element in Dumézil's work. This element has been used to great effectiveness in G. Duby, *The Three Orders: Feudal Society Imagined* (Chicago, 1980), 5–6, 9, 63, *et passim*.

89. Durkheim, *Les formes élémentaires*, 178–80; *Elementary Forms*, 148–49. It is difficult to credit W. Doroszewski's attempt to historically link Durkheim to Saussure in "Quelques remarques sur les rapports de la sociologie et de la linguistique: Durkheim et F. de Saussure," *Journal de psychologie* 30 (1933): 82–91, although archival research may make the link more plausible. See also R. Godel, "Addendum," to his *Les sources manuscrites du cours de linguistique général de F. de Saussure* (Geneva, 1957), 282. C. Lévi-Strauss is clearly pushing his role as Durkheim's "inconstant disciple" when he attempts to establish some parallel between Saussure and the Durkheimian enterprise. See C. Lévi-Strauss, *Structural Anthropology* (New York, 1963–76), 2:17–18.

90. É. Durkheim, *De la division du travail social: Étude sur l'organization des sociétés supérieures*, 1st ed. (Paris, 1893); English translation by J. Simpson, *The Division of Labor in Society* (New York, 1933). Cf. Durkheim's characterization of the "simplicity" of "primitive societies" in *Les formes élémentaires*, 7–8; *Elementary Forms*, 18.

91. This is the persistent point of Schwartz's suggestive monograph, *Vertical Classification*.

92. Compare Schwartz, *Vertical Classification*, 160–61.

93. C. Lévi-Strauss, "Les organisations dualistes existent-elles?" *Bijdragen tot de Taal-, Land-, en Volkenkunde* 112 (1956): 99–108; English translation in Lévi-Strauss, *Structural Anthropology* 1:132–63. This article gave rise to an important controversy between Maybury-Lewis and Lévi-Strauss. See D. Maybury-Lewis, "The Analysis of Dual Organizations: A Methodological Critique," *Bijdragen tot de Taal-, Land-, en Volkenkunde* 116 (1960): 17–44, and Lévi-Strauss's rejoinder in the same publication, "On Manipulated Social Models," 45–54. The latter has been reprinted in Lévi-Strauss, *Structural Anthropology* 2:71–81.

94. P. Radin, "The Winnebago Tribe," *Annual Report of the Bureau of American Ethnology* 37 (1915–16): 33–500. The monograph has recently been reissued as a separate monograph, P. Radin, *The Winne-*

bago Tribe (Lincoln, Neb., 1970), which I cite. Compare Radin's earlier formulations of this topic: "The Clan Organization of the Winnebago," *American Anthropologist* 12 (1910): 209–19, and "The Social Organization of the Winnebago Indian," *Museum Bulletin of the Canadian Department of Mines* (Geological Survey), 10 (1915): 1–40. In what follows, although deeply indebted to Lévi-Strauss's analysis, I have largely followed Radin's account, especially, *The Winnebago Tribe*, 133–58.

95. On the basis of Radin's ethnography, it is curiously impossible to determine any orientational significance to this scheme. For example, in rituals, the Thunderbird is consistently associated with the west. See Radin, *The Winnebago Tribe*, 399, 407, 423, *et passim*.

96. Radin, *The Winnebago Tribe*: 140–41 and figs. 33–34. Compare Lévi-Strauss, *Structural Anthropology* 1:133–35 and figs. 6–7.

97. Lévi-Strauss, *Structural Anthropology* 1:134–35.

98. Ibid., 1:139–40.

99. Radin, *The Winnebago Tribe*, 136, 143, 202.

100. Lévi-Strauss, *Structural Anthropology* 1:154–55, cf. 1:151–52 for the model. In suggesting, above, that Lévi-Strauss's "deductive model" of the Winnebago (*Structural Anthropology* 2:76) is not "fully supported" by the ethnographic record, I am not challenging the overall deduction of a tripartition concealed within the dualism.

(1) I would question whether Lévi-Strauss has not been overly symmetrical in his description. For example, he writes that there are "twelve clans divided into three groups," that "the lower moiety contains two groups of *four clans each* ('earth' and 'water')," and that the upper moiety "contains one group of four clans ('sky')" (Lévi-Strauss, *Structural Anthropology* 1:155, emphasis added). I find Radin's distinctions less clear. Rather than four, he presents only two groups that are unambiguously identified with water: the Water-spirit and the Fish. I presume that Lévi-Strauss is identifying the Snake as water-related, although he provides no list, and nothing in Radin's brief report on Winnebago taxonomy would support this classification (Radin, *The Winnebago Tribe*, 138). Even if the Snake be granted for purposes of the argument, which group represents the fourth? At best, there appear to be five earth clans (Bear, Wolf, Deer, Elk, Buffalo) and three water groups (Water-spirit, Fish, Snake [?]). Note that T. Michelson, "Some Notes on Winnebago Social and Political Organization," *American Anthropologist* 37 (1935): 446, 448–49, attempts to demonstrate, inconclusively, the existence of a Turtle clan among the Winnebago on the basis of an 1829 traveler's report and Siouan parallels. Radin had insisted that the Winnebago "never had a Turtle clan" (*The Winnebago Tribe*, 50).

(2) There is a "restlessness" within native accounts of their classification precisely at the level of the water group. Radin, in addition

to the list of twelve groups he obtained from Jasper Blowsnake (one of his three main informants and a member of the Thunderbird clan [*The Winnebago Tribe*, xvi, 399]), supplies a second list of ten groups, from another informant, John Harrison, with the Fish and Snake clans omitted (Radin, *The Winnebago Tribe*, 143, cf. Radin, "The Clan Organization of the Winnebago," 210). Furthermore, as Radin goes on to note, L. H. Morgan (*Ancient Society* [1st ed. London, 1877; I cite a reprint, Chicago, n.d.], 161) provides a list of eight, omitting the Fish and Water-spirit clans along with the Warrior and Pigeon; J. O. Dorsey, "Siouan Sociology," *Annual Report of the Bureau of American Ethnology* 15 (1894): 240–41, provides a list of eleven, omitting the Fish. Taking all the lists together, it is one member (or more) of the water group that is most consistently omitted—the Fish clan in all three alternative catalogues.

(3) In his subsequent article on the Winnebago dual, Lévi-Strauss quotes Radin, *The Winnebago Tribe*, 193: "One informant . . . said . . . that the clans were arranged in three groups, one over which the Thunderbird clan ruled, another over which the Water-spirit ruled and a third over which the Bear clan ruled" (Lévi-Strauss, *Structural Anthropology* 2:77). This, Lévi-Strauss suggests, "is proof enough that a ternary system existed at least in a latent state." True enough. This would accord well with Winnebago demographics. As Radin noted, the Thunderbird, Bear, and Water-spirit clans were "the most important and numerous in the tribe" (*The Winnebago Tribe*, 50). Nevertheless, the ellipsis points in Lévi-Strauss's quotation of Radin's text mark two omissions of interest. The first identifies the informant as a member of the Bear clan and, thus, of the *B* moiety. The second omission is the phrase, "that the Water-spirit clan was the chief of the lower phratry." The passage in Radin continues, after the sentence quoted by Lévi-Strauss, still citing the same Bear clan informant, "He insisted, however, that just as the Thunderbird clan rules over the whole tribe in a general way, so the Water-spirit clan ruled over the clans of the lower phratry." This is an odd report from a Bear clan informant. It is generally agreed that the Thunderbird and Bear clans are the paramount ones. What is here predicated of the Water-spirit is usually predicated of the Bear (Radin, *The Winnebago Tribe*, 178). It would appear that the informant is working with a Thunderbird/Water-spirit dualism and is inserting his own clan as forming a triad. This supposition is strengthened by the continuation of the passage in Radin (*The Winnebago Tribe*, 193): "Other informants claimed that the Water-spirit clan originally ruled over the entire tribe and that its place was subsequently usurped by the Thunderbird clan. It might be best to regard the function of the Water-spirit clan as akin but subsidiary to that of the Thunderbird clan"—a notion he does not return

to. Elsewhere, however, Radin notes that the mythological figure of the Thunderbird was considered to be in "eternal enmity" with the Water-spirit (Radin, *The Winnebago Tribe*, 240). Is this dualism— Thunderbird/Water-spirit—reflected both in the mythology and in the ideological arrangements of the tribe? This question raises another possibility. The Winnebago appear to have maintained a five-fold taxonomic scheme that has not been employed in Radin's discussion of a dual or in Lévi-Strauss's postulation of a triad: above-the-sky, sky, earth, water, below-the-water (Radin, *The Winnebago Tribe*, 138). The dualism Thunderbird/Water-spirit reflects the extremities of this division: "Among the Winnebago the thunderbird belongs to the empyrean . . . and the water spirit, below the water" (ibid.). Thus, there would appear to be three possible schemata for the Winnebago system:

(a) Above (four groups)
     Below (four groups)

(b)   Sky (four groups)
     Earth (six groups, or five)   Water (two groups, or three)

(c) Above-the-Sky (one group)
     Sky (three groups)
     Earth (six groups, or five)
     Water (two groups, or three)
     Below-the-Water (one group)

In an unpublished manuscript by J. O. Dorsey, quoted by Radin (*The Winnebago Tribe*, 143), yet a fourth schema is proposed, although Radin insists that the list "was scarcely intended as an enumeration of the clans":

(d) Invisible Thunderbird People (one group)
     Visible Thunderbird People (three groups)
     Land (six groups, or five)
     Water (two groups, or three)

101. Radin, "The Clan Organization of the Winnebago," 211.
102. Radin, *The Winnebago Tribe*, 272, cf. 152 *et passim*.
103. Ibid., 136.
104. Ibid., 163.
105. Ibid., 152–53.
106. Ibid., 178.
107. Ibid., 178–79.
108. The ethnographic details have been reviewed in note 100, above.

109. See note 100 (1), above.

110. I am using the term *fuzzy* in a manner akin to the mathematical usage *fuzzy sets*. In Mac Lane's critical description, "Recall that a set S is completely determined by knowing what things x belong to S (thus $x \varepsilon S$) and what things do not so belong. But sometimes, it is said, one may not know whether or not $x \varepsilon S$. So for a fuzzy set F one knows only the likelihood . . . that the thing x is in the fuzzy set F." S. Mac Lane, *Proof, Truth, and Confusion* (Chicago, 1982), 26. See, further, W. J. M. Kickert, *Fuzzy Theories in Decision Making: A Critical Review* (Leiden, 1978).

111. See note 100(2), above. Radin, with his historicistic approach, notes that Snake and Fish are "regarded by all as being of recent origin" (Radin, *The Winnebago Tribe*, 143).

112. Radin, *The Winnebago Tribe*, 152–53.

113. Ibid., 153. Note, however, the claim that the Water-spirit clan once exercised the paramount chiefship. See note 100(3), above.

114. In his lexical note on *opposition*, Dumont shrewdly observes that the distinction between symmetrical and asymmetrical opposition is most significant with respect to inversion. L. Dumont, *Essais sur l'individualisme: Une perspective anthropologique sur l'idéologie moderne* (Paris, 1983), 264, cf. 217). Thus, to take an example from the Winnebago (see note 100[3], above), the Thunderbird and the Water-spirit, as the extremities of the system in schema (c), can be inverted with respect to rulership without any apparent intellectual consequences. Informants report that either the one or the other is or was the paramount chief. But to suggest that the leader of a subordinate segment, the Bear-clan, can be considered a co-equal chief is to propose a cognitive revolution that alters, thoroughly, the social topography.

115. *The American Heritage Dictionary of the English Language* (Boston, 1980), 1001, s.v. *place*. "*Place* (verb) always implies care or precision in bringing something to a desired position. When this sense of exactness is not appropriate, *put* is used as a more general term."

116. See the important essay (no. 12.11) on the word *place* in C. D. Buck, *A Dictionary of Selected Synonyms in the Principle Indo-European Languages* (Chicago, 1949), 2:830–31. Of particular interest: the Greek *topos*, in the sense of the Lithuanian *tapti*, or Lettish *tapt*, "to become"; the Latin *locus*, French *lieu*, in the sense of **stel*, "to set up," as in Old High German *stellen*; the Avestan *gātu*, Old Persian *gāthu*, meaning both "place" and "throne."

117. Roger Bacon, *Opus maius* 1.1.5, in the translation by R. B. Burke, *The Opus Majus of Roger Bacon* (Oxford, 1928), 1:159.

Three

1. J. F. Blumrich, *The Spaceships of Ezekiel* (New York, 1974), 2.

2. Ibid., 92–100, 105–9, 121–22.

3. In what follows, I shall base my observations on the text of Ezekiel established by J. A. Bewer (1937), as reprinted and emended in R. Kittel, ed., *Biblia Hebraica*, 9th ed. (Stuttgart, 1954), and on the text by K. Elliger (1977) in *Biblia Hebraica Stuttgartensia*, ed. K. Elliger and W. Rudolph (Stuttgart, 1977), taking into account newer readings (especially from LXX[967]) and those proposed in the commentaries cited below. I have freely emended the translation of the Revised Standard Version (1952), which has consistently served as the base. I have drawn most heavily on three commentaries: G. A. Cooke, *A Critical and Exegetical Commentary on the Book of Ezekiel* (Edinburgh, 1936), in the series International Critical Commentary; W. Eichrodt, *Der Prophet Hesekiel* (Göttingen, 1970), in the series Das Alte Testament Deutsch; English translation, *Ezekiel: A Commentary* (London, 1970), in the series The Old Testament Library; and, above all, the magisterial work of W. Zimmerli, *Ezechiel* (Neukirchen, 1955–69), in the series Biblisches Kommentar Altes Testament, 13.1–2; English translation, *Ezekiel* (Philadelphia, 1979–82), 1–2, in the series Hermeneia. In critical matters, I have depended constantly on H. Gese, *Der Verfassungsentwurf des Ezechiel (Kap. 40–48): Traditionsgeschichtlich Untersucht* (Tübingen, 1957), in the series Beiträge zur historischen Theologie, 25; and I have been in constant dialogue (more than these notes testify) with K. Elliger, "Die grossen Tempelsakristeien im Verfassungsentwurf des Ezechiel," *Festschrift A. Alt* (Tübingen, 1953), 79–103, in the series Beiträge zur historischen Theologie, 16. I have made no attempt, in these notes, to engage the totality of biblical criticism on Ezekiel; I shall note counterpositions only when essential to the interpretative tasks of this chapter.

4. C. Geertz, *Negara: The Theatre State in Nineteenth-Century Bali* (Princeton, 1980), 123.

5. The phrase $k^e mibn\bar{e}h$ '$\hat{i}r$ is a hapax legomenon. I have omitted both the MT "in the south" and the LXX "opposite me" as glosses.

6. Much ink has been spilled on the precise unit of measurement; see Zimmerli, *Ezekiel* 2:348–49. Whatever system is followed, the figure of approximately ten feet appears correct.

7. The criterion wall = city is most frequently employed in archeological reports. For a general statement, see L. Mumford, *The City in History* (New York, 1961), 37, 63.

8. See J. H. Tigay, *The Evolution of the Gilgamesh Epic* (Philadelphia, 1982), 6, 140–49.

9. On Psalm 48, in relation to elements in the Zion tradition, see

J. H. Hayes, "The Traditions of Zion's Invulnerability," *Journal of Biblical Literature* 82 (1963): 419–26.

10. For example, the Hammurapi and Samsuilina chronicles in J. B. Pritchard, *Ancient Near Eastern Texts Relating to the Old Testament*, 2d ed. (Princeton, 1955), 270–71.

11. For example, Shulgi B (line 379) and Shulgi C (lines 27–31) in G. R. Castellino, *Two Šulgi Hymns* (Rome, 1972), 69, 263, in the series Studi Semitici, 42.

12. For example, Sargon of Agade (Pritchard, *Ancient Near Eastern Texts*, 267), Ashurnasirpal II (ibid., 275); Shalmaneser III (ibid., 278, 279); Sargon II (ibid., 285); Esarhaddon (ibid., 291, 293).

13. For Ur, see the Sumerian, "Lamentation over the Destruction of Ur" (line 66), in Pritchard, *Ancient Near Eastern Texts*, 456. For Jerusalem, see 2 Kings 25.8; Ezra 4.13, 16; Nehemiah 2.13; 4.7; and compare Sennacherib in Pritchard, *Ancient Near Eastern Texts*, 288. See, further, the royal "negative confession" from the Babylonian *akitu* festival: "I watched out for Babylon. I did not smash its walls," as interpreted in J. Z. Smith, *Imagining Religion* (Chicago, 1982), 90–93.

14. This is the central theme of the long-neglected classic study by H. Nissen, *Das Templum: Antiquarische Untersuchungen* (Berlin, 1869). For a more recent, typical statement, see M. Eliade, *Patterns in Comparative Religion* (New York, 1958), 371: "The enclosure, wall, or circle of stones surrounding a sacred place—these are among the most ancient of known forms of man-made sanctuary. . . . The enclosure does not only imply and indeed signify the continued presence of a kratophany or hierophany within its bounds; it also serves the purpose of preserving profane man from the danger to which he would expose himself by entering it without undue care. . . . The same is the case with city walls: *long before they were military erections*, they were a magic defence, for they marked out from the midst of a 'chaotic' space . . . an enclosure, a place that was organized, made cosmic, in other words, provided with a 'centre.'" (Emphasis added.) Cf. E. Cassirer, *The Philosophy of Symbolic Forms* (New Haven, 1955), 2:99–104, for another particularly eloquent expression of this notion.

15. J. Bird, *Centrality and Cities* (London, 1977), 34. The economic understanding of "center" owes its origin to the seminal work of W. Christaller, *Die zentralen Orte in Suddeutschland* (Jena, 1933), English translation, *Central Places in Southern Germany* (Englewood Cliffs, N.J., 1966), as developed in major theoretical studies such as A. Lösch, *The Economics of Location* (New Haven, 1944); W. Isard, *Location and the Space Economy* (New York, 1956); P. Haggett, *Locational Analysis in Human Geography* (London, 1965). Central to such approaches is the assumption that hierarchy is the essential character of human organization—however, the literature is ambiguous as to whether hierarchy is an observed phenomenon or a derivative postu-

late from central-place theory (see B. J. L. Berry and W. L. Garrison, "Recent Developments in Central-Place Theory," *Proceedings of the Regional Sciences Association* 9 [1958]: 107–20; idem, "The Functional Bases of the Central Place Hierarchy," *Economic Geography*, 34 [1958]: 145–54). For an overview, see B. J. L. Berry and A. Pred, *Central Place Studies: A Bibliography of Theory and Applications* (Philadelphia, 1961); B. J. Garner, "Models of Urban Geography and Settlement Location," in *Socio-Economic Models in Geography*, ed. P. J. Chorley and P. Haggett (London, 1968), 303–60; R. E. Blanton, "Anthropological Studies of Cities," *Annual Review of Anthropology* 5 (1976): 249–64.

16. In what follows, I shall draw on the following works: P. Wheatley, "What a City Is Said to Be," *Pacific Viewpoint* 4 (1963): 163–88; idem, *The City as Symbol* (London, 1969); idem, *The Pivot of the Four Quarters: A Preliminary Enquiry into the Origins and Character of the Ancient Chinese City* (Chicago, 1971); idem, "The Concept of Urbanism," in *Man, Settlement, and Urbanism*, ed. P. J. Ucko, R. Tringham, and G. W. Dimberly (London, 1972), 601–37; Wheatley, "The Suspended Pelt," in *Geographic Humanism and Social Action: Proceedings of a Symposium Celebrating a Half Century of Geography at Michigan*, ed. D. R. Deskins, Jr., G. Kish, J. D. Nystuen, and G. Olsson (Ann Arbor, 1977), 47–108, in the series Michigan Geography Publications, 17; Wheatley and T. See, *From Court to Capital: A Tentative Origin of the Japanese Urban Tradition* (Chicago, 1978); K. S. Sandhu and Wheatley, eds., *Melaka: The Transformation of a Malay Capital* (Kuala Lumpur, 1982), 1–2; Wheatley, *Nāgara and Commandery: Origins of the Southwest Asian Urban Traditions* (Chicago, 1983), in the series University of Chicago Department of Geography Research Papers, 207–8.

17. Wheatley, *Pivot*, 8.

18. Ibid., xviii, 374, *et passim*.

19. Ibid., 225–26.

20. Ibid., 267, cf. 281.

21. Ibid., 303, 311, 319.

22. Ibid., 305.

23. One might question, for example, the evidence for the primary specialization of the priesthood; the applicability of the Polanyi redistributive model; or whether Wheatley has employed a sufficiently supple model of stratification.

24. This latter is even more pronounced in Wheatley, *The City as Symbol*, and Wheatley, "The Suspended Pelt."

25. R. N. Bellah, "Religious Evolution," *American Sociological Review* 29 (1964): 358–74, reprinted in idem, *Beyond Belief: Essays on Religion in a Post-Traditional World* (New York, 1970), 20–50. See Wheatley, *Pivot*, 318–21 *et passim*.

26. See, especially, J. H. Steward, *Theory of Culture Change: The Methodology of Multilinear Evolution* (Urbana, 1955); R. M. Adams,

The Evolution of Urban Society: Early Mesopotamia and Prehispanic Mexico (Chicago, 1966). See also Wheatley, *Pivot*, 262–82 *et passim*.

27. K. V. Flannery, "The Cultural Evolution of Civilizations," *Annual Review of Ecology and Systematics* 3 (1972): 399–426. The relevance of this article to cities was, to my knowledge, first suggested by Blanton, "Anthropological Studies of Cities," 251.

28. See the essays collected in R. A. Rappaport, *Ecology, Meaning and Religion* (Richmond, Calif., 1979). Wheatley draws upon Rappaport, "Sanctity and Adaptation," Werner-Gren Symposium Paper (1969); "The Sacred in Human Evolution," *Annual Review of Ecology and Systematics* 2 (1971): 23–44; and "Ritual, Sanctity and Cybernetics," *American Anthropologist* 73 (1971): 59–76.

29. Flannery, "The Cultural Evolution of Civilizations," 409, as quoted in Wheatley and See, *From Court to Capital*, 12.

30. I have, in the above, summarized Wheatley and See's summary of Flannery in *From Court to Capital*, 11–14. Cf. Wheatley, *Nāgara and Commandery*, 23–27.

31. Rappaport, "The Sacred in Human Evolution,": 36. Cf. Wheatley and See, *From Court to Capital*, 15–16; Wheatley, *Nāgara and Commandery*, 27–28.

32. Wheatley, *Nāgara and Commandery*, 273, 327–29, 423.

33. C. Geertz, *Negara: The Theatre State in Nineteenth Century Bali* (Princeton, 1980), 13 and 102. For an early, supple formulation by Geertz, see his remarks on the interrelationship between "The Doctrine of the Exemplary Center," "The Doctrine of Graded Spirituality," and "The Doctrine of the Theatre State," in Geertz, *Islam Observed: Religious Development in Morocco and Indonesia* (New Haven, 1968), 36–38.

34. For Durkheim, see Wheatley, *Pivot*, 317, 390–92, *et passim*; cf. Wheatley and See, *From Court to Capital*, 8. For Friedman, Wheatley relies most heavily, in his later work, on J. Friedman, "Tribes, States and Transformations," in *Marxist Analysis and Social Anthropology*, ed. M. Bloch (London, 1973), 161–202. See Wheatley, *Nāgara and Commandery*, 279–84 *et passim*.

35. See the useful review of the state of the question by F. Cancian, "Social Stratification," *Annual Review of Anthropology* 5 (1976): 227–48, and the generous anthology by A. Béteille, ed., *Social Inequality* (Baltimore, 1969). In using the term "social reality," I have been most influenced by L. A. Fallers, *Inequality: Social Stratification Reconsidered* (Chicago, 1973), esp. 3–29.

36. L. Dumont, *Homo hierarchicus: Essai sur le système des castes*, 1st ed. (Paris, 1966), 2d ed. (Paris, 1979). I cite the first French edition. The second French edition, which adds a new "Preface" and a "Postface," is unavailable to me. English translation, Dumont, *Homo Hier-*

archicus: The Caste System and Its Implications, 2d ed. (Chicago, 1980). I cite this translation hereafter as *Homo Hierarchicus* (ET).

37. Dumont, *Homo hierarchicus,* 14–17, 305–23, *et passim; Homo Hierarchicus* (ET), 2–4, 247–266, *et passim.* Cf. *Homo Hierarchicus* (ET), xx.

38. Dumont, *Homo hierarchicus,* 63–68; *Homo Hierarchicus* (ET), 42–46.

39. The theoretical force of this distinction is somewhat vitiated by Dumont's assumption that India may be a special case in this respect. See *Homo hierarchicus,* 66 n. 24^e, 100 n.32^h, 102, 268–69, *et passim; Homo Hierarchicus* (ET), 356, 364, 74, 212–13, *et passim.*

40. Dumont, *Homo hierarchicus,* 79–80, 83–84, 268–69, *et passim; Homo Hierarchicus* (ET), 56, 59, 74, 212, *et passim.*

41. *Homo hierarchicus,* 195, 213, *et passim; Homo Hierarchicus* (ET), 153, 167, *et passim.*

42. Dumont, *Homo hierarchicus,* 99–101, 213–16, *et passim; Homo Hierarchicus* (ET), 71–72, 167–70, *et passim.* Compare the important discussion in S. J. Tambiah, *World Conqueror and World Renouncer: A Study of Buddhism and Polity in Thailand Against a Historical Background* (Cambridge, 1976), 19–31, 73–131, *et passim.*

43. Dumont, *Homo hierarchicus,* 92; *Homo Hierarchicus* (ET), 66.

44. L. Dumont, "La communauté anthropologique et l'idéologie," *L'homme* 18 (1978): 83–110, esp. 101–9, reprinted in idem, *Essais sur l'individualisme: Une perspective anthropologique sur l'idéologie moderne* (Paris, 1983), 187–221, esp. 210–20.

45. Dumont, *Homo Hierarchicus* (ET), 239–40.

46. Ibid., 241. He attributes this formulation to an unpublished dissertation by Raymond Apthorpe.

47. Dumont, *Homo Hierarchicus* (ET), 242.

48. Dumont, *Homo hierarchicus,* 100 n. 32^h; *Homo Hierarchicus* (ET), 364–65, cf. xxxviii–xxxix. See, further, L. Dumont and D. Pocock, "Pure and Impure," *Contributions to Indian Sociology* 3 (1959): 9–39, and Dumont, "On Putative Hierarchy and Some Allergies to It," *Contributions to Indian Sociology,* n.s. 5 (1971): 58–78. Compare V. Valeri, *Kingship and Sacrifice: Ritual and Society in Ancient Hawaii* (Chicago, 1985), 89–90.

49. Note that in making these preliminary distinctions as to maps, I make no presumptions as to literary sources and raise no vexing questions as to *Grundtext* and *Nachinterpretation.* I would note, however, that there is an additional map in Ezekiel 40–48, namely, Ezekiel 47.1–12. That map seems to reflect a quite different ideological perspective that cannot be homologized to the other maps. For this reason, I have omitted it. All other verses in Ezekiel 40–48 have been taken into account in the interpretations proposed below.

50. See the detailed discussion of this principle of "segmentation" in C. Geertz, *Negara: The Theatre State*, 112–13.

51. Ibid., 109. I would note that the enterprise of such a "vocabulary of walls, gates, passageways, sheds and furniture" is even more characteristic of the P mapping of the Tabernacle, a tradition that Ezekiel 40–48 stands extremely close to. Without accepting its implications for the dating of P, see the description of the mapping of P in M. Haran, *Temples and Temple Service in Ancient Israel: An Inquiry into the Character of Cult Phenomena and the Historical Setting of the Priestly School* (Oxford, 1978), 150–87 *et passim*.

52. See the discussion in Zimmerli, *Ezekiel* 2:352.

53. I am aware of the argument by D. Neiman ("A Canaanite Cult Object in the Old Testament," *Journal of Biblical Literature* 67 [1948]: 55–60) that *pgr* can be translated as memorial stelae. Although this understanding has gained favor (for example, Zimmerli, *Ezekiel* 2: 417), the philological evidence is not overwhelming. The fact that no archeological evidence supporting royal burials next to the temple precinct can be found is scarcely probative. There is little archeological evidence for much of Ezekiel's depictation of the temple. Note the contrast to Christian cathedrals, where corpses of kings and martyrs confer sanctity rather than pollution (P. Brown, *The Cult of the Saints* [Chicago, 1981], 4–6 *et passim*). But this is the idiom of the hierarchy of power, not the hierarchy of status.

54. Many editors emend the Hebrew at this point and substitute, "he [the angel]" for YHWH. It is YHWH who announces the problem in Ezekiel 43.6, and it is YHWH who, here, gives the solution. The least of the problems with Ezekiel's Hebrew text is that of having YHWH speak of himself in the third person!

55. Literally: "only the prince, the prince, may sit in it." For the problems with this construction, see J. Botterweck, "Textkritische Bemerkungen zu Ezechiel 44:3a," *Vetus Testamentum* 1 (1951): 145–46, and Zimmerli, *Ezekiel* 2:438. Much energy has been expended but little gained in the protracted discussion of Ezekiel's preference for *nāśî* rather than *melek*. Suffice it to say that *nāśî* appears to be the preferred term within the Priestly tradition; the reasons are no longer recoverable. See the review of the scholarship in J. D. Levenson, *Theology of the Program of Restoration of Ezekiel 40–48* (Missoula, 1976), 57–69, in the series Harvard Semitic Monograph Series, 10.

56. In Ezekiel 46.1–13, the question is *not* that of the "prince in relation to YHWH's royal function. In what follows, I have abstained from commenting on the "prince's" meal, as Ezekiel provides no context. I am hesitant about identifying it with other priestly sacrificial traditions of "eating before YHWH," as is done in most commentaries.

57. Eichrodt, *Ezekiel*, 560.

58. Levenson, *Program of Restoration in Ezekiel 40–48*, 140, cf.69 and 113.

59. Zimmerli, *Ezekiel* 2:546.

60. This is, of course, in sharp contrast to the notion of the temple as a "royal chapel."

61. 11Q *Temple Scroll* 56.12–60.15. See Y. Yadin, *Megillat Ha-Miqdash* (Jerusalem, 1978), 1:264–7; 2:177–93.

62. The Hebrew of Ezekiel 44.5 reads: "with regard to the entrance to the house through all the exits of the sanctuary."

63. The characterization of the "foreigners" as ʿarlê-lēb wᵉ ʿarlê bāśār is unusually harsh. Compare Jeremiah 9.25–26 and see Smith, *Imagining Religion*, 8–15.

64. This is *not* to imply the presence within the Hebrew Bible of the Indic *varṇa*-system or the Indo-European "tripartite ideology." See the facetious proposal to this effect by J. Brough, "The Tripartite Ideology of the Indo-Europeans: An Experiment in Method," *Bulletin of the School of Oriental and African Studies* 22 (1959): 85–97, and G. Dumézil's immediate, savage, and decisive response, "L'idéologie tripartie des Indo-Européens et la Bible," *Kratylos* 4 (1959): 97–118, reprinted in his *Mythe et epopée* (Paris, 1973), 3:338–61.

65. For other elements of what Gese terms the "Zadokite stratum" (Gese, *Der Verfassungsentwurf des Ezechiel*, 57–67), see Ezekiel 40.46; 43.19; 45.4–5; 46.19–21; 46.24; 48.11.

66. S.J. Tambiah, *World Conqueror and World Renouncer*, esp. 102–58.

67. Despite the alleged etymology of Benjamin as "son of the right," that is, the south (cf. Psalm 89.13), Benjamin is often classed as northern in royal texts (for example, 1 Kings 4.18; 11.32). Note, in the Chronicler, the double "Judah-Benjamin" (2 Chronicles 11.1, 3, 10, 12, 23, among others).

68. Cf. Levenson, *Program of Restoration in Ezekiel 40–48*, 118, who makes a similar point.

69. Here, the tendentious Hebrew text must be corrected by the Greek (esp. LXX⁹⁶⁷). In both Ezekiel 45.1 and 48.9, the figure of 20,000 cubits for the "consecrated area" has been reduced to 10,000 to identify the "holy place" solely with the (Zadokite) priests. See Zimmerli, *Ezekiel* 2:465, 468, 522, 533–34.

70. Ezekiel 45.1–5 provides further details about the temple and an additional contrast between the Zadokite and the Levitical land. The temple precincts form a square, 500 cubits on each side, with an additional band of pasture land surrounding it. The total area of temple lands (in the strict sense) is less than one-tenth of one percent of the total area.

Emending verses 4–5 (see Zimmerli, *Ezekiel* 2:466) the territory of the temple priests is for houses and for pasture lands for their cattle; the Levitical lands are for cities to live in. This latter appears to be a centralization of the old notion of widely scattered Levitical cities.

71. It must be admitted that this second view of the city (Ezekiel 48.30–35) has a number of puzzling details with respect to the mapping of the gates of the twelve tribes. In part, these are the result of cartographic difficulties in shifting a bidirectional map (north–south) to one employing the four cardinal directions; in part, because here Levi is treated as one of the twelve tribes.

72. I have been helped here by S. J. Tambiah's discussion of the "emulsion-type globular model" in *World Conqueror and World Renouncer*, 153–55.

73. Wheatley and See, *From Court to Capital*, 16.

74. I have followed the text as established by A. Pelletier, *Lettre d'Aristée à Philocrate* (Paris, 1962), in the series Sources chrétiennes, 89; and the English translation by M. Hadas, *Aristeas to Philocrates* (New York, 1951), in the series Dropsie College Edition, Jewish Apocryphal Literature. I have profited most from the extensive commentary by R. Tramontano, *La lettura di Aristea a Filocrate* (Naples, 1931), and from the topographical comments in H. Vincent, "Jérusalem d'après la lettre d'Aristée," *Revue Biblique*, n.s. 5 (1908): 520–32; ibid., 6 (1909): 555–75. See, further, the masterful review of the scholarly literature on Aristeas in S. Jellicoe, *The Septuagint and Modern Study* (Oxford, 1968), 29–73.

75. The sole exception is an opaque reference in *Aristeas* 106 that appears to imply that some individuals use the upper roads in the city; others, the lower; and the two groups keep apart from each other because of purity rules, so that they "touch nothing improper."

76. *Aristeas* 139–66 is most relevant. Here, the purity regulations are wholly disconnected from the cult.

77. This problem plagues contemporary urban geographers in their discussions of the notion of center and fringe. See R. E. Pahl, ed. *Readings in Urban Sociology* (London, 1968), 263–97, and Bird, *Centrality and Cities*, 101–14, for reviews of the theoretical literature.

FOUR

1. C. Geertz, *Islam Observed: Religious Development in Morocco and Indonesia* (New Haven, 1968), 36–38.

2. The pre-Iconoclastic, early Byzantine ritual of Constantinople has proven exceedingly difficult to reconstruct. The most convincing account, focusing on the eucharistic service, is that by T. F. Matthews, *The Early Churches of Constantinople: Architecture and Liturgy* (University Park, Pa., 1971), 111–76. Matthews places particular im-

portance on the evidence offered by the liturgical commentaries, especially the seventh century work of Maximus, *Mystagoga* (Migne, *PG* 91:657–717) and the earliest recension of the eighth century *Historia ecclesiastica* attributed to Germanus of Constantinople (N. Borgia, *Il commentario liturgico di S. Germano patriarcha constantinopolitano* [Grottaferrata, 1912], which replaces the later recension of the text in Migne, *PG* 98:384–453). See Matthews, *Early Churches of Constantinople*, 112–16.

3. For the later, imperial ritual, see especially the works by J. Ebersolt, *Sainte-Sophie de Constantinople: Étude de topographie d'après les cérémonies* (Paris, 1910); idem, *Le Grand Palais de Constantinople et le livre des cérémonies* (Paris, 1910); idem, *Constantinople: Recueil d'études d'archéologie et d'histoire* (Paris, 1951). See, further, A. Vogt, ed., *Constantin VII Porphyrogénete: Le livre des cérémonies* (Paris, 1935–40), 1–3, 2d ed. (Paris, 1967), 1–2; R. Guilland, *Études de topographie de Constantinople* (Berlin, 1969); D. A. Miller, *Imperial Constantinople* (New York, 1969).

4. F. de Saussure, *Course in General Linguistics* (New York, 1966), 122–27.

5. See the inscription from Termessos in Pisidia, as cited in N. H. Baynes, *Constantine the Great and the Christian Church*, 2d ed. (London, 1972), 96, 101 n. 3. Baynes reminds us that "new" is a "hypothetical insertion." The solar symbolism of Constantine has been much discussed; see the still classic treatment by T. Preger, "Konstantinos-Helios," *Hermes* 36 (1901): 457–69.

6. For a profound meditation on this theme, see E. H. Kantorowicz, *The King's Two Bodies: A Study in Medieval Political Theology* (Princeton, 1957), 83. The meaning of the term "new Rome" is carefully delineated in E. Gerland, "Byzantion und die Gründung der Stadt-Konstaninopel," *Byzantinisch-neugriechische Jahrbücher* 10 (1934), 103. For Constantinople as the "new Jerusalem," see E. Fenster, *Laudes Constantinopolitanae* (München, 1968), 121, in the series Miscellanea byzantina Monacensia, 19.

7. Sozomen, *Historia ecclesiastica* 2.3 (J. Bidez and C. C. Hansen, *Sozomenos Kirchengeschichte* [Berlin, 1960], 51, in the series, *GCS*, 50). For the same tradition in an anti-Christian source, see Zosimus, *Historia nova* 2.30 (R. T. Ridley, trans., *Zosimus: New History* [Melbourne, 1982], 37). Compare the later identification of Justinian as the "new Achilles"; see Procopius, *Buildings* 1.2 with the valuable appendix in the LCL edition and translation by H.B. Dewing and G. Downey (London, 1959), 395–98; cf. G. Downey, "Justinian as Achilles," *Transactions and Proceedings of the American Philological Association* 71 (1940): 68–77.

8. For the Palladium, see Procopius, *De bello gothico* 1.15 (in the Loeb Library edition and translation by H. B. Downey [London,

1961], 152–53); *Chronicon paschale* (L. Dindorf, ed. [Bonn, 1832], 1:528). For the Cross, see Socrates, *Historia ecclesiastica* 1.17 (Migne, *PG* 67:120); Paulus Deaconus, *Historia miscella* 11 (Migne, *PL* 95: 911). See, further, D. Lathoud, "La consécration et la dédicace de Constantinople (1)," *Échos d'orient* 23 (1924): 299, 311; E. Gren, "Zu den Legenden von der Gründung Konstantinopels," *Serta Kazaroviana* (Sofia, 1950), 1:161–62; G. Dagron, *Naissance d'une capitale: Constantinople et ses institutions de 330 à 451* (Paris, 1974), 30, 39, in the series Bibliothèque byzantine, Études, 7. Over time, the column is depicted as a veritable museum of religious antiquities, allegedly containing, according to one or more Byzantine chroniclers, pieces of the crosses of the two thieves, the basket from the multiplication of loaves, the jar containing the ointment with which Jesus was anointed, the head of the ax of Noah, the stone from which Moses drew water, and a variety of relics from sundry saints. See the texts cited in A. Frolow, "La dédicace de Constantinople dans la tradition byzantine," *Revue de l'histoire des religions* 127 (1944):77 n. 1. See, further, R. Janin, *Constantinople byzantine*, 2d ed. (Paris, 1964), 77–80; A. Cameron and J. Herrin, *Constantinople in the Early Eighth Century: The Parastaseis Syntomoi Chronikai* (Leiden, 1984), 198, in the series Columbia Studies in the Classical Tradition, 10. As a mixture of old and new, there is also the widespread notion that the statue of Constantine was originally that of Apollo with the head struck off and the emperor's substituted. See E. Legrand, "Description des œuvres d'art et de l'église des Saints-Apôtres de Constantinople: Poème en vers iambiques par Constantin le Rhodien," *Revue des études grecques* 9 (1896):71 (citing T. Reinach), and the discussion in D. Lathoud, "La consécration (2)," *Échos d'orient* 24 (1925):190; Frolow, "La dédicace," 64; Dagron, *Naissance d'une capitale*, 38–39 *et passim*; Cameron and Herrin, *Constantinople in the Early Eighth Century*, 263–64 *et passim*.

9. Philostorgus, *Historia ecclesiastica* (Migne, *PG* 65:472). For the archaic sense of *mundus*, see the definitive article by S. Weinstock, "Mundus patet," *Rheinisches Museum* 45 (1930):111–23. For the Constantinian ritual, see Lathoud, "La consécration (1)," 299–300, and L. Voekl, *Die Kirchenstiftungen des Kaisers Konstantin im Lichte des römisches Sakralrechts* (Köln and Opladen, 1964), 17, in the series Arbeitsgemeinschaft des Landes Nordrhein-Westfalen, 17.

10. This point is forcefully argued by R. Krautheimer, *Three Christian Capitals: Topography and Politics* (Berkeley, 1983), 26–31, 40, 50–52, 130 n. 19.

11. R. Krautheimer, *Early Christian and Byzantine Architecture*, 2d ed. (Harmondsworth, 1975), 27–30, 37–51. See, further, idem, "The Constantinian Basilica," *Dumbarton Oaks Papers* 21 (1967):117–40; J. B. Ward Perkins, "Constantine and the Origin of the Christian Ba-

silica," *Papers of the British School at Rome* 22 (1954):69–90; M. H. Shepherd, Jr., "The Earliest Christian Basilicas," *Yearbook of Liturgical Studies* 7 (1966):73–86.

12. F. Gabuieli, *Arab Historians of the Crusades* (Berkeley, 1969), 148 n. 1. See G. Le Strange, *Palestine under the Moslems* (London, 1890), 202–9, for a brief conspectus of Muslim views of the shrine.

13. See this phrase in the various accounts of the speech by Urban II to the Council of Clermont, 27 November 1095 (translations in E. Peters, *The First Crusade* [Philadelphia, 1971], 3, 5).

14. The most careful study of the Gospel accounts remains F.-M. Braun, "La sépulture de Jésus," *Revue biblique* 45 (1936):34–52, 184–200, 346–63.

15. See, among others, J. B. Hennessy, "Preliminary Report of Excavations at the Damascus Gate, Jerusalem 1964–66," *Levant* 2 (1970):22–27; R. H. Smith, "The Tomb of Jesus," *Biblical Archeologist* 30 (1967):74–90; M. Avi-Yonah, "The Third and Second Walls of Jerusalem," *Israel Exploration Journal* 18 (1968):98–125; K. M. Kenyon, *Digging Up Jerusalem* (London, 1974), 226–34, 261–67; R. E. Brown, *The Gospel According to John* (Garden City, 1970), 2:899; C. Coüasnon, *The Church of the Holy Sepulchre in Jerusalem* (London, 1974), 8–10. A review of the state of the questoin is provided by E. M. Laperrousiz, "Le problème du 'premier mur' et du 'deuxieme mur' de Jérusalem," in *Festschrift G. Vadja*, ed. G. Nahon and C. Touat (Louvain, 1980), 13–35.

16. The most complete account is given by H. Windisch, "Die ältesten christlichen Palästinapilger," *Zeitschrift des deutschen Palästina-Vereins* 48 (1925):145–58.

17. A claimed exception is Melito of Sardis, *Peri Pascha* 72, 93–94 (S. G. Hall, *Melito of Sardis: On Pascha and Fragments* [Oxford, 1979], 38–39, 52–53). The thrice-repeated charge that Jesus was killed *en mesō Ierousalēm* has been taken as a topographical reference. See A. E. Harvey, "Melito and Jerusalem," *Journal of Theological Studies*, n.s. 17 (1966):401–4; Brown, *The Gospel According to John* 2:899; Hall, *Melito of Sardis*, 53 n. 55; E. D. Hunt, *Holy Land Pilgrimage in the Later Roman Empire: AD 312–480* (Oxford, 1982), 3. I must concur with O. Parler, *Méliton de Sardes: Sur la pâque et fragments* (Paris, 1966), 177, in the series *SC*, 123—this is a rhetorical device and not a matter of topography. See the chain in *Pascha*, 94 (lines 704–5): Jesus was murdered "in the middle of the street, in the middle of the city, in the middle of the day—for all to see." This needs to be related to the bitter polemic which dominates *Pascha*, 72–99; see K. W. Noakes, "Melito of Sardis and the Jews," *Texte und Untersuchungen* 116 (1975):244–49.

18. See the data supplied by C. Erdmann, *The Origin of the Idea of the Crusade* (Princeton, 1977), 300–301 and nn. 121–22, a work trans-

lated from idem, *Die Entstehung des Kreuzzugsgedankens* (Stuttgart, 1935). In accepting Erdmann's linguistic data, I do not imply acceptance of his argument vis-à-vis Jerusalem and the Crusades. The only exceptions I am familiar with have an eschatological reference, for example, the "holy land" as the "promised land" (Origen, *Contra Celsum* 7.28). In Christian discourse, the *topoi* were, par excellence, grave sites or relic shrines. See, H. Delehaye, "Loca sanctorum," *Analecta Bollandiana* 48 (1930):5–65.

19. P. Brown, *The Cult of the Saint: Its Rise and Function in Late Antiquity* (Chicago, 1981), 9–10.

20. Eusebius, *Oratio de laudibus Constantini* 11.3 (in the English translation by H. A. Drake, *In Praise of Constantine: A Historical Study and New Translation of Eusebius' Tricennial Orations* [Berkeley, 1975], 103).

21. Arius, *Epistula ad Eusebium Nicomediensem* = Theodoret, *Historia ecclesiastica* 1.5 = Epiphanius, *Panarion* 69.6, in H. G. Opitz, *Urkunden zur Geschichte des arienischen Streits, 318–28* (Berlin, 1935), 1.1:1–3, which forms volume 3 of his edition of *Athanasius: Werke*.

22. H. Chadwick, "Faith and Order at the Council of Nicaea: A Note on the Background of the Sixth Canon," *Harvard Theological Review* 53 (1960):174; compare the whole discussion, pp. 173–75. The argument by Z. Rubin ("The Church of the Holy Sepulchre and the Conflict Between the Sees of Jerusalem and Caesarea," *Cathedra* 2 [1982]:79–105), which seeks to find echoes of the Jerusalem-Caesarea conflict in Eusebius's account of the discovery and construction of the edifice in *Vita Constantini*, is tempting but unconvincing.

23. C. Nicaea, canon 7, in E. J. Jonkers, *Acta et symbola conciliorum quae saeculo quarto habit sunt* (Leiden, 1954), 42, in the series Textus minores, 19.

24. See E. Honigmann, "Juvenal of Jerusalem," *Dunbarton Oaks Papers* 5 (1950):211–79.

25. C. Chalcedon, act 7, in E. Schwartz, *Acta Conciliorum Oecumenicorum* (Berlin-Leipzig, 1924–40), 2.1.3:5, line 23.

26. See the masterful review of the state of the question in F. Winkelmann, "Zur Geschichte des Authentizitätsproblem der Vita Constantini," *Klio* 40 (1962):187–243.

27. (1) There is one reference that *might* precede the Constantinian construction in Jerusalem reporting a topographical tradition concerning the general location of the grave site; it is in Eusebius, *Onomastikon* (E. Klostermann, *Eusebius: Das Onomastikon des Biblische Ortsnamen* [Leipzig, 1904], 74, lines 20–21, in the series GCS 11.1) that Golgotha, the place of the skull where Jesus was crucified, is located "in Aelia, to the north of Mount Sion." Both terms are notorious for their lack of specificity. For the dating of the *Onomastikon* to

the last decade of the third century, see T. D. Barnes, *Constantine and Eusebius* (Cambridge, Mass., 1981), 110–11.

(2) During the ceremonies dedicating the Constantinian memorial at the site of the grave, Eusebius gave the main address (*Vita Constantini* 4.46). During the same period, he gave several other addresses in Jerusalem as well, "at one time explaining through scriptural descriptions the beauties wrought by the sovereign, at another applying pertinent prophetic views to its symbolic significance" (*Vita Constantini* 4.45). The latter were delivered before Constantine on an unspecified date. Although Eusebius promises to publish them (*Vita Constantini* 4.46), they are now lost.

(3) There is, however, a growing agreement that the inaugural speech has been preserved, attached by his posthumous editor to another speech, now forming chapters 11–18 of *De laudibus Constantini*. If so, this is the text Eusebius mentions as having been delivered (or redelivered) before Constantine himself: "For when, at one time, emboldened by [Constantine's] piety . . . we asked permission to deliver an account of the Savior's memorial in his hearing, he lent his ears most eagerly, and, surrounded by a large audience in the palace itself, listened while standing up . . ." (*Vita Constantini* 4.33). Although the chronology is far from secure (in general, I follow the chronology and placement of Constantine in T. D. Barnes, *The New Empire of Diocletian and Constantine* [Cambridge, Mass., 1982], 68–80), I am persuaded by Drake's arguments that would place the date of this second delivery in the winter of 335–36. Alas, though it is an intriguing homily, dealing with the "tabernacling" of the Logos, idolatry and false temples, and with Constantine's general policies of church construction, there is only one possible reference to the memorial at the tomb site. Indeed, the general portions of the address appear to have been borrowed from another work, Eusebius's apologetic *Theophaneia*, composed ten years earlier. (See H. Gressmann, *Eusebius: Theophaneia* [Leipzig, 1904], xiii–xx, in the series *GCS* 11.2.)

(4) In *De laudibus Constantini* 9, most likely delivered before Constantine on 25 July 336, there are a few lines describing the significance of the memorial. For the text of *De laudibus Constantini*, see I. A. Heikel, *Eusebius Werke* (Leipzig, 1911), 1:195–259, in the series *GCS* 7; English translation, H. E. Drake, *In Praise of Constantine* (Berkeley, 1976), 83–127. On the question of the two texts in *De laudibus* and their connection with the church dedication, see H. E. Drake, "When Was the 'De Laudibus Constantini' Delivered?" *Historia* 24 (1975):345–56; T. D. Barnes, "Two Speeches By Eusebius," *Greek, Roman and Byzantine Studies* 18 (1977):341–45.

28. *De laudibus Constantini* 11.2 (Drake, *In Praise of Constantine*, 103); 9.16–17, 19 (ibid., 101).

29. For the text of the *Vita Constantini,* see I. A. Heikel, *Eusebius Werke* (Leipzig, 1902), 1:1–148, esp. 89–95, and the more recent edition, F. Winkelmann, *Uber das Leben des Kaisers Konstantin* (Berlin, 1975):94–101, in the series *GCS.* Two inadequate English translations exist. One appears anonymously in the S. Bagster & Sons edition of *The Greek Ecclesiastical Historians of the First Six Centuries* (London, 1845), 6:1–234, esp. 136–47, and the other in E. C. Richardson, *A Select Library of the Nicene and Post-Nicene Fathers* (New York, 1890), ser. 2, vol. 1: 481–559, esp. 526–30. Both of these are based on the 1830 edition by F. A. Heinichen (*non vidi*). There is a better, though abbreviated, translation of the relevant portions of 3.25–40 in J. Wilkinson, *Egeria's Travels to the Holy Land,* 2d ed. (Jerusalem, 1981), 164–71. I have profited from the discussion and partial translation in French in H. Vincent and F. M. Abel, *Jérusalem: Recherches de topographie, d'archéologie, et d'histoire* (Paris, 1912–14), 2:154–64, 206–8, and the discussion and full translation in German with important philological notes in A. Heisenberg, *Grabskirche und Apostelkirche: Zwei Basiliken Konstantins* (Leipzig, 1908), 1:16–44.

30. For Constantine's building policy, see, among others, L. Voelkl, "Die konstantinischen Kirchenbauten nach Eusebius," *Rivista di archeologia cristiana* 29 (1953):49–66; W. Telfer, "Constantine's Holy Land Plan," *Studia Patristica* 1 (1957):696–700 (= *Texte und Untersuchungen,* 63); G. T. Armstrong, "Imperial Church Building and Church State Relations, A.D. 313–363," *Church History* 36 (1967):3–17; D. J. Geanakopolos, "Church Building and 'Caesaropapism,' A.D. 312–565," *Greek, Roman, and Byzantine Studies* 7 (1966):167–86; G. T. Armstrong, "Imperial Church Building in the Holy Land in the Fourth Century," *The Biblical Archeologist* 30 (1967):90–102; idem, "Constantine's Churches: Symbol and Structure," *Journal of the Society of Architectural History* 33 (1974):5–16; U. Suessenbach, *Christuskult und kaiserliche Baupolitik bei Konstantin* (Bonn, 1977), in the series Abhandlungen zur Kunst-, Musik-, und Literarischewissenschaft, 241. For the economic impact, see, especially, M. Avi-Yonah, "The Economics of Byzantine Palestine," *Israel Exploration Journal* 8 (1958), esp. 41–43.

Ironically, it would appear that one of the motivations behind Julian's ill-fated attempt to rebuild the Jewish temple in Jerusalem was, through a process quite parallel to Constantine's construction, "to reverse Constantine's foundation of his new Christian Jerusalem." See Hunt, *Holy Land Pilgrimage,* 157.

31. The standard monograph on the Easter Fire remains G. Klameth, *Die Karamstagfeuerwunder der heiligen Grabskirche* (Vienna, 1913), in the series Studien und Mitteilungen aus dem kirchengeschichtlichen Seminar in Wien, 13. Compare the synoptic study in E. W. Hopkins, "The Cult of Fire in Christianity," in *Festschrift C. E. Pavry,*

ed. J. D. C. Pavry (Oxford, 1933), 142–50. B. McGinn ("*Iter Sancti Sepulchri*: The Piety of the First Crusaders," in *The Walter Prescott Webb Memorial Lectures: Essays on Medieval Civilization*, ed. B. K. Lackner and K. R. Philp [Austin, 1978], 33–71) has written an extraordinary essay about the failure of the fire in 1101. R. Curzon (*Visits to Monasteries in the Levant* [London, 1850], 230–50) provides a gripping account of the Easter Fire Riot of 1834; A. P. Stanley (*Sinai and Palestine* [London, 1864], 354–58) has written one of the better eyewitness accounts based on his visit in 1853.

For the ritual of the new light and the paschal candle, see H. A. P. Schmidt, *Hebdoma Sancta* (Rome, 1956–57), 2:809–26, and the interpretation by O. B. Hardison, Jr., *Christian Rite and Christian Drama in the Middle Ages* (Baltimore, 1965), 145–54.

32. For the coinage, see J. Maurice, *Numismatique constantinienne* (Paris, 1908–12), 2:506–13; A. Alföldi, "On the Foundation of Constantinople: A Few Notes," *Journal of Roman Studies* 37 (1947):14; P. Bruun, "The Christian Signs of the Coins of Constantine," *Arctos*, n.s. 3 (1962):21–22; idem, *Constantine and Licinius, A.D. 313–337* (London, 1966), 62, 64, 567 n. 2, which serves as volume 7 of *The Roman Imperial Coinage*, ed. C. H. V. Sutherland and R. G. Carson; and the important interpretative article by P. Courcelle, "Le serpent à face humaine dans la numismatique imperiale de Ve siècle," in *Festschrift A. Piganiol*, ed. R. Chevallier (Paris, 1966), 1:343–53. On the tablet, see C. Mango, *The Brazen House: A Study of the Vestibule of the Imperial Palace of Constantinople* (Copenhagen, 1959), 23–24, 108–9, *et passim*.

33. On this passage, see especially the interpretation by R. Lassus, "L'empereur Constantin, Eusèbe et les lieux saints," *Bulletin de la Société Ernest Renan*, n.s. 15 (1966), 28–36 = *Revue de l'histoire des religions* 171 (1967), 135–44.

34. See the insistence on this point in H. A. Drake, "A Coptic Version of the Discovery of the Holy Sepulchre," *Greek, Roman, and Byzantine Studies* 20 (1979):383–86.

35. See A. Holder, *Inventio sanctae Crucis* (Leipzig, 1889); J. Staubinger, *Die Kreuzauffindungslegende* (Paderborn, 1912), in the series Forschungen zur christlichen Literatur- und Dogmengeschichte, 2.3; H. Leclercq, *Dictionnaire d'archéologie chrétienne et de liturgie* (Paris, 1903–15), 3.2:3131–39; C. Cecchelli, *Il trionfo della croce* (Rome, 1954); J. Vogt, *Reallexikon für Antike und Christentum* (Stuttgart, 1950–), 3:372–74, cf. idem, "Helena Augusta, the Cross, and the Jews," *Classical Folia* 31 (1977):135–51; A. Frolow, *La relique de la vraie croix* (Paris, 1961), esp. 55–72, 155–58, in the series Archives de l'orient chrétien, 7; Hunt, *Holy Land Pilgrimages*, 28–49.

36. Cyril of Jerusalem, *Catecheses illuminandorum* 4.10; 10.19; 13.4 (Migne, *PG* 33:469, 688, 776).

37. John Chrysostom, *Homiliae in John* 85.1 (Migne, *PG* 59:461);

Ambrose, *De Obitu Theodosii* 40–48 (D. Callau, *Ambrosi opera omnia* [Paris, 1844], 8:133–36). See C. Favez, "L'episode de l'invention de la croix dans l'oraison funèbre de Théodose," *Revue des études latines* 10 (1932):423–49; W. Steidle, "Die Leichenrede des Ambrosius für Kaiser Theodosius und die Helena-Legende," *Vigiliae Christianae* 32 (1978):94–112.

38. Rufinus, *Historia ecclesiastica* 10.7–8 (in T. Mommsen, *Rufinus Kirchengeschichte* = E. Schwartz, *Eusebius Kirchengeschichte* [Leipzig, 1908], 2.2:969–70, in the series *GCS* 9.3).

39. Paulinus of Nola, *Epistle* 31.4–5 (Migne, *PL* 61:327–29).

40. Socrates, *Historia ecclesiastica*, 1.17 (Migne, *PG* 67:117–19); Sozomen, *Historia ecclesiastica* 2.1 (Bidez and Hanssen, *Sozomenus Kirchengeschichte*, 47–50); Theodoret, *Historia ecclesiastica* 1.18 (L. Parmentier and F. Scheidweiler, *Theodoret Kirchengeschichte* [Berlin, 1954], 63–65, in the series *GCS*).

41. See Voelkl, *Die Kirchenstiftungen des Kaisers Konstantin*, 33–34 and n. 84.

42. The following selective bibliography on the Church of the Holy Sepulchre includes items that are important either for illustrating major stages in the ongoing debate over the architecture and reconstruction of the complex or for the textual, legendary, or iconographic details they contain. J. F. Plessing, *Über Golgotha und Christi Grab* (Halle, 1769); R. Willis, *The Architectural History of the Church of the Holy Sepulchre*, 2d ed. (London, 1849); M. de Vogüé, *Les églises de la Terre Sainte* (Paris, 1860), 118–63; J. Fergusson, *The Holy Sepulchre and the Temple at Jerusalem* (London, 1865); F. W. Unger, *Die Bauten Constantins des Grossen am heiligen Grabe zu Jerusalem* (Göttingen, 1866); P. Schegg, *Die Bauten Konstantins über dem heiligen Grab zu Jerusalem* (Freizing, 1867); F. Adler, *Der Felsendom und die heilige Grabskirche* (Berlin, 1873); G. C. Warren, *The Temple and the Tomb* (London, 1880); H. Lewis, *The Churches of Constantine at Jerusalem* (London, 1891); E. M. Klos, *Kreuz und Grab Jesu* (Kempten, 1898); C. Mommert, *Die heiligen Grabskirche zu Jerusalem in ihren ursprunglichen Zustande* (Leipzig, 1898); idem, *Golgotha und des heilige Grab zu Jerusalem* (Leipzig, 1900); H. Leclerq, "Saint-Sépulchre," in *Dictionnaire d'archéologie chrétienne et de liturgie* (Paris, 1903–15), 15.1:518–38; A. Baumstark, "Die Heiligtümer des byzantinischen Jerusalem nach einer übersehenen Urkunde," *Oriens christianus* 5 (1905):227–89; C. W. Wilson, *Golgotha and the Holy Sepulchre* (London, 1906), cf. idem, "Sepulchre, Holy," in *Encyclopaedia Britannica*, 11th ed. (1910), 24:656–58; U. de Nuncio, *Il sanctuario Constantiniano del Calvario e del S. Sepolcro* (Rome, 1907); A. Heisenberg, *Grabeskirche und Apostelkirche: Zwei Basiliken Konstantins* (Leipzig, 1908); L. H. Vincent and F. M. Abel, *Jérusalem: Recherches de topographie, d'archéologie et d'histoire*, vol. 2, *Jérusalem nouvelle* (Paris, 1912–14), 89–300; A. Baumstark, *Die Modestienischen*

und die Konstantinischen Bauten am heiligen Grab zu Jerusalem (Paderborn, 1915); K. Schmaltz, *Mater ecclesiarum: Die Grabskirche zu Jerusalem* (Strasbourg, 1918); L. H. Vincent, "'Garden Tomb,' L'histoire
d'une mythe," *Revue biblique* 34 (1925): 401–37; W. Harvey, *Church of
the Holy Sepulchre: Structural Survey, Final Report* (London, 1935);
G. Dalman, *Sacred Sites and Ways* (London, 1935), 346–81; D. Baldi,
Enchiridion locorum sancti (Jerusalem, 1935), 784–986; G. Stuhlfaut,
"Konstantins Bauten am heiligen Grabe in Jerusalem," *Theologische
Blatter* 16 (1937): 177–88; H. G. Evers, "Zu den Konstantinsbauten
am heiligen Grab in Jerusalem," *Zeitschrift für ägyptische Sprache und
Altertumskunde* 75 (1939): 53–60; E. Dyggve, *Gravkirken i Jerusalem*
(Copenhagen, 1941), in the series Studien fra Sprog- og Oldtids
forskning, 186; J. W. Crowfoot, *Early Churches in Palestine* (London,
1941), 9–21; A. Piagnol, "L'hémisphairon et l'omphalos des lieux
saints," *Cahiers archéologiques* 1 (1945): 7–14; G. Testa, ed., *Il Santo
Sepolcro di Gerusalemme* (Bergamo, 1949); E. Wistrand, *Konstantins
Kirch am heiligen Grab in Jerusalem* (1952, see note 43, below); A. Par-
rot, *Golgotha or the Church of the Holy Sepulchre* (London, 1957); J. G.
Davies, "Eusebius' Description of the Martyrium at Jerusalem,"
American Journal of Archaeology 61 (1957): 171–73; J. Conant, "The
Original Buildings at the Holy Sepulchre in Jerusalem," *Speculum* 31
(1956): 1–48; G. Downey, "Constantine's Churches at Antioch, Tyre
and Jerusalem: Notes on Architectural Terms," *Mélanges de l'Univer-
sité Saint-Joseph* 38 (1962): 191–96; R. H. Smith, "The Church of the
Holy Sepulchre," *The Yale Review* 55 (1965): 34–56; R. H. Smith, "The
Tomb of Jesus," *Biblical Archeologist* 30 (1967): 74–90; L. E. C. Evans,
"The Holy Sepulchre," *Palestine Exploration Quarterly* 100 (1968): 112–
36; V. Corbo, *La basilica del S. Sepolcro* (Jerusalem, 1969, see note 44,
below); A. Ovadiah, *Corpus of Byzantine Churches in the Holy Land*
(Bonn, 1970), 75–77; J. Wilkinson, "The Tomb of Christ," *Levant* 4
(1972): 83–97; C. Coüasnon, *The Church of the Holy Sepulchre in Jerusa-
lem* (London, 1974), cf. Coüasnon's earlier report, *Akten der VII inter-
national Kongress fur christlichen Archeologie* (Vatican, 1969), 447–63;
J. E. Phillips, *The Site of the Church of the Holy Sepulchre in Jerusalem: Its
PreConstantinian and Constantinian Phases*, Ph.D. diss., University of
Texas (Austin, 1977), *non vidi*; B. Bagatti and E. Testa, *Il Golgota e la
Croce* (Jerusalem, 1978); E. L. Nitowski, *Reconstructing the Tomb of
Christ from Archeological and Literary Sources*, Ph.D. diss., University
of Notre Dame (Notre Dame, 1979), *non vidi*; D. Chen, "A Note
Pertaining to the Design of the Rotunda Anastasis in Jerusalem,"
Zeitschrift des deutschens Palästina-Vereins 95 (1979): 178–81.

43. Wistrand, *Konstantins Kirche am Heiligen Grab in Jerusalem nach
den ältesten literarischen Zeugnissen* (Göteborg, 1952), in the series
Acta Universitatis Gotoburgensis, 1952.1.

44. V. Corbo, "Gli edifici della santa Anastasis a Gerusalemme,"

Studi Biblici Franciscani Liber Annus 12 (1961–62):231–316; idem, "Nuove scoperte archeologiche nella basilica del S. Sepolcro," ibid. 14 (1963–64):293–338; idem, "Scavo della cappella dell'Invenzione della S. Croce e nuovi reperti archeologici nella basilica del S. Sepolcro a Gerusalemme," ibid. 15 (1964–65):318–66; idem, "La basilica del S. Sepolcro a Gerusalemme," ibid. 19 (1969):65–144 and plate I. Corbo's work is most accessible in English in Coüasnon, *The Church of the Holy Sepulchre,* but see Corbo's review, "Problemi sul Santo Sepolcro di Gerusalemme in una recente pubblicazione," *Studi Biblici Franciscani Liber Annus* 29 (1979):279–92.

45. Pseudo-Kodinos, *Narratio de aedificatione templi Sanctae Sophiae,* in *Scriptore originum Constantinopolitanarum,* T. Preger (Leipzig, 1901), 1:105.

46. The late, post-exilic Chronicler transformed the Deuteronomistic story of judgment (2 Samuel 24) into a "*hieros logos*" (K. Rudolph, below) of the foundation of the Temple site (1 Chronicles 21.1–22.1). The central editorial alternation, transforming David's temporary altar constructed to avert a plague (2 Samuel 24.25) into the proleptic site of the sanctuary, besides the implication of David's continual sacrificial activity at the place (1 Chronicles 21.28b), is the emphatic "Here shall be (*zeh hû*ʾ) the house of the Lord God and here the altar of burnt offerings for Israel" (1 Chronicles 22.1). Other temple motifs added to the narrative include the angel "standing between earth and heaven" (1 Chronicles 21.16) and yhwh's "answering" David's sacrifice "with fire from heaven upon the altar of burnt offerings" (1 Chronicles 21.26b). On 2 Samuel 24, see the important analysis in R. A. Carlson, *David the Chosen King: A Traditio-historical Approach to the Second Book of Samuel* (Uppsala, 1964), 194–222. On 1 Chronicles 21.1–22.1, see K. Rudolph, *Chronikbücher* (Tübingen, 1955), 141–49, in the series Handbuch zum Alten Testament, 21; R. Mosis, *Untersuchungen zur Theologie des chronistischen Geschichtswerkes* (Freiburg im Breisgau, 1973), 104–24; H. G. M. Williamson, *1 and 2 Chronicles* (Grand Rapids, 1982), 142–52, in the series New Century Bible Commentary.

In 2 Chronicles 3.1, there is an additional aetiological note. See Rudolph, *Chronikbücher,* 201, and Williamson, *1 and 2 Chronicles,* 203–5. While the primary function of this verse is to relate the site of Solomon's temple back to the narrative in 1 Chronicles 21.1–22.1, the passage introduces the geographical designation Moriah. "Then Solomon began to build the house of the Lord in Jerusalem on Mount Moriah, where the Lord had appeared to David his father, at the place that David had appointed, on the threshing floor of Ornan the Jebusite." If this is an allusion to the "land of Moriah" (Genesis 22.2) and the "mountain of yhwh" (Genesis 22.14) in the narrative of Abraham's offering of Isaac, then this marks the beginning of the process of connecting the Temple site with significant events in biblical history (see note 48, below). Whatever the Chronicler's intentions, within a few centuries, the identification was secure. Thus, Josephus refers to Abraham going with Isaac "to that mount on which David later erected the temple" in his paraphrase of Genesis 22 (*Antiquities* 1.226); Jubilees 18.13 identifies the locale of the Akedah as the Jerusalemite "Mount Zion." The identification is continued in later rabbinic and Christian traditions; see L. Ginzberg, *Legends of the Jews* (Philadelphia, 1909–46), 5:253 n. 253; S. Spiegel, *The Last Trial: On the Legends and Lore of the Command to Abraham to Offer Isaac as a Sacrifice* (New York, 1967), 43–44 *et passim;* B. Grossfeld, "The Targum to Lamentations 2.10," *Journal of Jewish Studies* 28 (1977):60–64. The Chronicler, however, may have had some other location in mind, or the reference in Genesis 22.2 may be secondary, that is, derivative from the Chronicler. See the lengthy discussion in R. Kilian, *Isaaks Opferung: Zur Überlieferungsgeschichte von Genesis 22* (Stuttgart, 1970), 31–46, in the series Stuttgarter Bibelstudien, 44; and compare C. Westermann, *Genesis* (Neukirchen, 1974–), 1.16:437, in the series Biblischer Kommentar Altes Testament, 1.

Note that in later Christian legend, the site of Abraham's offering of Isaac is transferred to Golgotha or to the "Chapel of Abraham" in the precincts of the Church of the Holy Sepulchre. See C. Coüasnon, *The Church of the Holy Sepulchre,* 52–53, and R. A. S. MacAlister, "Moriah," *Encyclopaedia Britannica,* 11th ed. (1911), 18:836 n. 1.

47. For this mythology, see, among others, M. Michlin, "Der Tempelberg oder Eben Shettija," *Yerushalayim* 11–12 (137–236); J. Horovicz, *Geschichte des Sch'thija-steines* (Frankfurt am Main, 1927); R. Patai, *Man and Temple in Ancient Jewish Myth and Ritual* (London, 1947); K. L. Schmidt, *Der heilige Fels in Jerusalem* (Tübingen, 1933).

48. (1) j. *Sanhedrin* 29a; *Genesis R.* 3.4. (2) *Genesis R.* 3.4; *Pesikta d.R. Kahana* 21. (3) *Midrash Tanhuma,* Ked. 10 (Buber: 78). (4) Palestinian Targum ad Genesis 2.7; *Pirke d.R. Eliezer* 12. (5) Jerusalem Targum ad Genesis 3.20; *Pirke d.R. Eliezer* 31. (6) *Apocalypsis Mosis* 40.6 (?), cf. the later tradition in J. Fabricius, *Codex Pseudepigraphus Veteris Testamenti* 2d ed. (Hamburg, 1722), 1:73. (7) Jerusalem Targum ad Genesis 8.20; b. *Zevahim* 115b; *Genesis R.* 24.9; *Pirke d.R. Eliezer* 23. (8) *Yalkut Reuveni ad Genesis* 1.1 (9) Jerusalem Targum ad Genesis 8.20; b. *Zevahim* 115b; *Genesis R.* 24.9; *Pirke d.R. Eliezer* 23 (10) *Pirke d.R. Elizer* 24. (11) See the *Baedeker Guide to Palestine and Syria,* 1876 ed., p. 173, which quotes "Jewish tradition" to this effect. (12) Jerusalem Targum ad Genesis 22.15. Compare the chains in *Genesis R.* 56.10; *Pesikta R.* 31; *Pirke d.R. Eliezer* 31. (13) *Pirke d.R. Eliezer* 35; *Genesis R.* 69.7. (14) See the collection of texts in E. Abbot, "A Specimen of Research," *Diatessarica,* ed. E. Abbot (London, 1907), 11:xi–lxii. (15) Targum ad 1 Chronicles 21.15; b. *Berakhot* 62b. See, further, the com-

plex set of Davidic traditions in Patai, *Man and Temple*, 54–57; cf. L. Ginzberg, *Legends of the Jews* (Philadelphia, 1909–38), 4:96–97.

49. Events 1, 2, 7, 9, 12, and 15 are placed as occurring on Passover in some of the traditions cited above.

50. See, especially, C. D. Matthews, *Palestine: Mohammedan Holy Land* (New Haven, 1949), in the Yale Oriental Series, Researches, 24.

51. The most important work is J. Jeremias, *Golgotha* (Leipzig, 1926), in the series Angelos: Archiv für neutestamentliche Zeitgeschichte und Kunst, 1. See, further, A. Couret, *Les legendes du Saint-Sepulchre* (Paris, 1893); G. Klameth, *Die neutestamentlichen Lokaltraditionen Palästinas* (Münster, 1914), 1:88–138; E. Roth, *Der volkreiche Kalvarienberg in Literatur und Kunst des Spätmittelalters* (Berlin, 1958), in the series Philologische Studien und Quellen; E. Testa, "Il Golgota, porto della quiete," in *Festschrift P. Bellarmo Bagatti*, ed. I. Mancini (Jerusalem, 1976), 1:197–244, in the series Studium Biblicarum Franciscanum, Collectio maior, 22.

52. This may be an attempt in *Aristeas* to argue Hellenistic notions of mystical behavior; see O. Casel, *De philosophorum graecorum silentio mystico* (Giessen, 1919). It remains a fact, however, that no ritual formulae for the Temple cult are presented anywhere in the Hebrew Bible. Y. Kaufmann (*Toledot ha'emunāh hayyisre elit* [Tel Aviv, 1942–46], 2:476–77, cf. the abridged translation, Y. Kaufmann, *The Religion of Israel* [London, 1961], 302–4) has noted that "the priestly temple is the kingdom of silence," and he has attempted to draw a contrast between Israel's "soundless worship" and the ritual utterances of "paganism." The accuracy of the observation is to be accepted even as the polemics are rejected. The various descriptions of cult practice in the Priestly literatures are systemic, they are not to be confused with the actual cult books of the Temple, which are lost.

53. R. Jakobson, *Six Lectures on Sound and Meaning* (Cambridge, Mass., 1978), 66.

54. C. Lévi-Strauss, *La pensée sauvage* (Paris, 1962), 152. Note that the first edition of the English translation, *The Savage Mind* (Chicago, 1966), 115, has misdrawn the diagram. It has been corrected in subsequent editions.

55. A. P. Stanley, *Sinai and Palestine in Connection with Their History*, 2d ed. (New York, 1870), 451.

56. Cyril of Jerusalem, *Catecheses mystagogicae* 2.4 (text and translation in F. L. Cross, *St. Cyril of Jerusalem's Lectures on the Christian Sacraments* [Crestwood, 1977], 19, 60).

57. For churches built on the model of the Church of the Holy Sepulchre, see G. Dalman, *Das Grab Christi in Deutschland* (Leipzig, 1922), in the series Studien über christliche Denkmäler, 14. See, most recently, G. Bresc-Bautior, "Les imitations du Saint-Sépulcre de

Jérusalem," *Revue de l'histoire de la spiritualité* 50 (1974):319–42.
R. Krautheimer (*Studies in Early Christian, Medieval and Renaissance Art* [New York, 1969], 115–50) has elucidated the notion of medieval "architectural imitation" using copies of the *Anastasis* as a prime example. The earliest example of such imitation was the Apostoleion, Constantine's burial site in Constantinople (idem, *Early Christian and Byzantine Architecture,* 72–74); one of the latest, the mausoleum constructed for Emperor Frederick III at Potsdam in 1888 (idem, *Studies,* 141 n. 9).

A second type of reproduction is that of scaled models, built as side chapels or as small, independent chapels, most frequently in cemeteries. See N. C. Brooks, *The Sepulchre of Christ in Art and Liturgy* (Urbana, 1921), 88–91, in the series University of Illinois Studies in Language and Literature, 7.2. See, further, J. Lauffray, "La Memoria Sancti Sepulchri du Musée de Narbonne et le Temple Rond de Baalbeck," *Mélanges de l'Université St. Joseph* 38 (1962):199–217.

An important review of the archeological and iconographic materials, with attention given to the question of liturgical drama (see note 59, below), is provided by W. H. Forsyth, *The Entombment of Christ: French Sculptures of the Fifteenth and Sixteenth Centuries* (Cambridge, Mass., 1970), 9–21.

58. J. A. Jungmann, *Pastoral Liturgy* (London, 1962), 223–37. Compare idem, "Die Andacht der vierzig Stunden das heilige Grab," *Liturgisches Jahrbuch* 2 (1952):184–98; idem, "Des Gebet beim heiligen Grab und die Auferstehungsfeier," *Theologisch-praktische Quartalschrift* 100 (1952):72–77.

59. These three practices have been of special interest to students of medieval liturgical drama. See, in general, E. K. Chambers, *The Medieval Stage* (Oxford, 1903), 2:11–36. For the Easter Sepulchre (whether focused on a permanent construction or a prop fabricated for the occasion), see A. Heales, "Easter Sepulchres," *Archaeologia* 42 (1869):263–308; H. P. Feasey, "The Easter Sepulchre," *Ecclesiastical Review* 32 (1905):337–55, 468–99; J. Brand, *Observations on Popular Antiquities,* rev. ed. (London, 1913), 83–85; K. Young, *The Dramatic Associations of the Easter Sepulchre* (Madison, 1920), in the series University of Wisconsin Studies in Language and Literature, 10; Brooks, *The Sepulchre of Christ,* 30–87; K. Young, *The Drama of the Medieval Church* (Oxford, 1933), 2:500–513, cf. 1:112–48, 239–410; O. B. Hardison, Jr., *Christian Rite and Christian Drama in the Middle Ages* (Baltimore, 1965), 173–75, 231–32, *et passim.*

60. For example, Hardison, *Christian Rite and Christian Drama,* 192–94.

61. On the ritual, see J. A. Jungmann, *The Mass of the Roman Rite* (New York, 1950), 2:266–67, 310–11. For the address, see Amalarius,

in J. M. Hanssen, *Amalarii episcopi opera liturgica omnia* (Vatican, 1948–50), 2:346–49, 367–68. For the general symbolism of the alter as *Sepulchri Christi*, see Young, *Drama of the Medieval Church* 1:219–20.

62. For example, Hardison, *Christian Rite and Christian Drama*, 228–32. The association of the font and the tomb is archaic. See note 56, above. Compare W. Bedard, *The Symbolism of the Baptismal Font in Early Christian Thought* (Washington, 1951), in the series Catholic University of America, Studies in Sacred Theology, 2.45.

63. *Missale mixtum* (Migne, *PL* 85:418–19, 432–35); compare the interpretation by Amalarius (Hanssen, *Amalarii* 2:468–69); *Decreta Authentica Congregationis Sacrorum Rituum* (Rome, 1898–1927), 4:419–21. See Young, *Dramatic Associations of the Easter Sepulchre*, 10–18; Brooks, *The Sepulchre of Christ*, 49–52. For the controversy, see H. Thurston, "Easter Sepulchre or Altar of Repose?" *The Month*, ser. 3, 29 (1903):304–14; A. Dolezal, "Was machen wir mit dem heiligen Grab?" *Bibel und Liturgie* 23 (1955–56):130–31.

64. For the detail concerning the "Little Jerusalems," see K. A. Kneller, *Geschichte der Kreuzwegandacht* (Freiburg im Breisgau, 1908), 56.

65. See H. Thurston, *The Stations of the Cross* (New York, 1906); Keller, *Geschichte der Kreuzwegandacht;* M. Sleutjes, *Instructio de stationibus S. Viae Crucis*, 5th ed. (Quaracchi-Florence, 1927). The practice can be dated to the fifteenth century. It became widely distributed through the efforts of the eighteenth century Franciscan, Leonard of Port Maurice.

66. See the items in Hunt, *Holy Land Pilgrimages*, 129–30; R. H. Smith, "The Tomb of Jesus," *Biblical Archeologist* 30 (1967):84. See, further, the seventeenth century account of C. Deshayes reproduced in F. de Chateaubriand, *Itinéraire de Paris à Jérusalem* (1st ed. Paris, 1811), in the edition of E. Malakis (Baltimore, 1946), 2:94–95.

67. A. Frolow, *La relique de la vraie croix*, 55–152, presents the history of the expansion. See the chart on p. 111.

68. Ibid., 57–58.

69. See the important study by S. G. Nichols, Jr., *Romanesque Signs: Early Medieval Iconography and Narrative* (New Haven, 1983), 66–94, esp. the formula on p. 73, "Holy Sepulchre: Constantine : : Holy Sepulchre: Charlemagne."

70. F. L. Cross, "Introduction," in his *St. Cyril of Jerusalem's Lectures*, xix.

71. Text: O. Prinz, *Itinerarium Egeriae*, 5th ed. (Heidelberg, 1960), in the series Sammlung vulgärlateinischer Texte. English translations: G. E. Gingras, *Egeria, Diary of a Pilgrimage* (New York, 1970), in the series Ancient Christian Writers; J. Wilkinson, *Egeria's Travel to the Holy Land*, 2d ed. (Jerusalem, 1981). Also, H. Pétré, *Éthérie: Journal de voyage* (Paris, 1948), in the series, Sources chrétiennes, 21.

There is a full bibliography: M. Starowieyski, "Bibliografia Egeriana," *Augustinianum* 19 (1979):297–318.

72. P. Devos, "La date du voyage d'Egérie," *Analecta Bollandiana* 85 (1967):165–94. See, *contra*, B. Bagatti, "Ancore sulla data di Eteria," *Bibbia e Oriente* 10 (1968):73–75. There is a careful discussion of the date in Wilkinson, *Egeria's Travels*, 237–39, 330–31.

73. *Itinerarium Burdigalense* in P. Geyer and O. Cuntz, *Itineraria et alia Geographica* (Turnholt, 1965), 1:1–26, in the series *CCSL* 175.

74. See J. Ziegler, "Die *Pereginatio Aetheriae* und die heilige Schrift," *Biblica* 12 (1931):162–98; idem, "Die Peregrinatio Aetheriae und das *Onomastikon* das Eusebius," ibid., 70–84.

75. L. Spitzer, "The Epic Style of the Pilgrim Aetheria," *Comparative Literature* 1 (1949):239.

76. *Egeria* 4.3 requires emendation as per P. Geyer, *Itinera hierosolymitana saeculi IIII–VII* (Vienna, 1898), 41.

77. *Egeria* 20 is more complex than this extract suggests. In addition to the building being a "memorial" to the patriarch, it is also a "shrine to the martyr" Helpidus (otherwise unknown), who is buried there and who is, himself, the object of pilgrimage (*Egeria* 20.5). Furthermore, Egeria observes, "Just as we [Christians] venerate . . . the place where the house of Abraham originally stood . . . so the pagans venerate . . . the place where the tombs of Nachor and Bethuel are located, about a mile from the city" (*Egeria* 20.8)—an observation which touches off a learned discussion (*Egeria* 20.9–10).

78. See W. van Oorde, *Lexicon Aetherianum* (Amsterdam, 1930), 41–42, 145.

79. See the reconstructions in R. Zerfass, *Die Schriftlesung im Kathedraloffizium Jerusalems* (Münster, 1968), in the series Liturgiewissenschaftliche Quellen und Forschungen, 48; and in Wilkinson, *Egeria's Travels*, 260–77.

80. A. Baumstark, *Liturgie comparée* (Chevetogne, 1940), 6, 149–61, 178–79, *et passim*. Compare the striking formulation in F. Cabrol, *Les origines liturgiques* (Paris, 1906), 187.

81. See W. J. Swaans, "A propos des Catecheses Mystagogiques attribuées à S. Cyrille de Jérusalem," *Le muséon* 55 (1942):1–43.

82. For a brief overview of the progress made since D. Baldi, *La liturgia della chiesa di Gerusalemme dal IV al IX secolo* (Jerusalem, 1939), see G. Kretschmer, "Die frühe Geschichte der Jerusalemer Liturgie," *Jahrbüch für Liturgik und Hymnologie* 2 (1956):22–46. To date, the most important studies are those by Zerfass, *Die Schriftslesung*, and the introductory monograph by A. Renoux to his edition, *Le Codex Arménien Jérusalem 121* (Paris, 1969–71), 1:5–215, in the series Patrologia orientalis, 35. For the Armenian, Renoux's edition is the most important new find. For the Old Palestinian, see M. S. Black, *A Christian Palestinian Syriac Horologion* (Cambridge, 1954); for the Old Georgian,

G. Garitte, *Le calendrier palestino-géorgien du Sinaiticus 34* (Brussels, 1958); for the Old Iberian, T. Tarchnišvili, *Le grande lectionnaire de l'église de Jérusalem, V^e–VIIIe siècle* (Louvain, 1959–60), 1–2.

83. Best studied of the stational liturgies is the Roman praxis, first witnessed in the late seventh century *Ordo Romanus* I (M. Andrieu, *Le pontifical romain au Môyen-Age* [Vatican, 1938–41], 1:67–108). For a full study, see G. G. Willis, "Roman Stational Liturgy," *Further Essays in Early Roman Liturgy* (London, 1968), 3–87, in the series Alcuin Club Collections, 50. See, further, the older studies by J. P. Kirsch, *Die Stationskirchen des Missale Romanum* (Freiburg im Breisgau, 1925); idem, "L'origine des stations liturgiques du Missel Romain," *Ephemerides Liturgicae* 41 (1927):137–50; R. Hierzegger, "Collecta und Statio: Die römischen Stationsprozessionen im frühen Mittelalter," *Zeitschrift für Katholische Theologie* 60 (1936):511–54. For the stational liturgy at Constantinople, see J. Baldwin, "Le liturgie stationelle à Constantinople," *La Maison-Dieu* 140 (1981):85–94. For the Jerusalem stational liturgy, in addition to the references in note 87, below, see Renoux, *Le codex Arménien* 1:33–55 and 2:193–207.

84. G. Dix, *The Shape of the Liturgy*, 2d ed. (London, 1960), 593.

85. See note 80, above. The point is put bluntly by Dix, *The Shape of the Liturgy*, 348.

86. See notes 79 and 82, above.

87. F. Cabrol. *Étude sur la Peregrinatio Silviae: Les églises de Jérusalem, la discipline et la liturgie au IVe siècle* (Paris-Poitiers, 1895), esp. 33–34; H. Leclercq, "La liturgie a Jérusalem," *Dictionnaire d'archéologie chrétienne et de la liturgie* (Paris, 1907–53), 7:2374–90; A. Bludau, *Die Pilgerreise der Aetheria* (Paderborn, 1927), 43–190; Pétré, *Éthérie*, 57–64; Zerfass, *Die Schriftslesung*, 20–24.

88. As described in the text, *Egeria* 31, the Palm Sunday ritual, which is a literal reenactment of the entrance into Jerusalem, cannot be exported. Other dramatic reenactments (lacking the locale) were developed, however. See E. Wiepen, *Palmsonntagsprozession und Palmesel* (Bonn, 1903). There are other, more minor examples, such as *Egeria* 39.5, perhaps the most intensively local passage in the text.

89. Dix, *The Shape of the Liturgy*, 303–98 *et passim*.

90. S. Czarnowski, *Le culte des héros et ses conditions sociales: Saint Patrick, héros national de l'Ireland* (Paris, 1919; reprint, New York, 1975). A Polish translation, *Kult bohaterów i jego spoleczne podloze: Swięty Patryk, bohater narodowy Irlandii*, was published in the edition of Czarnowski's works, *Dziela* (Warsaw, 1956), 4:11–236.

91. Czarnowski, *Le culte des héros*, 325–29 *et passim*. Compare F. A. Isambert, "At the Frontier of Folklore and Sociology: Hubert, Herz and Czarnowski, Founders of a Sociology of Folk Religion," in P. Besnard, *The Sociological Domain* (Cambridge, 1983), 164–65.

FIVE

1. C. Middleton, *A Letter from Rome Shewing an Exact Conformity between Popery and Paganism: or, The Religion of the Present Romans to be derived entirely from that of their Heathen Ancestors* (London, 1729), 9. Although the copy I have is of the same date and by the same printer as the first edition, it appears to be a second printing.

2. Ibid., 11.

3. Ibid., 12.

4. Ibid., 13.

5. Ibid., ii (the second, unpaginated page of the Preface).

6. Ibid., 13.

7. Ibid., 16.

8. Ibid., 23.

9. Ibid., 13–14.

10. Ibid., 69–70.

11. Incense and altars (ibid., 15–16); altar boys (16); holy water (16–21); lamps and candles (21–22); votive offerings (22–29); devotion to the saints and their statues (29–43); roadside shrines, altars, and crosses (44–49); pomps and processions (50–52); miracles and relics (52–64); notion of sanctuary (64–65); priesthood (65–67).

12. Ibid., ii.

13. Ibid., 26.

14. Ibid., 31.

15. Ibid., 33; see, further, 36–37.

16. Middleton was later to achieve considerable fame with the publication of his *Life of Cicero* (London, 1741), until it was demonstrated that it was heavily plagiarized from W. Bellenden, *De tribus luminibus Romanorum* (Paris, 1633). The majority of the copies of this work were lost in transit to England. One of the few survivors was deposited at the Cambridge Library, where Middleton was University Librarian. See *Encyclopaedia Britannica*, 11th ed., 3:698, s.v. *Bellenden.*

17. C. Lévi-Strauss, *Structural Anthropology* (New York, 1963–76), 2:55.

18. J. P. S. Uberoi, *Science and Culture* (Delhi, 1978), 25.

19. Uberoi, *Science and Culture*, 31, 28, 33.

20. The question whether the eucharist was to be understood as *figura* or *ueritas* was first raised in strong form in the ninth century controversy between Paschasius Radbertus and Ratramnus and gained classical formulation in the eleventh century work of Berengar. It is in a retort to the latter that one finds one of the earliest expressions of the notion of "merely a symbol," in the response of Peter, a deacon of Rome at the Council of Vercelli in 1050: "If up till now we hold only the symbol, when shall we have the thing itself?"

(Berengar, *De sacra coena adversus Lanfrancum*, 9, in the edition by
A. F. Vischer and F. T. Vischer [Berlin, 1834], 43; in the new, and far
from satisfactory, edition by W. H. Beekenkamp [The Hague, 1941],
in the series Kerkhistorische Studien, 2, the passage occurs on p. 13,
lines 2–3).

For the debate, see the standard treatments by J. R. Geiselmann,
Die Eucharistielehre der Vorscholastik (Paderborn, 1926); A. J. Mac-
Donald, *Berengar and the Reform of Sacramental Doctrine* (New York,
1930), cf. idem, ed., *The Evangelical Doctrine of Holy Communion*
(Cambridge, 1930); C. E. Sheedy, *The Eucharistic Controversy of the
Eleventh Century* (Washington, D.C., 1947); J. de Montclos, *Lanfranc et
Berengar: La controverse eucharistique du XIᵉ siècle* (Louvain, 1971), in
the series Spicilegium sacrum Lovaniense, Études et documents, 37;
and G. Macy, *The Theologies of the Eucharist in the Early Scholastic Period*
(Oxford, 1984). The article by N. M. Haring, "Berengar's Definitions
of *Sacramentum* and Their Influence on Mediaeval Sacramentology,"
Mediaeval Studies 10 (1948):109–146, is particularly helpful in showing the wide semantic range of *sacramentum* and Berengar's attempt
to stipulate a restrictive definition. Two recent works review the eucharistic controversies in a manner refreshingly different from the
usual histories of dogma: B. Stock, *The Implications of Literacy: Written
Language and Models of Interpretation in the Eleventh and Twelfth Centuries* (Princeton, 1983), 241–315; R. Wagner, *Symbols that Stand for
Themselves* (Chicago, 1986), 96–125.

21. Among other references, see H. Zwingli, *On the Lord's Supper*
3 (translation in G. W. Bromiley, *Zwingli and Bullinger* [Philadelphia,
1953], 185–238, esp. 233–35). The Marburg debate, on which Uberoi
lays so much emphasis, has been reconstructed by W. Köhler, *Das
Marburger Religionsgespräch 1529: Versuch einer Rekonstruktion* (Leipzig,
1929), in the series Schriften des Vereins für Reformationsges-
chichte, 48:1 (no. 148); pp. 7–38 of Köhler's work has been translated into English by D. J. Ziegler, *Great Debates of the Reformation*
(New York, 1969), 71–107, esp. 82–83: "We must take the word 'is' in
the Lord's Supper to mean 'signifies' . . . [Melanchthon agrees] with
me that something is only 'signified' by the words." Curiously, the
concession by Zwingli that "we have no scriptural passage that says,
'This is the sign [*figura*] of my body'" (Ziegler, *Great Debates*, 80)
echoes an early polemic by Theodore of Mopsuestia, "Christ did not
say , 'This is the symbol [*symbolon*] of my body and blood,' but
rather, 'This is my body and blood'" (*Fragmenta in Mt.* 26.26, Migne,
PG 66:713).

22. See the texts from Beza cited in the important study by
J. Raitt, *The Conversion of the Elements in Reformed Eucharistic Theory
with Special Reference to Theodore Beza*, Ph.D. dissertation, University

of Chicago (Chicago, 1970), 208–9. Raitt's study of the issue among the Reformers is the most searching to date.

23. Text quoted in ibid, 157.

24. In the following paragraphs, all the dated, but otherwise un-identified, quotations, are taken from the *Oxford English Dictionary,* s.vv. *ceremony, custom, rite, ritual, symbol.*

25. For example, Duncan Forbes, *Some Thoughts Concerning Religion Natural and Revealed and the Manner of Understanding Revelation: Tending to Shew that Christianity is, Indeed very near, as Old as the Creation* (London, 1735), 34, "Almost all the Jewish religious Service consisted in external, emblematical acts, rites and observances which, in themselves, and but for the institution and what was intended to be represented by them, served for no good purpose." (The copy I cite, in Special Collections of the Joseph Regenstein Library of the University of Chicago, is bound together with Middleton's *A Letter from Rome.*) The usual term for empty ritualization is "Pharasaic," as in "The causes of Superstition are . . . Excesse of Outward and Pharisicall Holinesse" (1625), which allows the combination, "Pharisaically and Papistically" (1655).

26. J. Corbet, *A Discourse of the Religion of England* (London, 1667), 17. On pagano-papism, see H. Pinard de la Boullaye, *L'étude comparée des religions* (Paris, 1922–25), 1:151–56; L. Stephen, *History of English Thought in the Eighteenth Century,* 3d ed. (New York, 1949), 1:253–62; M. T. Hodgen, *Early Anthropology in the Sixteenth and Seventeenth Centuries* (Philadelphia, 1964), 325–30 *et passim.*

27. P. Mussard, *Les conformitez des cérémonies modernes avec les anciennes. Où il est prouvé par des autoritez incontestables que les cérémonies de l'église romaine sont empruntées des pagans* (London [?], 1667). I have not seen the English translation, *Roma antiqua et recens,* or the *Conformity of antient and modern Ceremonies, shewing from indisputable Testimonies that the Ceremonies of the Church of Rome are borrowed from the Pagans* (London, 1732). It has been charged that Middleton took parts of *A Letter from Rome* from Mussard (Stephen, *History of English Thought,* 1:256 n. 11). I doubt it. (See notes 5 and 16, above.)

28. P. Smart, *A Sermon Preached in the Cathedral Church of Durham, 1628,* 2d ed. (London, 1640), 18.

29. J. Toland, *Letters to Serena* (London, 1704), 130.

30. Erasmus, *Enchiridion militis Christiani* (1503), in J. P. Dolan, *The Essential Erasmus* (New York, 1964), 68.

31. For a profound meditation on the notion of "decipherment," see M. V. David, *Le débat sur les ecritures et l'hieroglyphique aux XVIIᵉ et XVIIIᵉ siècles et l'application de déchiffrement aux écritures mortes* (Paris, 1965).

32. See the study of this terminology and its implications in M. T.

Hodgen, *The Doctrine of Survivals: A Chapter in the History of Scientific Method in the Study of Man* (London, 1936).

33. [C. de Brosses], *Du culte des dieux fétiches* ([Geneva], 1760), 267. The first edition, which I cite, was published anonymously, without indication of the author, publisher, or place of publication.

34. See the critique of Adolf Jensen and the presuppositions of the Frobenius School in J. Z. Smith, *Imagining Religion* (Chicago, 1982), 42–44.

35. In the formulations in this and the following three paragraphs, I am relying on, and modifying, my earlier set of statements in ibid., 54–56.

36. Herodotus, 2.172. I have adapted the standard translation by G. Rawlinson, 1st. ed. (London, 1858–60).

37. [Norman Anonymous] *De consecratione pontificum et regium* in *Libelli de lite imperatorum et pontificum saeculis XI et XII conscripti*, H. Bömer (Hanover, 1891–97), 3:664, in the series *Monumenta Germaniae historica*. I have followed the English translation by E. H. Kantorowicz, *The King's Two Bodies* (Princeton, 1957), 46.

38. See H. Bouillard, "Le categorie du sacré dans la science des religions," in *Le sacré: Études et recherches*, ed. E. Castelli (Paris, 1974), esp. 33–38.

39. See E. Benveniste, *Le vocabulaire des institutions indo-européennes* (Paris, 1969), 2:179–207.

40. Isaiah 44.14–17; Horace, *Satires* 1.8.1–3. Compare, Wisdom of Solomon 13.11–14.8; Tertullian, *De idolatria* 8.

41. Tertullian, *Apologia* 13.4.

42. See the use of the Amasis story in Minucius Felix, *Octavius* 22.4; Theophilus, *Ad Autolycum* 1.10. Compare Philo, *De Vita Contemplativa* 7; Justin, 1 *Apologia* 9.3; Arnobius, *Adversus nationes* 6.12.

43. E. Durkheim, *Les formes élémentaires de la vie religieuse*, 6th ed. (Paris, 1979), 167–80; English translation by J. W. Swain, *The Elementary Forms of the Religious Life* (London, 1915; reprint, New York, 1965), 140–49. On this topic, see the useful article by M. Singer, "Emblems of Identity: A Semiotic Exploration," in *On Symbols in Anthropology*, ed. J. Maquet (Los Angeles, 1982), 73–133, esp. 80–90, which compares Durkheim and Lévi-Strauss.

44. Durkheim, *Les formes élémentaires*, 172; *Elementary Forms*, 144. I am aware, *as was Durkheim* (*Les formes élémentaires*, 168 n. 3; *Elementary Forms*, 140 n. 101) that not all *tjurunga* are marked. See T. G. H. Strehlow, *Aranda Traditions* (Melbourne, 1947; reprint, New York, 1968), 57, 73. This has been emphasized by C. Lévi-Strauss (*La pensée sauvage* [Paris, 1962], 318) in attacking Durkheim's formulation. A few counterexamples do not necessarily destroy a theory if they can be explained. Strehlow provides ample explanation. The first example (Strehlow, *Aranda Traditions*, 54–55) represents a native Northern

Aranda distinction between the stone *tjurunga ṭalkara,* which is the metamorphized body of the ancestor, and the wooden (always engraved) *tjurunga ititjangariera,* which are thought to be representations of the original *tjurunga ṭalkara.* If these are engraved, "they are not engraved by the hand of man." The second example comes from the outer border of the Aranda-*tjurunga* culture: "[From that point]" onwards, sea-shells, known as *poṭṭ' irkara* had taken their [the tjurunga's] place as objects of worship" (Strehlow, *Aranda Traditions,* 73).

45. Durkheim, *Les formes élémentaires,* 178–79; *Elementary Forms,* 148–49.

46. See above, p. 40.

47. C. Lévi-Strauss, "Introduction à l'œuvre de Marcel Mauss," which serves as a preface to Lévi-Strauss's collection *Sociologie et anthropologie par Marcel Mauss* (Paris, 1950), ix–lii. See Lévi-Strauss's remarks on the relationship between Durkheim and Mauss, p. xli.

48. Lévi-Strauss, "Introduction," xlii–xliii. I have profited from D. Pocock's translation of some paragraphs of this essay in his "Foreword" to the English translation of M. Mauss, *A General Theory of Magic* (London, 1972), 1–6.

49. Lévi-Strauss, "Introduction," xliii. The passage is cited from Tesa, *Studi del Thevenet* (Pisa, 1881), 17 (*non vidi*), in Mauss, *A General Theory of Magic,* 114. Both Thevenet's examples and those provided by Lévi-Strauss refer to new objects introduced by trade and culture contact. See, further, J. Z. Smith, *Map Is Not Territory* (Leiden, 1978), 298–99.

50. Lévi-Strauss, "Introduction," xliv.

51. Ibid., xlvii, xlix.

52. Ibid., xlix.

53. Ibid., i. In his text, Lévi Strauss uses the analogy of the number zero; in a footnote, he refers to the linguistic notion developed by R. Jakobsen of "un phoneme zéro."

54. Lévi-Strauss, "Introduction," i n. 1.

55. See above, pp. 85–86.

56. I am much taken with the suggestion by G. G. Porton ("Defining Midrash," in *The Study of Ancient Judaism,* ed. J. Neusner [New York, 1981], 1:64–65) of the existence "during the intertestamental period . . . [of] two possible sources of authority, two parallel but possibly conflicting paths . . . the priesthood/priestly traditions and the Torah."

57. Smith, *Imagining Religion,* 63.

58. J. C. Heestermann, *The Inner Conflict of Tradition: Essays in Indian Ritual, Kingship and Society* (Chicago, 1985), 3.

59. A. van Gennep, *Les rites de passage* (Paris, 1909), 16; English translation, *The Rites of Passage* (London, 1960), 12.

60. S. Freud, "Zwangshandlungen und Religionsübungen" (1907),

in *Gesammelte Werke,* S. Freud (London, 1940–), 7:129–39; English translation, "Obsessive Acts and Religious Practices," in *The Standard Edition of the Complete Psychological Works of Sigmund Freud,* ed. J. Strachey (London, 1953–), 9:117–27.

61. C. Lévi-Strauss, *L'homme nu* (Paris, 1971), 596–603; English translation by J. and D. Weightman, *The Naked Man* (New York, 1981), 667–75.

62. Lévi-Strauss, *La pensée sauvage,* 17.

63. See W. E. H. Stanner (*On Aboriginal Religion* [Sydney, 1966], 14, in the series The Oceania Monographs, 11), who speaks of "the great split of the pristine unity."

64. See pp. 11–12, above. There, as well as in what follows, I have been much influenced by N. Munn, "The Transformation of Subjects into Objects in Walbiri and Pitjantjatjara Myth," in *Australian Aboriginal Anthropology,* ed. R. M. Berndt (Nedlands, 1970), 141–63. Though taking a different tack, the question I raise here is that raised by Lévi-Strauss in *La pensée sauvage,* 302–23.

65. I have been influenced in these formulations by, in addition to Munn (see above, note 64), W. E. H. Stanner, "Religion, Totemism, and Symbolism," in *Aboriginal Man in Australia,* ed. R. M. Berndt and C. H. Berndt (Sydney, 1965), 207–37, as reprinted in *Religion in Aboriginal Australia: An Anthology,* ed. M. Charlesworth et al. (Queensland, 1984), esp. 164.

66. Stanner, *Aboriginal Religion,* 11.

67. M. Charlesworth, "Introduction: Change in Aboriginal Religion," in Charlesworth et al., eds., *Religion in Aboriginal Australia,* 113.

68. Stanner, *Aboriginal Religion,* 63.

69. Smith, *Imagining Religion,* 56.

70. Strehlow, *Aranda Traditions,* 120, cf. 84–172.

71. Stanner, *Aboriginal Religion,* 32.

72. See the crisp formulation of this in H. A. Drake, "A Coptic Version of the Discovery of the Holy Sepulchre," *Greek, Roman, and Byzantine Studies* 20 (1979):384–85.

73. A. Baumstark, *Comparative Liturgy* (London, 1958), 182.

74. See the treatment by A. Frolow, "La vraie croix et les expéditions d'Héraclius en Perse," *Festschrift M. Jugie* (Paris, 1953):89–105 = *Revue des études byzantines* 11 (1953).

75. On Khosrau = Lucifer, see H. P. L'Orange, *Studies on the Iconography of Cosmic Kingship* (Oslo, 1953), 114–84, in the series Forelesninger av det Instituttet for sammenlignende Kulturforskning, ser. A, 12. Note that in the *Chronicum venetum* (Altinate), edited by H. Simonsfeld, *Monumenta Germaniae historica,* series *Scriptores* (Hanover, 1826–), 14:49–50, Constantine's and Heraclius's campaigns have been combined into a single event.

76. The standard monograph remains W. Meyer, *Die Geschichte der*

Kreuzholzes vor Christus (Munich, 1882) in the series Abhandlungen der philosophisch-philologischen Classe der Königlich Bayerischen Akademie der Wissenschaften, 16.2 (1882):103–160. E. C. Quinn, *The Quest of Seth for the Oil of Life* (Chicago, 1962) is the most recent full treatment.

77. See the important treatment of this in M. Halbwachs, *La topographie légendaire des évangiles en Terre sainte* (Paris, 1941). I find most helpful his notions of "concentration" and "doubling" (pp. 185–86).

78. This density is revealed at the level of chapels, not to speak of individual relics. See, among others, the description by C. Deshayes, *Voyage du Levant fait par le commandement du Roy* (Paris, 1624), 392–402, as reproduced in F. A. de Chateaubriand, *Itinéraire de Paris à Jerusalem* (1811). I cite the critical edition by E. Malakis, *Chateaubriand: Itinéraire de Paris à Jerusalem* (Baltimore, 1946), 2:92–97.

> Upon entering the Church, you come to the Stone of Unction on which the body of Our Lord was anointed with myrrh and aloes. . . . Some say that it is of the same rock as mount Calvary, others assert that it was brought to this place by Joseph and Nicodemus. . . . The Holy Sepulchre is thirty paces from this Stone. . . . At the entrance to the door of the Sepulchre, there is a stone about a foot and a half square . . . upon this stone was seated the angel when he spoke to the two Marys. . . . The first Christians erected before it a little chapel which is called the Chapel of the Angel. Twelve steps from the Holy Sepulchre, turning north, you come to a large block of gray marble . . . placed there to mark the spot where our Lord appeared to the Magdalene in the form of a gardener. Further on is the Chapel of the Apparition where, according to tradition, Our Lord first appeared to the Virgin after his resurrection. . . . Continuing your walk around the Church, you find a small vaulted chapel . . . the Prison of Our Lord where he was held while the hole was dug for the erecting of the Cross. . . . Very near is another chapel . . . standing on the very spot [*au même lieu*] where Our Lord was stripped by the soldiers before being nailed to the Cross. . . . Leaving this chapel . . . going down thirty steps, you come to a chapel . . . commonly called the Chapel of St. Helena because she prayed there before bringing about the search for the Cross. You descend eleven more steps to the place where it was discovered, along with the nails, the crown of thorns, and the head of the lance. . . . Near the top of this staircase . . . is a chapel . . . underneath the altar [of which] is a pillar of gray marble. . . . It is called the pillar of *Impropere* because Our Lord was forced to sit there in order to be crowned with thorns. Ten paces from this chapel [is the

staircase by which you ascend] to Mount Calvary. . . . You still see the hole dug in the rock. . . . Near this is the place where stood the two crosses of the two thieves."

79. See note 78, above. For the "Stone of Unction," see M. A. Graeve, "The Stone of Unction in Caravaggio's Painting for the Chiesa Nuova," *The Art Bulletin* 40 (1958):230. Compare A. Millet, *Recherches sur l'iconographie de l'Évangile aux XIVe, XVe et XVIe siècles*, 2d ed. (Paris, 1960), 479. For the "prison," see G. Dalman, *Sacred Sites and Ways: Studies in the Topography of the Gospels* (London, 1935), 336.

80. For the biographical details, see I. Iparraguirre, *Practica de los Ejercicios de San Ignaci de Loyola en Vida de su autor* (Rome, 1946), 34*– 40*, in the series Bibliotheca Instituti Historici Societatis Jesus, 3.

81. The scheme is pre-Ignatian. The most immediate influence on Ignatius was the fourteenth century *Vitae Christi* by Ludolfus of Saxony. See M. I. Bodenstedt, *The Vitae Christi of Ludolphus the Carthusian* (Washington, D.C., 1944), and C. A. Conway, Jr., *The Vitae Christi of Ludolph of Saxony: A Descriptive Analysis* (Salzburg, 1976), in the series Analecta Carthusiana. For earlier exemplars, see the anonymous, thirteenth century *De meditatione passionis Christi per septem diei horas* (Migne, *PL* 94:561–68), and the popular, late thirteenth century Tuscan text, falsely attributed to Bonaventure, *Meditationes vitae Christi*. On the latter, see the study by L. Oliger, "Le meditationes vitae Christi del pseudo-Bonaventura," *Studi Francescani*, n.s. 7 (1921):143–83; 8 (1922):18–47; and the translation of the text and reproduction of an illustrated version by I. Ragusa and R. B. Green, *Meditations on a Life of Christ: An Illustrated Manuscript of the Fourteenth Century, Paris, Bibliothèque Nationale, Ms. Ital. 115* (Princeton, 1961), in the series Princeton Monographs in Art and Archaeology. The instructions for meditating over a period of a week include the detail "feeling yourself present in those places as if the things were done in your presence" (Ragusa and Green, *Meditations*, 387).

82. Ignatius of Loyola, *Ejercicios espirituales*, 150–51, in the critical edition by J. Calveras, *Sanctii Ignatii de Loyola, Exercitia spiritualia* (Rome, 1969), 250–53, in the series Monumenta historica societatis Jesu, 100. In the enumeration of the convenient edition by J. Roothan (*Los ejercicios espirituales de San Ignacio de Loyola*, 3d ed. [Zaragoza, 1959], 192–93), the passages appear as numbers 191–92. Although the meditations were designed to produce a mental picture, in the sixteenth century, Jeronimo Nadal was commissioned by the Jesuits to supply illustrations for the Gospels keyed to Ignatius's *Ejercicios* (the *Evangelicae historiae imagines* [Antwerp, 1596]); by the eighteenth century, illustrated editions of the *Ejercicios* themselves were common in Europe.

To the passages quoted from the *Ejercicios* should be compared other texts, such as the *Zardino de Oration* 16, a fifteenth century manual of devotion for young girls, which instructs the girls to mentally "place" the figures of the actors in the Passion narrative in Jerusalem, "taking for this purpose a city that is well-known to you" (quoted in M. Baxandall, *Painting and Experience in Fifteenth Century Italy* [Oxford, 1972], 46).

For a full discussion of Ignatius's "application of the senses," see H. Rahner, *Ignatius the Theologian* (London, 1968), 181–213. Both R. Barthes (*Sade, Fourier, Loyola* [New York, 1976], 39–75) and J. Spence (*The Memory Palace of Matteo Ricci* [New York, 1984], 12–22 *et passim*) have contributed strikingly original views on the Ignatian enterprise of visualization.

Index

Achilpa. *See* Tjilpa
Adams, R. McC., 52
Anastasis. *See* Jerusalem, Church of the Holy Sepulchre
Aranda, 1–15; ancestors, 5, 7, 22, 112–14; and Christian syncretism, 5; sacred poles among, 6; *tjurunga*, 5
Aristeas, 71–73, 85
Aristotle, 26
Arunta. *See* Aranda
Australian aborigines: ancestors among, 11–12; high gods, 5; alleged primitivity of, 15. *See also* Aranda, Pitjantjara, Tjilpa, Walbiri

Bacon, R., 46
Baumstark, A., 91, 116
Bellah, R., 52
Beza, T., 100
Bird, J., 50
Blumrich, J. F., 47–48
Brosses, C. de, 98, 102
Brown, P., 77

Caesarea, 78
Center: in Eliade, 2, 10, 14, 22; and galactic polity, 66; in Geertz, 74–75; in Jerusalem Temple, 58–60; as a political notion, 19; in Wheatley, 51–52
Chalcedon, Council of, 78

City: definition of, 50, 53; and urbanization in Wheatley, 50–54
Classification: dual, 39–45; in Durkheim and Mauss, 35–39
Comparison: theory and method of, 13–14; and the unique, 34–35
Concentric structures, 42–45, 65, 68
Constantine, 75–76, 78–80
Constantinople, 75–76, 86
Corbo, V., 83
Corpse pollution, 55, 60–61, 63, 77
Cross, F. L., 88
Cross: discovery of, 82, 115–16; exaltation of, 116; relics of, 82, 87–88; stations of, 87; wood of, 116
Cyril of Jerusalem, 86, 91
Czarnowski, S., 94

Diametric structures, 42–45, 68
Dix, G., 94
Dumézil, G., 40–41
Dumont, L., 54–56, 60, 62
Durkheim, É., 35–40, 105–7

Easter fire, 80
Egeria, 88–94
Eichrodt, W., 61
Eliade, M., 1–10, 14
Enuma elish, 19–20
Erasmus, 101
Eusebius, 77–83
Ezekiel, 47–71, 73

Flannery, K., 52
Freud, S., 24–25, 110–11
Friedman, J., 54
Fuzzy structures, 42–45

Geertz, C., 46, 48, 53–54, 57, 74–75
Gennep, A. van, 110
Geography: environmental determinism, 30–31; exceptionalism, 31–35; humanistic, 28–31; theory in, 28–35
Glacken, C. J., 31
Goyen, W., 29
Gussow, A., 30

Hadrian, 79
Hartshorne, R., 32–35
Heidegger, M., 21
Helena, 82, 115
Herodotus, 104
Hettner, A., 33
Hierarchy, 41–46, 50, 52, 54–56; and egalitarian structures, 66–71; of power, 54, 56–62; of status, 62–65
Holy Saturday, 80, 87
Holy Sepulchre, Church of the. See Jerusalem, Church of the Holy Sepulchre
Howitt, A. W., 4
Hume, D., 98
Hypocoherence, 53, 65

Ideology, 40–42
Ignatius Loyola, 117
Isaac, E., 21

Jakobson, R., 85, 108
Jerusalem: Aelia Capitolina, 79–80; Christian, 76–83, 86–95; Church of the Holy Sepulchre, 76–95, 115–16; Golgotha, 85; prestige of, 78; Temple in, 47–73, 83–86, 108–12
Juvenal, 78

Kant, I., 27–28; geographical theories of, 31–34; French Neo-

Kantianism, 39; German Neo-Kantianism, 33–34

Levenson, J., 61
Lévi-Strauss, C.: on mana, 107–8; nature of anthropology, 98–99; ritual theory, xii, 85–86, 111–12, 114; on the Winnebago, 42–45
Licinius, 81
Liturgical year, 88–95
Locke, J., 26

Macarius, 77–78
Mauss, M. See Durkheim, É.
Meddling, 53, 69
Memory and memorialization, 7, 9–10, 13, 25–26, 93–94, 113–14
Middleton, C., 96–98
Mishnah, xii–xiii, 86, 95
Munn, N., 11–12, 113
Mussard, P., 101
Myth: Near Eastern, 18–21; theories of, 101–2

Needham, R., 38
Neusner, J., xii–xiii
Nicaea, Council of, 77
Norman Anonymous, 105
Numbakulla, 1–2, 4–5

Pagano-papism, 100–101
Pan-Babylonian School, 15–16
Pilgrimage, Christian, 76, 87, 89
Pitjantjara, 11–12
Place: as arbitrary, 83–86; and hierarchy, 45–46; as home place, 28–29; as human construct, 26–28
Priestly function, 55, 57–58, 63, 68, 72
Prince: in relation to Temple in Ezekiel, 60–62, 70
Promotion, 53, 70

Radin, P., 42–45
Rappaport, R., 52–53
Reid, T., 26
Relations of difference, 85–86
Replication, 73, 83–84, 87–88, 94–95

Rickert, H., 33
Ritual: in Christian Jerusalem, 88–94; and difference, 109–12; and historicity, 73, 86–95, 114–17; in relation to myth, 112–14; in relation to myth in Christianity, 114–17; Reformation theories of, 98–103; theories of, 52–53; theory of, 102–8
Róheim, G., 11, 17–18
Rome, 75
Royal function, 55, 60, 63, 68, 79–81

Sacred poles: among the Aranda, 6; Tjilpa myths of, 1–13
Segmentation, 56–57
Sopher, D., 30
Space. See Place
Spencer, B., and F. J. Gillen, 1–10
Spencer, J., 98
Stanner, W. E. H., 113–14
Stational liturgy, 91–94, 115
Steiner, G., 30
Steward, J., 52
Strehlow, T. G. H., 12–13
Symmetry and asymmetry, 39–40, 69

Tambiah, S. J., 66
Temple in Jerusalem. See Jerusalem, Temple in
Temples: Near Eastern, 18–21; Near Eastern and Indic compared, 2, 14, 22
Tertullian, 105–6
Tjilpa: ancestors, 17; myth of broken pole, 1–13; tjurunga, 15
Tjurunga, 5, 15, 106–7
Tuan, Y.-F., 28

Uberoi, J. P. S., 99–100

Walbiri, 11–12
Walls, symbolism of, 49–50
Wheatley, P., 46, 50–54, 69
Windelband, W., 33
Winnebago, 42–45, 49
Wistrand, E., 83
World-mountain, 15

Yates, F., 26

Zion traditions, 48, 60
Zwingli, U., 99–100